Rational Expectations
and the
New Macroeconomics

Rational Expectations and the New Macroeconomics

PATRICK MINFORD and DAVID PEEL

Martin Robertson · Oxford

First published in 1983 by
Martin Robertson & Company Ltd.,
108 Cowley Road, Oxford OX4 1JF.

British Library Cataloguing in Publication Data

Minford, Patrick
    Rational expectations and the new macroeconomics.
    1. Rational expectations (Economic theory)
    —Mathematical models
    I. Title   II. Peel, David
    330   HB199

    ISBN 0-85520-713-2
    ISBN 0-85520-714-0   Pbk

Typeset by Santype International, Salisbury, Wilts.
Printed and bound in Great Britain by
Redwood Burn Ltd, Trowbridge, Wiltshire

To our wives,
Rosie and Janet

Contents

List of Tables and Figures

Preface

This book is designed as an introduction to the use of rational expectations methods in macroeconomics. It will be suitable both for third-year undergraduate courses and for postgraduate teaching. It has arisen out of a course of lectures in macroeconomics we have been giving to third-year economics undergraduates at Liverpool for the last three years.

While this course covers some topics not dealt with in this book, its main emphasis is on rational expectations. It is taken by all economics students and optionally by some accounting and business studies students; our treatment has been conditioned by this. We have tended to use concrete examples of simple macroeconomic models to put across our points rather than to attempt generalization and abstraction. We also use discrete time throughout, since stochastic difference equations are now in the toolkit of economics students, while differential stochastic methods are not. We have found from experience that students are best able in this way both to follow the argument and then to use rational expectations methods themselves on simple models relevant to a variety of problems; while there are no class problems included as such, the chapters lend themselves easily to class discussion and problem-solving.

The level of difficulty is fairly consistent throughout, given the audience we have in mind. Our principal assumption is that the reader has mastered basic econometric concepts, as set out in a standard text such as Johnston (1972). We do not, however, assume that he has reached a high level of attainment in econometrics. Because of the organization by topics each chapter is fairly self-contained, though Chapter 2 on solution methods is required reading for all the rest. The book is a 'text', but, presumably like most texts, it contains some new and some controversial material; we think this adds to its interest and value, and have not tried to put a *cordon sanitaire* around these thoughts of ours.

We have aimed to cover the topics that an applied macro-economist would need to understand, whether he is in teaching, business or government. Within the confines of space, this has led us to emphasize conceptual and policy issues and to give little space to the technical complexities either of estimation or of numerical solution. We justify this on the grounds that the applied macroeconomist who wants to carry out estimation and solution of a model on the computer should always seek expert advice on the details of his problem, and will in practice be guided to available software packages; and we do also include in Chapter 11, which describes our own work on a model of this sort, some preliminary hints that he may follow.

This book is not regrettably accessible to the layman, but it is accessible to economists in all walks of life, provided that they have a working knowledge of standard econometric techniques. We anticipate that it will therefore be useful to those economists whose training does not include the rational expectations methods so prevalent in macroeconomics today.

Our reason for writing this book is simple and compelling: the topic is of great importance to the applied macro-economist of today and central in particular to forecasting and policy making, yet teachers and students of it have been handicapped by the difficulty of most of the material available and understanding of it appears to us to have been correspondingly held back, limited mainly to some rather simple propositions in the literature which have given a quite misleading impression of its implications. We hope they will find this book useful, and the true implications of rational expectations – at least as we see them – as exciting as we do.

We have incurred a number of debts in writing this book. We have had fruitful discussions over the years with Mike Beenstock, Matt Canzoneri, Ken Wallis and Mike Wickens on many of the issues we have covered: notably, solution, estimation, model building and stabilization policy. Ken Cleaver assisted in interpreting the work of George Shackle, Peter Pope commented helpfully on the draft of the chapter on market efficiency, and Martyn Hill did the same for the appendix to Chapter 9 on wealth effects, contributing the empirical section. The Liverpool work used in this book owes a great deal that is not explicitly cited to other members of the Liverpool Research Group in Macroeconomics, notably Chris Ioannidis, Satwant Marwaha, and Kent Matthews. They, and other members of the Liverpool department, have also contributed to an ongoing seminar on the topics of this book. Simon Blackman prepared the references and the index. The manuscript was typed often under considerable pressure by Jackie Fawcett and Maureen Kay. We thank – without implicating – these friends and colleagues for their help in this venture. We also gratefully acknowledge the continuing financial support – since 1977 – of the Social Science Research Council for the work on the Liverpool model described in Chapter 11 and other related work referred to elsewhere in this book. Our thanks, too, go to the fine team at Martin Robertson for their usual efficiency, speed and charm. Finally, we thank our students over the past six years for acting as (mostly) friendly critics of our efforts; ultimately, they provided the spur, even if we had the whip hand.

Patrick Minford and David Peel
Liverpool July 1983

1

Introductory Ideas

Expectations are fundamental in economics. Every economic decision is about the *future*, given the existing situation. Even decisions apparently only involving the current situation, such as choosing to buy apples rather than pears, implicitly involve a view of the future; in this case it is a view both about future income which underlies the budget one is prepared to allocate to apples and pears, and about future prices of apples and pears, which dictates whether it is worthwhile storing them in place of future purchases.

By definition the future is unknowable. Economics, the study of economic decision making, therefore is concerned with how people deal with the unknowable.

The Liverpool University economist, George Shackle, made this a constant theme of his work. In his view (e.g. Shackle (1958)) each individual constructs in his imagination different scenarios or possible outcomes following on the different actions he is contemplating. He knows *now* the pleasure given by the consequences imagined for each course of action. The course which gives him the most pleasure when its consequences are imagined spurs him to action. So Shackle envisages a hedonistic calculus of the imagination as the basis for economic choice.

For Shackle the pleasure involved in a course of action will depend, not only on the 'expected pleasure' if the consequences anticipated were to occur, but also on the 'chances' of them occurring. A fine outcome will normally give less pleasure when imagined if it is fraught with uncertainty. But this will not always be true. For example, for some people the same outcome may seem the sweeter if it is accompanied by the challenge of possible failure. Too easy a victory may

1

not inspire a sense of triumph at all and may not attract the decision taker.

Shackle therefore regards economic decisions as entirely subjective, because the product of the individual's imagination interacting with the known facts of the past and present.

Nor does he feel that we can predict how people will act except in matters where nature reproduces herself with regularity. For example, in inventory control where the product has a reliable distribution, the manager can and will stop production when a sample has a proportion of defective products higher than some percentage.

In such cases Shackle says there is 'uncertainty', the rules of probability can be applied by people and we can infer what they will do from a knowledge of their objectives and of the probability distributions.

However, for many decisions the major elements in the future outcome are not subject to reliable distributions. For example what the voters of Warrington would do, faced with a Social Democratic candidate in July 1981, could not be described by a probability distribution. It was not a regular event. No sense could be given to 'the' probability distribution.

Such elements Shackle termed sources of 'potential surprise'. In evaluating future outcomes with such elements, each person will make his individual assessment and we cannot say what he will do without a complete knowledge of his psychology, even if we have access to exactly the same facts as he has.

Shackle's perceptions appear to be quite devastating to the use of statistical models in economics (i.e. econometrics). For these models assert that economic behaviour is predictable and regular. Their implication is that economic agents take decisions about future outcomes which are predictable and subject to well-defined probability distributions. For the models are supposed to be derived from assumptions about agents' preferences, technologies and the probability distributions they face.

The keystone of econometrics is the implicit assertion that, in the mass, individual decisions exhibit regularity, even though each individual decision will be quite unpredictable.

Suppose we could define the probability distribution of future outcomes. Then econometrics asserts that there is a 'typical' individual who, faced with this distribution, will decide in a certain way; we might in particular say that he 'maximizes an expected utility function', where the utility function is a mathematical representation of his preferences. Individuals, when aggregated in a large sample, will behave like many typical individuals.

This assertion is supported up to a point by the Central Limit Theorem, according to which the distribution of the mean of a sample of random variables will tend to normality as the sample gets larger, regardless of the distributions of each variable in the sample (see e.g. Hoel, 1962, p. 145). But, though supported in this way, it is still required that an individual decision can be regarded as a random variable with a defined mean, generated by a systematic decision process. Shackle denies this, while econometrics asserts it. Furthermore, it was supposed in the above argument that the future outcomes had a probability distribution. But for this to be the case it is necessary that individuals do behave in the aggregate in the regular manner just described. For the distribution of future outcomes is the product of the inter-action of individuals' behaviour – e.g. the distribution of future prices and quantities for sugar results from the inter-action of individuals' supplies and demands for sugar.

Thus the linchpin of the whole edifice of econometrics is the postulate of regularity in aggregate behaviour by individuals faced with regularities in economic nature. That postulate in turn justifies the assumption that they face regularities. Whether this postulate is 'true or false' can only be settled empirically, by evaluating the success and failure of econometrics in attempting to apply this basic assertion. But it is important to realize that the whole foundation of econometrics could be wrong. Indeed many economists regard it (as did Keynes – see e.g. Keynes, 1939) as an unfortunate development which has perverted policy on many important issues because of a false perception that numerical estimates of likely outcomes from different policies can be generated.

Some of the early hopes of econometricians were that econometrics would enable complex problems of decision making by governments, firms, and individuals to be reduced to the mere application of known techniques to models of the relevant economic environment. But these hopes have been cruelly dashed. Nowhere has this been more so than in macroeconomics. Macroeconomic models were built in great profusion in the 1960s for most major countries and used, especially in Britain and the United States, as the basis for forecasting and policy. Crude forms of 'optimal control' were used by governments; typically governments made forecasts, using their models, of inflation and unemployment over a horizon of a year or two and then adjusted their policy instruments to obtain better outcomes according to these models. By the mid-1970s disillusion with these methods was widespread, as the Western world grappled with a combination of high inflation and high unemployment which had, in general, neither been predicted by econometric models, nor had responded to policy in the manner predicted by these models.

The reaction to this disillusion has been varied, with the result that the consensus in macroeconomics that had appeared in the late 1960s had abruptly disappeared by the late 1970s. To some this was a vindication of their scepticism about econometrics. Others, however, have searched for reformulations of the models which failed in the 1970s.

RATIONAL EXPECTATIONS

In this book we are concerned with one particularly radical reformulation, rational expectations. Rational expectations takes one step further the basic assertion of econometrics that individuals in the aggregate act in a regular manner as if each was a typical individual following a systematic decision process. The step is to assert that in this decision process he utilizes efficiently the information available to him in forming expectations about future outcomes.

By 'efficient utilization' it is meant that the typical individual's perception of the probability distribution of future outcomes (his 'subjective distribution'), conditional on the available information, coincides with the actual probability distribution conditional on that information.

It cannot be stressed too heavily – since this is a source of repeated misunderstanding – that this is an assertion about the 'typical' individual; in other words, it is to be used operationally with reference to the aggregate behaviour of individuals. It cannot be falsified by examples of behaviour by any actual individual. Clearly particular individuals may behave in ways that exhibit no systematic rational behaviour or expectations-formation according to normal criteria, and yet if the behaviour of other individuals, who contributed a dominant proportion of the variability in aggregate behaviour, were rational in this sense, this would be sufficient to generate aggregate behaviour that exhibited rationality.

A further point is that, like all assertions in econometrics, it is to be judged by statistical criteria which will be relative. Whether a relationship asserted to operate for the behaviour of a group 'exists' or not will depend upon how reliable it is statistically, relative to the uses to which it may be put. Such uses in turn may themselves evolve from the discovery of new relationships.

There is therefore no such thing as an objective criterion for judging whether an econometric assertion is valid. Rather there is a joint and interactive evolution of models and their uses. The 1970s crisis in macroeconomic policy and modelling described earlier arose because the uses to which models were being put required properties that those models turned out not to have. The question therefore that the rational expectations research programme has to answer is: can models based on rational expectations be developed that are useful in application? If so, what are these uses, and how do they compare to the uses available for other modelling approaches?

The assertion (or 'hypothesis') of rational expectations in one sense vindicates Shackle's basic perception that expectations are at the centre of economic behaviour. For on this view behaviour reacts to expected future behaviour which in turn depends on current behaviour; the capacity exists therefore for changes in the environment to affect current behaviour sharply as individuals react to their perceptions of the changed environment and its implications for the future. Expectations are therefore completely integrated into behaviour.

In previous theories of expectations, this integration was incomplete. Econometric models used 'proxies' for expectations of particular types of outcome. These proxies were based on what had been found in the past to correlate well with behaviour in a way that could reasonably be attributed to the operation of expectations rather than actual events. Hence for any particular problem in hand a proxy would be sought *ad hoc problema.* It is obvious enough that if changes in the environment disturbed the previous relationship between the proxy's behaviour and expectations, this would affect behaviour in a way that would be inaccurately captured by the effect of changes in the proxy. Hence only under the restricted set of circumstances where the previous relationship is unaffected will the proxies be useful. Unfortunately the restricted set excludes most of the policy experiments of interest to governments.

Yet in another sense the rational expectations hypothesis conflicts with Shackle's vision in that it is an attempt to use econometrics to capture the integration of expectations into behaviour. As such, it could be rated as even more foolhardy than basic econometrics. For, whereas in well settled times, patterns of behaviour might conceivably evolve which could give rise to some econometric relationships, in times of change when expectations are being disturbed in an unfamiliar way, then surely to model the effect of the changes on expectations and their interactions with behaviour must be a mad attempt. For there is the capacity for immense diversity of imagined outcomes from the changes taking place; the 'typically' imagined outcome will be a useless construct in this diversity where different individuals will be behaving in unrelated and possibly conflicting ways.

This reaction correctly identifies the way in which rational expectations is a programme for pushing econometrics to the limits of its possibilities in the prediction of behaviour. At the same time the reaction correctly notes the ambition of this attempt. It is possible that the attempt is hopelessly over-ambitious. If it is proved to be so, then at least the limits of econometrics will have been clearly defined. For it will be the case that econometric relationships can at best only be useful in the restricted circumstances where the environment shows considerable stability. This would imply that they could be used to forecast existing trends in an unchanged environment, but not to predict the effects of changes in the environment, especially policy changes. If this were so, then it would equally invalidate attempts to use econometric models to design 'optimal' policy rules. Hence the implications flowing from a proper exploration of the potentialities of rational expectations are substantial and important. While our own view is that these potentialities are considerable, it will only be a decade or so before we will know with reasonable clarity just what can be delivered from this approach.

INTELLECTUAL HISTORY OF THE HYPOTHESIS – AN OVERVIEW

As so often in economics, it turns out that early economists propounded ideas at different stages that bear a striking resemblance to the hypothesis. For example, Marshall (1887), in his evidence to a Royal Commission, argued that an increase in the supply of money would affect economic activity by lowering interest rates, increasing loans, expenditure and finally prices. However, he also added that if the increase in the supply of money was well known, then individuals would anticipate the consequent expansion in demand and the effect on prices would be much faster.[1]

Modigliani and Grunberg (1954) are credited by Robert Shiller (1978) with the earliest post-war promulgation of the ideas behind the hypothesis. It was one of Modigliani's collaborators, John Muth who, however, truly created the hypothesis (Muth, 1961) in the sense that he set it down in precise form and showed how it could be applied to specific problems.

Muth's article was written partly in order to defend the prevailing fashion of the 1960s in expectations modelling, adaptive expectations, according to which expectations of a variable are an exponentially weighted average of past values of this variable. It turns out that under certain circumstances this is the same as the rational expectation. These were the circumstances to which Muth seemed to draw attention. His other work published at the time was exclusively devoted to the use of exponentially weighted averages (Muth, 1960; and Holt, Modigliani, Muth and Simon, 1960).

The use of a particular modelling technique depends as much on its perceived tractability by economists as on its inherent plausibility. It was in fact the best part of a decade before economists started to use Muth's concept in its own right in applied and theoretical work. Adaptive expectations seemed in the 1960s the best tool, partly perhaps because still new and relatively unexplored (it made its first journal appearance in Nerlove, 1958), partly because of its most convenient econometric transformation (due to L. M. Koyck, 1954) into a single lagged value of the dependent variable. By contrast, the techniques for using rational expectations (RE) were not widely available; the solution of models with RE presented difficulties, overcome by Muth in very simple models, but not readily dealt with in the larger models being developed in that decade. As we shall see, solution of larger models (and also estimation) requires substantial computing power; and it may well be that the rapid quickening of interest in RE modelling from the mid-1970s has been due to the explosion in the capability of the electronic computer.

The earliest published work in macroeconomics using Muth's concept seriously, if only to a limited extent, is that of Walters (1971), and Lucas (1972a). Walters showed that the effect of money on prices would be substantially quickened by RE. Lucas argued that under RE (unlike adaptive expectations) monetary expansion could not raise output above the natural rate on average (the 'natural rate hypothesis') though the responses of money to lagged output and prices (feedback responses) could affect the time path of output in response to shocks. Notice that neither author in these articles argued for the ineffectiveness of monetary policy feedback responses for influencing the time-path of output.

Another early paper was by Black (1973) who applied rational expectations to the foreign exchange market, an area which has seen many further and productive applications of the concept. Some of this subsequent work used Muth's original model in a partial equilibrium treatment of the market treating macroeconomic variables exogenously (e.g. Minford 1978; Bell and Beenstock, 1980). Other work (e.g. Frankel, 1979), has estimated reduced form models of the exchange rate derived from a monetary model with rational expectations. Shiller (1979) applied it to the term structure of interest rates; here too a separate but closely related body of work has been extremely fruitful.

This has taken the form of tests of the 'efficient market hypothesis'. This is a combination of the rational expectations hypothesis and some hypothesis about market behaviour, which thus makes it possible to test rational expectations through the behaviour of market prices. Eugene Fama (e.g. 1970, 1976) and his collaborators at Chicago have been prolific in this area, and have covered not only financial markets but also a variety of commodity markets, with results which have at the least substantially revised the popular notions of the early post-war period that markets were irrational and highly inefficient.

Work on general macroeconomic applications (i.e. to inflation and output) in the early 1970s is substantially due to Lucas (1972a,b), Sargent and Wallace (1975). Lucas' concern was to develop a rationale for fluctuations in money supply to affect output, his problem being that if information on money is available, then movements in money should immediately be discounted in prices, as everyone seeks to maintain relative prices unchanged. He developed a theme due to Milton Friedman (1968) that individuals perceive economy-wide data such as money and the general price level with an information lag, and are forced to estimate whether the price changes they currently perceive at the market level are relative price changes or merely reflect general price movements (inflation). A positive relationship between output and money or price movements (a 'Phillips curve') can occur because of mistakes made by individuals in estimating current inflation; they supply more output mistakenly thinking that the relative price of their product has risen.

This 'surprise' supply function is an essential component of the small-scale macro models used by Sargent and Wallace to illustrate the potential implications for policy making of RE. They showed that in a 'Keynesian' model, if the Phillips curve (a standard Keynesian construct) is interpreted as a surprise supply function, then only monetary surprises can affect output, monetary plans, whatever they are, can only affect prices. Hence, in particular, sophisticated feedback rules (which, for example, raised money supply in response to a poor past output performance) would be ineffective in their output stabilization objective. However Lucas and Sargent (1978) have pointed out that this work was not intended to imply that monetary policy was *in general* ineffective for output, merely that in a particular 'standard' model (which they did not in any case endorse) to which 'optimal' monetary control techniques were routinely applied, such techniques were in fact useless. The lesson they drew was cautionary: monetary policy rules should carefully allow for the reactions of private agents to the rules themselves.

Lucas (1975) and Sargent (1976a) have proceeded in the later 1970s to develop an alternative to the standard model, the so-called 'equilibrium business cycle' model. In this model the information lag story is maintained, but all markets are treated as if they are auction markets in which all agents are atomistic competitive units. Households are consumers and suppliers of labour and, period by period, compute optimal intertemporal plans for consumption and work based on the price sequences they perceive themselves as facing. Firms, on the other side of the labour and goods markets from households, similarly compute (given their technology) optimal plans for hiring labour and producing goods based on the same price sequences. The price sequences that *are* perceived are the rational expectations equilibrium sequences that clear the markets today and are expected to clear them in the future. Because firms and households, once they have made a plan, incur 'sunk costs', there is an adjustment cost in changing plans as these past decisions are unwound. This imparts the correlation of prices and quantities over time that is a feature of business cycles. But the impulse to the cycle comes from shocks to the economy, whether from monetary policy, technological innovations, or surprise shifts in household preferences. Models motivated in this way or parts of such models have been estimated by Sargent (e.g. 1976a) and Barro (e.g. 1977).

However, such a model is by no means mandatory in the rational expectations research programme. The underpinning of the 'surprise' supply function has been questioned (B. Friedman, 1978; Minford and Peel, 1980). Also, while the 'as if' assumption of auction markets and atomistic agents may work well for economies with highly competitive structures, monopoly power, in labour markets particularly, is widespread in Western economies, markedly so in Europe, and could require explicit modelling. Furthermore the role of long term contracts – in goods, labour and financial markets – may be inadequately captured by this 'as if' assumption; this assumption would imply that contracts were approximately 'fully contingent' (i.e. such that prices and quantities altered in response to shocks in just the manner that optimal plans would call for if there were no contracts), yet this apparently is not generally the case, for reasons that are not well understood but may well be entirely consistent with rationality.

Work by Phelps and Taylor (1977) and Fischer (1977) has taken non-contingent contracts in goods and labour markets as *given* and set up simple models to explore the implications. The influential model of an 'overshooting' foreign exchange market in an open economy by Dornbusch (1976) centres around the interaction of 'sticky' prices in goods and labour markets with an auction foreign exchange market. The effect of changes in financial asset values due to the presence of financial contracts (such as long-term bonds) has similarly played an important role in the models of Blanchard (1981) and Minford (1980). Integration of labour monopoly power into these models has been carried out by Minford and Brech (1981). These developments imply a model different in many aspects from the narrowly defined equilibrium model of Lucas and Sargent, though it should be stressed that a model with contracts and monopolies where agents have rational expectations could perhaps most naturally be described as an equilibrium model in that contracts have been voluntarily entered into and monopolies have agency rights on behalf of their members (and if the state legitimizes a closed shop, their non-members also). The policy properties differ substantially; there is in general more scope for stabilization, though whether it would be beneficial is another matter, requiring careful welfare analysis (see Chapter 5).

There are yet other strands in the ongoing RE research programme. B. Friedman (1979) and Brunner, Cukierman and Meltzer (1980) have attempted to introduce the modelling of learning about the model, notably about the evolving 'permanent' elements in the model's structure. Long and Plosser (1983) have suggested that business cycles may be modelled without an appeal to information lags or the surprise supply function; they may stem from real shocks to consumer wealth which generate equilibrium cycles in consumption, production and relative prices. Correlations between money and output may be explainable by implication in terms of reverse causation (King and Plosser, 1981). Finally there is an influential school led by Sims (1979) that despairs of modelling the economy's structure, but is interested in time series analysis for predictive purposes within stable structures, using the vector autoregression (i.e. the regression of a *group* of variables on the past of *all* members of the group).

Such is in outline the history of this concept and the current tendencies in the RE research programme. In the rest of this book we shall be elaborating on those details of this research that are of crucial importance, after describing some necessary techniques.

THE PLAN OF THE BOOK

The book is designed as a guide for the applied macro-economist. It therefore begins by describing the apparatus necessary for solving RE models; this is the subject of Chapter 2. The rest of the book deals with topics which have pre-eminently exercised macroeconomists.

Chapters 3–5 deal with government policy to stabilize output, a topic on which RE has newly aroused vigorous debate. Chapter 3 considers how RE affects its *feasibility*;

Chapter 4 extends this to situations where economic agents have access to partial current information about macro-economic variables. Chapter 5 considers the *desirability* of stabilization policy.

In Chapter 6, we investigate the theoretical basis of the 'Phillips curve' relationship between unexpected inflation and output. In virtually all RE macroeconomic models to date, this has been the mechanism by which shocks to the money supply caused output responses; it is therefore central to the role of money in the business cycle.

Chapter 7 discusses the behaviour of asset markets, and in particular their 'efficiency'. We look at some widely-used models of the exchange rate and interest rates; these have figured prominently in discussion of asset price 'volatility'.

Chapter 8 extends the discussion of macroeconomic policy by introducing public choice considerations; as compared to Chapters 3–5, which examine government policy from an essentially normative viewpoint (should/can governments stabilize output?), this chapter examines it from a positive viewpoint – how *will* governments act, given the 'potential' pressures on them? This is an important topic, since government reactions have a dominant role in RE models.

Chapter 9 explores the constraints binding fiscal and monetary policy (or how far can budget deficits be bond-financed?); one set of constraints is binding when there are wealth effects, and in an appendix we discuss the theory and evidence for such effects. We also consider what other constraints may be binding in their absence. This topic has been central to the debate on the feasibility of effective monetarist counter-inflation policy in the presence of substantial budget deficits.

In Chapter 10, we review the problems of testing RE models through reduced form regressions. Much empirical work of this kind has been carried out and has been widely cited as evidence for RE. The chapter is cautionary on this large literature.

Chapter 11 is an account of the Liverpool Model, a full-scale forecasting model of the UK economy. This makes use of much of the book's material, and so illustrates its practical implications for the UK.

The book ends – Chapter 12 – with a tentative assessment of where the RE research programme is and might be going.

We think these are the topics which an applied macro-economist today *cannot* ignore; this has guided our selection from a vast literature. The reader should ideally treat the book as a complete unit; but within limits, he may take individual topics and treat the relevant chapter as a self-contained unit. The main limits are defined by the fact that Chapter 2 is a uniform prerequisite, while Chapter 11 is very difficult without having also read Chapters 6, 7 and 9.

NOTE

1. This reference was pointed out to us by Richard Harrington.

2

Solving Rational Expectations Models

In the last chapter we defined the rational expectations hypothesis (REH) as the assumption that peoples' subjective probability distributions about future outcomes are the same as the actual probability distributions conditional on the information available to them. In practice we will be concerned with moments of these distributions, most frequently the mean, but also occasionally the variance, and very rarely the higher moments (the skewness, etc.). The mathematical term for the mean of a distribution is its 'expected value'; and it is usual for applied work on the REH to identify the 'expectation of x_{t+i} (x at time $t + i$)' with the mathematically expected value of x_{t+i}. In this book we will use the notation $\underset{j}{E} x_i$ is defined as $E(x_i | \Phi_j)$ where Φ_j is the set of generally of information generally available at time $t + j$; j, i can be positive or negative. E is the mathematical expectations operator, meaning 'mathematically expected value of'. Formally $\underset{j}{E} x_i$ is defined as $E(x_i | \Phi_j)$ where Φ_j is the set of generally available information at time $t + j$. Of course, once x_i is part of the information set Φ_j, then $\underset{j}{E} x_i = x_i$ trivially.

If we wish to indicate that the information available to those framing expectations is restricted to a set θ_j at $t + j$, we will write $\underset{j}{E} (x_i | \theta_j)$, i.e. the expectation of x at $t + i$ framed on the basis of information set θ available at $t + j$. It is natural to think of $\underset{j}{E} x_i$ as 'expectations formed at $t + j$ of x at $t + i$'; this will do for some purposes but it is not quite accurate. It is not in fact the date at which expectations are formed that matters but rather the date of the information set on the

15

basis of which they are formed. Because of information lags, people may form expectations for this period on the basis of last period's information, and we would write this as $\underset{-1}{\text{E}}\,x$.

Suppose for extreme simplicity that the model of x is:

$$x_{+1} = x + \varepsilon_{+1} \tag{2.1}$$

where ε is normally distributed with a mean of 0, a constant variance of σ^2, independence between successive values, and independence of all previous events; i.e. ε: $N(0, \sigma^2)$, $\text{E}(\varepsilon_i \varepsilon_j) = 0$ $(i \neq j)$ and $\text{E}\varepsilon_i \Phi_j = 0$ $(i > j)$. (2.1) states that x follows a 'random walk' (the change in x is random).

The expectation of x_{+1} at t is x, if we assume that people know x then. They cannot know ε_{+1} because it has not yet occurred and as a random variable its expected value is zero. If we write Φ as the total information set at t, therefore:

$$\underset{0}{\text{E}}\,x_{+1} = \text{E}(x_{+1}\,|\,\Phi) = \text{E}(x + \varepsilon_{+1}\,|\,\Phi)$$

$$= x + \text{E}(\varepsilon_{+1}\,|\,\Phi) = x \tag{2.2}$$

$\underset{0}{\text{E}}\,x_{+1}$ will be an unbiased predictor of x_{+1}, i.e. the mean (or expected value) of the prediction error $\left(x_{+1} - \underset{0}{\text{E}}\,x_{+1}\right)$ is zero. Thus:

$$\text{E}\left(x_{+1} - \underset{0}{\text{E}}\,x_{+1}\right) = \text{E}(x + \varepsilon_{+1} - x) = \text{E}\varepsilon_{+1} = 0 \tag{2.3}$$

$\text{E}x_{+1}$ will also be the efficient predictor of x_{+1}, i.e. the variance of the prediction error is smaller than that of any other predictor. Thus:

$$\text{Variance}\left(x_{+1} - \underset{0}{\text{E}}\,x_{+1}\right) = \text{E}\left(x_{+1} - \underset{0}{\text{E}}\,x_{+1}\right)^2$$

$$= \text{E}(\varepsilon_{+1})^2 = \sigma^2 \tag{2.4}$$

This is the minimum variance possible in prediction of x_{+1} because ε_{+1} is distributed independently of previous events (the meaning of 'unpredictable'). Suppose we add any expression whatsoever, say γz, where z is a variable taken from Φ, to $\underset{0}{E} x_{+1}$, making another predictor $\hat{x}_{+1}$:

$$\hat{x}_{+1} = x + \gamma z \tag{2.5}$$

Then:

$$E(x_{+1} - \hat{x}_{+1}) = E(\varepsilon_{+1} - \gamma z)^2 = \sigma^2 + \gamma^2 E z^2 \tag{2.6}$$

The variance will be increased by the variance of the added expression, because this must be independent of ε_{+1}.

The unbiasedness and efficiency of their forecasts are the two key properties of rational expectations forecasts that we will constantly return to in this book. However for the time being, in this chapter, we shall restrict ourselves to explaining how the rational expectation of variables determined in more complex models is to be found, and how those models are accordingly to be solved.

THE BASIC METHOD

Now take an exceedingly simple macro model:

$$m = p + y \tag{2.7}$$

$$p = \underset{-1}{E} p + \delta(y - y^*) \tag{2.8}$$

$$m = \bar{m} + \varepsilon \tag{2.9}$$

where m, p, y, are the logarithms of money supply, the price level, and output respectively; y^* is normal output, $\bar{m}$ is the monetary target (both are assumed to be known constants). (2.7) is a simple money demand function with a zero interest elasticity and a unit income elasticity. (2.9) is a money supply function in which the government aims for a monetary target with an error, ε, which has the properties of our previous ε in (2.1). (2.8) is a Phillips curve as can be seen by subtracting p_{-1} from both sides; in this case it states that the rate of inflation equals last period's expectation of the inflation rate plus a function of 'excess demand'. We can think of the 'periods' as being 'quarters', and prices as being set, as quantities change, on the basis of last quarter's information about the general price level; hence we appeal to an information lag of one quarter, and $\underset{-1}{\text{E}}$ hence refers to this quarter's expectation but formed (the operative element) on the basis of last quarter's information.

This model is three linear equations with three endogenous variables, two exogenous variables, $\bar{m}$ and ε, and an expectation variable, $\underset{-1}{\text{E}}\, p$. Given the expectation, we can solve it normally, e.g. by substitution. So substituting for m and p from (2.8) and (2.9) into (2.7) gives us:

$$\bar{m} + \varepsilon = \underset{-1}{\text{E}}\, p + (1 + \delta)y - \delta y^* \qquad (2.10)$$

But we now need to find $\underset{-1}{\text{E}}\, p$, to get the full solution.

To do this, we write the model in expected form (i.e. taking expectations at $t - 1$ throughout) as:

$$\underset{-1}{\text{E}}\, m = \underset{-1}{\text{E}}\, p + \underset{-1}{\text{E}}\, y \qquad (2.7)^e$$

$$\underset{-1}{\text{E}}\, p = \underset{-1}{\text{E}}\, p + \delta\!\left(\underset{-1}{\text{E}}\, y - y^* \right) \quad \text{or} \quad \underset{-1}{\text{E}}\, y = y^* \qquad (2.8)^e$$

$$\underset{-1}{\text{E}}\, m = \bar{m} \qquad (2.9)^e$$

Substituting $(2.8)^e$ and $(2.9)^e$ into $(2.7)^e$ gives:

$$\underset{-1}{\text{E}}\, p = \bar{m} - y^* \qquad (2.11)$$

This is substituted into (2.10) to give:

$$y = y^* + \left(\frac{1}{1 + \delta} \right)\varepsilon \qquad (2.12)$$

Consequently from (2.8) and using (2.11):

$$p = \bar{m} - y^* + \left(\frac{\delta}{1 + \delta} \right)\varepsilon \qquad (2.13)$$

The solutions for y and p consist of an expected part (y^* and $\bar{m} - y^*$, respectively) and an unexpected part (factors of ε). Rational expectations has incorporated anything known at $t - 1$ with implications for p and y at time t into the expected part, so that the unexpected part is purely unpredictable.

This model, though simple, has an interesting implication, first pointed out by Sargent and Wallace (1975). The solution for y is invariant to the parameters of the money supply rule. Output would in this model be at its normal level in the absence of surprises, which here are restricted to monetary surprises. If the government attempts to stabilize output by changing the money supply rule to, say:

$$m = \bar{m} - \gamma(y - y^*)_{-1} + \varepsilon \qquad (2.14)$$

then still the solution for output is (2.12), because this money supply rule is incorporated into people's expectations at $t - 1$ and cannot cause any surprises. The only effect is on expected (and so also actual) prices:

$$\underset{-1}{\text{E}}\ p = \bar{m} - \gamma(y - y^*)_{-1} - y^*$$

$$= \bar{m} - y^* - \frac{\gamma}{1 + \delta}\,\varepsilon_{-1} \qquad (2.15)$$

$$p = \bar{m} - y^* - \frac{y}{1 + \delta}\,\varepsilon_{-1} + \frac{\delta}{1 + \delta}\,\varepsilon \qquad (2.16)$$

Notice that this will raise the variance of prices around their long-run value $(\bar{m} - y^*)$ by $[\gamma/(1 + \delta)]^2\sigma^2$.

Contrast this solution and its implications with those of the same model, had we assumed in accordance with the popular practice of the 1960s that expectations of the price level were formed adaptively. The adaptive expectations hypothesis is that:

$$x^e - x^e_{-1} = \lambda(x_{-1} - x^e_{-1}) \quad 0 < \lambda < 1 \qquad (2.17)$$

or that expectations of x change by some positive fraction, λ, of last period's error. This can be written equivalently as:

$$x^e = \lambda x_{-1} + (1 - \lambda)x^e_{-1}$$

$$= \lambda x_{-1} + (1 - \lambda)[\lambda x_{-2} + (1 - \lambda)x^e_{-2}] = \cdots$$

$$= \lambda \sum_{i=0}^{\infty} (1 - \lambda)^i x_{-1-i} \qquad (2.18)$$

by continuous substitution for $x^e_{-2}, x^e_{-3}, \ldots$.

Substituting p^e for $\underset{-1}{E} p$ in our simple model (2.7)–(2.9) turns it into an orthodox dynamic model to be solved by standard methods. (2.8) becomes:

$$p = \lambda \sum_{i=0}^{\infty} (1 - \lambda)^i p_{-1-i} + \delta(y - y^*) \qquad (2.8)^a$$

We can see that expected prices depend not on planned money supply but on events known to the government last period. Consequently the government can plan a money supply for this period confident that it will not be 'frustrated' by a response from expectations. They can set a target, m^*, such that $y = y^*$. This will be a target which 'accommodates' prices at their expected level, delivering $p = p^e$; for $(2.8)^a$ assures us that when $p = p^e$, $y = y^*$. By (2.7), when $p = p^e$ and $y = y^*$, then:

$$m^* = p^e + y^* = \lambda \sum_{i=0}^{\infty} (1 - \lambda)^i p_{-1-i} + y^* \qquad (2.19)$$

We now find that the solution for output depends on the deviations of money supply from this optimal target:

$$y = y^* + \frac{1}{1 + \delta} (m - m^*) \qquad (2.20)$$

These deviations may be due either to unpredictable errors, ε, as in the RE case, or to a policy failure to plan m at m^*; in other words:

$$m - m^* = \varepsilon + m^T - m^* \qquad (2.21)$$

where m^T is the actual policy target. But in this adaptive model both affect output, whereas in the RE version only ε, the error term, does. In other words, the monetary policy *chosen* affects output.

We shall in subsequent chapters be examining this RE model and a number of considerably more complex RE models whose properties will differ from this one substantially. Nevertheless, it is a common feature of all these models that there is an important difference between the effects of an anticipated and of an unanticipated change in any exogenous variable; in models where expectations are formed adaptively (or as any fixed function of past data), by contrast, it makes no difference. This is probably the most fundamental result of rational expectations. It is the nature of the difference of these effects that forms the detailed study of RE models.

The method of solution set out above (our 'basic' method) will suffice for all RE models in which there are expectations (at any date in the past) of current events only. To repeat, this method involves three steps:

(1) Solve the model, treating expectations as exogenous.
(2) Take the expected value of the equations at the date of the expectations, and solve for the expectations.
(3) Substitute the expectations solutions into the solution in (1), and obtain the complete solution.

RE MODELS WITH EXPECTATIONS OF FUTURE VARIABLES
(REFV MODELS)

However, it will very often, in fact almost invariably, be the case – in the nature of economic decisions which, as we have seen, involve a view of the future – that expectations of future events, whether formed currently or in the past, will enter the model. For these REFV models, our basic method must be supplemented and it can be replaced by more convenient alternatives.

For example, add to our previous simple model the assumption, made by Cagan (1956) in his influential study of hyperinflation, that the demand for money responds negatively to expected inflation. (We can think of this as approximating the effect of interest rates on money demand in less virulent inflations.) Let the model now be:

$$m = p + y - \alpha \left[\underset{-1}{E} \, p_{+1} - \underset{-1}{E} \, p \right] \quad (\alpha > 0) \qquad (2.22)$$

$$p = \underset{-1}{E} \, p + \delta(y - y^*) \qquad (2.8)$$

$$m = \bar{m} + \varepsilon \qquad (2.9)$$

We keep (2.8) and (2.9) as before. In (2.22) expectations of inflation in the current period are regarded as formed on the basis of last period's (quarter's) information; as in (2.8) we are appealing to an information lag.

Let us use our basic method and see how it has to be adapted for this model. Step (1) (solving, given expectations as exogenous) gives us:

$$\bar{m} + \varepsilon = p + \frac{1}{\delta}\left(p - \underset{-1}{\mathsf{E}}\, p\right) + y^* - \alpha\left(\underset{-1}{\mathsf{E}}\, p_{+1} - \underset{-1}{\mathsf{E}}\, p\right)$$

$$(2.23)$$

To find $\underset{-1}{\mathsf{E}}\, p$, $\underset{-1}{\mathsf{E}}\, p_{+1}$ we take expectations of the model at $t - 1$ (step 2) to yield:

$$\bar{m} - y^* = (1 + \alpha)\, \underset{-1}{\mathsf{E}}\, p - \alpha\, \underset{-1}{\mathsf{E}}\, p_{+1} \qquad (2.24)$$

(2.24) can solve for $\underset{-1}{\mathsf{E}}\, p$ in terms of $\bar{m}$, y^*, and $\underset{-1}{\mathsf{E}}\, p_{+1}$. But this is not a solution because $\underset{-1}{\mathsf{E}}\, p_{+1}$ is not solved out; we appear to have shifted the problem into the future.

To solve for $\underset{-1}{\mathsf{E}}\, p_{+1}$ we may lead the model by one period (e.g. write (2.22) as $m_{+1} = p_{+1} + y_{+1} - \alpha(\mathsf{E}p_{+2} - \mathsf{E}p_{+1})$) and take expectations of it at $t - 1$ as before. This yields analogously:

$$\bar{m} - y^* = (1 + \alpha)\, \underset{-1}{\mathsf{E}}\, p_{+1} - \alpha\, \underset{-1}{\mathsf{E}}\, p_{+2} \qquad (2.25)$$

We have now solved for $\underset{-1}{\mathsf{E}}\, p_{+1}$ in terms of $\bar{m}$, y^*, and $\underset{-1}{\mathsf{E}}\, p_{+2}$, again shifting the problem into the future.

In fact, we can carry on in this way indefinitely and it is easy to see that we obtain a series of equations which can be written as a sort of difference equation:

$$\bar{m} - y^* = (1 + \alpha)\, \underset{-1}{\mathsf{E}}\, p_{+i} - \alpha\, \underset{-1}{\mathsf{E}}\, p_{+i+1} \quad (i \geqslant 0) \quad (2.26)$$

This is actually a difference equation in a variable p^e_{+i}, defined to be p_{+i} as expected from $t - 1$:

$$p^e_{+i+1} - \frac{1 + \alpha}{\alpha} p^e_{+i} = -\left(\frac{\bar{m} - y^*}{\alpha}\right) \quad (i \geqslant 0) \quad (2.27)$$

The solution of this first order non-homogeneous difference equation is familiarly:

$$p^e_{+i} = \bar{m} - y^* + [p^e_0 - (\bar{m} - y^*)]\left(\frac{1 + \alpha}{\alpha}\right)^i \quad (i \geqslant 0) \quad (2.28)$$

$\bar{m} - y^*$ is the equilibrium of p (the 'particular' solution); $(1 + \alpha)/\alpha$ is the root and $p^e_0 - (\bar{m} - y^*)$ is the constant (determined by the initial value, p^e_0) in the 'general' solution.

CHOOSING A UNIQUE EXPECTED PATH

(2.28) gives an infinite number of solution paths for p^e_{+i} $(i \geqslant 0)$. For we are free to choose any value of p^e_0 we like; the model does not restrict our choice. Another way of looking at (2.28) is to say that we can choose any future value for any $p^e_{+i}\left(\underset{-1}{E} p_{+i}\right)$ we wish and work back from that to a solution for $p^e_0\left(\underset{-1}{E} p\right)$. We would already have guessed this would be so from (2.24), for, to obtain the expectation of a current value, we were compelled to take a view about $\underset{-1}{E} p_{+1}$. Any view of this future will then compel a present which is consistent with it; any set of expectations is therefore self-justifying.

REFV models (i.e. the vast majority) would be little better than *curiosa* if they did not carry with them additional restrictions sufficient to define a unique solution; for they would merely assert in effect 'anything can happen provided it is expected, but what is expected is arbitrary'. Worse still, as (2.28) illustrates, these paths for events can be unstable; in fact, our model here implies that all paths for prices except that for which $p^e_0 = \bar{m} - y^*$, explode monotonically. Thus our particular REFV model would assert that only by accident would an equilibrium price level be established, otherwise prices would be propelled into either ever-deepening hyperdeflation or ever-accelerating hyperinflation, even though money supply is held rigid! (Output in this model is always expected to be in equilibrium.) While such an assertion may appeal to some, it has not impressed those who have espoused RE models; they have looked instead for additional restrictions.

We have already hinted at the source of an additional restriction in our model by noting the instability of all but one path. It is clear that the unstable paths are in some sense absurd. The question is: what would prevent them?

It has to be the case that behaviour would alter in such a way as to prevent them.

Consider for example the path of ever-accelerating hyperinflation anticipated fully now (on the basis of last period's information). People deciding how much money to hold for transactions would expect now that in so many years they will need truck-fulls of money to buy the daily groceries; they would therefore find an alternative means of carrying out transactions to avoid the investment in trucks they will otherwise anticipate. They will use beans or cows or sophisticated forms of barter to replace the old money. Ultimately the old money would not be used at all; prices will be defined in the new money, say, beans.

But money has an issuer; it may be a bank or a government. This issuer derives profits from people's use of their money issue, and it will pay them to avoid its replacement. This they can only do by stopping any such hyperinflation 'bubbles' occurring. It turns out that a commitment on their part to put an end to any such inflation at *some* point, by decreasing the money supply at a sufficient rate to offset any decline in real money balances held, will do the trick.

For if people expect that inflation will stop at some period $t + N$ (at which the bank will 'step in'), then this implies an arresting of the very ongoing process that sustains the earlier path. Real money balances demanded in $t + N$ will be higher than anticipated in that path, so inflation must be lower in $t + N$. But if so, then real money balances in $t + N - 1$ will be similarly higher, so also inflation then; and so on. The whole path will be invalidated.

In fact we can show this formally by imposing on the difference equation (2.27) the condition that:

$$p^e_{+i} - p^e_{+i-1} = 0 \quad (i \geqslant N + 1) \tag{2.29}$$

and letting (2.27) run from $N \leqslant i \geqslant 0$, since $t + N$ is the period when the bank's new regime takes over. Using (2.27) for $i = N$, we have:

$$\bar{m} - y^* = p^e_{+N} + \alpha(p^e_{+N} - p^e_{+N+1}) = \text{by (2.29)} \ p^e_{+N} \tag{2.30}$$

By (2.28) this implies:

$$\bar{m} - y^* = \bar{m} - y^* + [p^e_0 - (\bar{m} - y^*)]\left(\frac{1 + \alpha}{\alpha}\right)^N \tag{2.31}$$

or:

$$p^e_0 = (\bar{m} - y^*) \tag{2.32}$$

It can be seen that (2.32) selects the unique stable path for p^e_{+i} so that:

$$p^e_{+i} = \bar{m} - y^* \quad (i \geqslant 0) \tag{2.33}$$

An analogous argument can be constructed for the path of ever-deepening hyperdeflation. In this case people will 'demand' infinite amounts of money because its return is infinite in the long term. The bank or government will have an incentive to issue money until the profit rate on the issue has returned to a normal level, i.e. the rate of deflation is zero. The knowledge that the issuer will go on issuing money until this occurs acts to impose the same condition (2.29) on the model.

We have constructed verbal arguments to justify the imposition of a 'terminal condition' such as (2.29) in our model. These arguments appeal to forces not explicitly in the model, but which would be brought into play by certain types of behaviour apparently allowed for by the model. These forces will differ from model to model; for example we may appeal to legal controls or supervisory agencies to ensure 'orderly markets', or to competitive forces[1], or to precepts upon government itself. But an RE model with expectations of the future (REFV model) is incomplete without some forces of this kind to supply additional restrictions, such as our terminal condition here.

Our terminal condition (2.29) has the effect in the model here of selecting the unique stable path. For REFV models with such a unique stable path (i.e. with the 'saddlepath' property, so called because any deviation from this path is unstable), the imposition of terminal stationarity as here on the expectations ensures the selection of this path. For such models, it is therefore only necessary to specify as a side-condition on the model that the solutions be stable or stationary; this condition is referred to variously in the literature as the 'stability' or 'stationarity' or 'convergence' condition, or 'ruling out speculative bubbles' or 'boundedness'. With other REFV models (i.e. without a unique stable path) this condition is either inadequate or over-strong and solution requires careful specification of the terminal conditions on the model. We revert to this issue, the 'uniqueness' problem, below.

Armed with our solution for p^e_{+i} in (2.33), we have now completed step (2) in our solution procedure, albeit in a more complex manner than before; call it step (2'). We proceed to step (3) and substitute for $\underset{-1}{E} p$, $\underset{-1}{E} p_{+1}$ into (2.23). It turns out in fact in this model that the solution is the same as for our earlier model, as the reader can easily verify.

We may now review our basic method for solving REFV models.

(1) Solve the model, treating expectations as exogenous.
(2') Take the expected value of the equations at the date of the expectations. If the model generates a unique stable path for the expectational variables, impose the stability condition, and derive this solution for the expectations.
(3) Substitute the expectations solutions into the solution in (1) and obtain the complete solution.

OTHER METHODS OF SOLUTION FOR REFV MODELS

Not surprisingly there are several other methods for finding the unique stable solution to an REFV model which has one.

We shall explain three in detail because they have been widely used; the Sargent method of forward substitution, the Muth method of undetermined coefficients, and the Lucas method of undetermined coefficients.

Sargent Method

The Sargent method, so called here because it has been used repeatedly by Thomas Sargent of the University of Minnesota in his RE work, uses step (1) as above, obtaining (2.23). It continues as in step (2′) to take expectations at $t - 1$, obtaining (2.24). Lead this one period to obtain (2.25) but write this as:

$$\mathop{E}_{-1} p_{+1} = \left(\frac{1}{1 + \alpha}\right)(\bar{m} - y^*) + \left(\frac{\alpha}{1 + \alpha}\right) \mathop{E}_{-1} p_{+2} \quad (2.25)$$

Substitute successively (forwards) for $\mathop{E}_{-1} p_{+2}, \mathop{E}_{-1} p_{+3},$ in (2.25) to obtain:

$$\mathop{E}_{-1} p_{+1} = \frac{1}{1 + \alpha} \sum_{i=0}^{N-1} \left(\frac{\alpha}{1 + \alpha}\right)^i (\bar{m} - y^*)$$

$$+ \left(\frac{\alpha}{1 + \alpha}\right)^N \mathop{E}_{-1} p_{+N+1} \quad (2.34)$$

Let $N \to \infty$ and apply the stability condition to $\mathop{E}_{-1} p_{+i}$, so that $\mathop{E}_{-1} p_{+N+1} \to 0$, as $N \to \infty$. Since $[\alpha/(1 + \alpha)]^N \to 0$ also as $N \to \infty$, (2.34) becomes:

$$\mathop{E}_{-1} p_{+1} = \frac{1}{1 + \alpha} \sum_{i=0}^{\infty} \left(\frac{\alpha}{1 + \alpha}\right)^i (\bar{m} - y^*) = \bar{m} - y^* \quad (2.35)$$

By the same argument but starting from (2.24), $\mathop{E}_{-1} p = \bar{m} - y^*$ also. We have therefore reached the same result as in step (2′) and proceed to step (3) as in the basic method.

The Sargent method is more difficult to apply in models where the exogenous variables are not constant as here and where there are lagged endogenous variables. Sargent has evolved techniques using the forward operator (the inverse of the standard backward, or lag, operator) to deal with these models; we will briefly explain these below.

The Muth Method of Undetermined Coefficients

The Muth method starts from the proposition that the general solution of our model can be written:

$$p = \bar{p} + \sum_{i=0}^{\infty} \pi_i \varepsilon_{-i} \qquad (2.36)$$

$$y = \bar{y} + \sum_{i=0}^{\infty} \phi_i \varepsilon_{-i} \qquad (2.37)$$

where $\bar{p}$, $\bar{y}$ are the equilibrium values of p, y.

Let us focus on the solution for p, since that for y follows easily enough. $\bar{y} = y^*$ and $\bar{p} = \bar{m} - y^*$ by setting $\underset{-1}{E} p = \underset{-1}{E} p_{+1} = p = \bar{p}$ and $y = \bar{y}$ in the model.

Having found the equilibrium in terms of the constants, we now drop these from the model and define (p, y) in deviations from equilibrium. The model can now be written in terms of p as:

$$\varepsilon = \left(1 + \frac{1}{\delta}\right)p + \left(\alpha - \frac{1}{\delta}\right) \underset{-1}{E} p - \alpha \underset{-1}{E} p_{+1} \qquad (2.38)$$

Using (2.36),

$$p = \sum_{i=0}^{\infty} \pi_i \varepsilon_{-i} \qquad (2.39)$$

$$\underset{-1}{E} p = \sum_{i=1}^{\infty} \pi_i \varepsilon_{-i} \qquad (2.40)$$

$$p_{+1} = \sum_{i=0}^{\infty} \pi_i \varepsilon_{-i+1} = \sum_{i=-1}^{\infty} \pi_{i+1} \varepsilon_{-i} \qquad (2.41)$$

$$\underset{-1}{E} p_{+1} = \sum_{i=1}^{\infty} \pi_{i+1} \varepsilon_{-i} \qquad (2.42)$$

(2.40) and (2.42) follow from (2.39) and (2.41) respectively because $\underset{-1}{E} \varepsilon = \underset{-1}{E} \varepsilon_{+1} = 0$.

Substituting (2.39)–(2.42) into (2.38):

$$\varepsilon - \left(1 + \frac{1}{\delta}\right) \sum_{i=0}^{\infty} \pi_i \varepsilon_{-i} - \left(\alpha - \frac{1}{\delta}\right) \sum_{i=1}^{\infty} \pi_i \varepsilon_{-i}$$

$$+ \alpha \sum_{i=1}^{\infty} \pi_{i+1} \varepsilon_{-i} = 0 \quad (2.43)$$

Each ε_i can be any number so that (2.43) can hold if, and only if, the set of coefficients on ε, on ε_{-1}, on ε_{-2}, ..., each individually sums to zero. These sets then must satisfy:

(on ε) $\qquad\qquad 1 - \left(1 + \frac{1}{\delta}\right)\pi_0 = 0 \qquad\qquad (2.44)$

(on ε_{-i}, $i \geqslant 1$) $\quad -(1 + \alpha)\pi_i + \alpha\pi_{i+1} = 0 \qquad (2.45)$

Equation (2.45) is a homogeneous difference equation in π_i with the same root as (2.27) above, and an analogous solution:

$$\pi_i = \pi_1 \left(\frac{1 + \alpha}{\alpha}\right)^{i-1} \quad (i \geqslant 1) \qquad (2.46)$$

In (2.46) again we see that there are an infinity of solutions chosen here by selecting π_1 arbitrarily, and that only one is stable, namely that where $\pi_1 = 0$.

Invoking the stability condition we set $\pi_1 = 0$, so that $\pi_i = 0$ $(i \geqslant 1)$.

From (2.44) we obtain $\pi_0 = \delta/(1 + \delta)$. Our solution for p is therefore:

$$p = \bar{m} - y^* + \left(\frac{\delta}{1 + \delta}\right)\varepsilon \qquad (2.47)$$

as before.

The Muth method becomes unwieldy for larger models where there are several errors like ε, for each of which a sequence of coefficients must be determined, but it is often convenient for small illustrative models, and we will use it frequently for this purpose.

Lucas Method of Undetermined Coefficients

A variant of the Muth method of undetermined coefficients has occasionally been used – e.g. Barro (1976), Lucas (1972a)

– whereby the solution for the endogenous variables, instead of being written in terms of the constants and the errors, is written in terms of the 'state' variables, i.e. current and past values of the exogenous variables (including the error terms of the model equations) and past values of the endogenous variables. The need to include all the state variables can make this method unnecessarily complicated, as the example of this model shows.

Write the solution for p (on which we focus) as:

$$p = \pi_1 \varepsilon + \pi_2 p_{-1} + \pi_3 y_{-1} + \pi_4 \varepsilon_{-1} + \pi_5 \bar{m} + \pi_6 y^* \quad (2.36)^L$$

We have:

$$\bar{m} + \varepsilon = p + \frac{1}{\delta}\left(p - \mathop{E}_{-1} p\right) + y^* - \alpha\left(\mathop{E}_{-1} p_{+1} - \mathop{E}_{-1} p\right)$$

$$(2.23)$$

Use $(2.36)^L$ to generate $\mathop{E}_{-1} p$, $\mathop{E}_{-1} p_{+1}$ and substitute for these and p in (2.23), obtaining:

$$\bar{m} + \varepsilon = \pi_1 \varepsilon + \pi_2 p_{-1} + \pi_3 y_{-1} + \pi_4 \varepsilon_{-1} + \pi_5 \bar{m} + \pi_6 y^*$$

$$+ \frac{1}{\delta}(\pi_1 \varepsilon) + y^* - \alpha[(\pi_2 - 1)(\pi_2 p_{-1} + \pi_3 y_{-1} + \pi_4 \varepsilon_{-1}$$

$$+ \pi_5 \bar{m} + \pi_6 y^*) + \pi_3 y^* + \pi_5 \bar{m} + \pi_6 y^*] \quad (2.38)^L$$

We used $\mathop{E}_{-1} y = y^*$ in this, from the Phillips curve. Now

by the same argument as with the Muth method, the terms in each of the state variables must equate. So we have:

(terms in ε) $\qquad 1 = \pi_1 + \frac{1}{\delta}\pi_1,$

yielding $\qquad\qquad \pi_1 = \dfrac{1}{1 + 1/\delta} = \dfrac{\delta}{1 + \delta}$

(terms in p_{-1}) $\quad 0 = \pi_2 - \alpha(\pi_2 - 1)\pi_2 = \pi_2(1 + \alpha) - \alpha\pi_2^2,$

from which there are two solutions for $\pi_2 = 0$, $(1 + \alpha)/\alpha$. Of these, $(1 + \alpha)/\alpha$ violates the stability condition and is ruled out, leaving $\pi_2 = 0$.

(terms in y_{-1}) $\quad 0 = \pi_3 - \alpha(\pi_2 - 1)\pi_3$, implying $\pi_3 = 0$

(terms in ε_{-1}) $\quad 0 = \pi_4 - \alpha(\pi_2 - 1)\pi_4$, implying $\pi_4 = 0$

Given these solutions, the terms in $\bar{m}$ and y^* yield $\pi_5 = 1$, $\pi_6 = -1$. Hence we have obtained, if by a somewhat round-about route, the solution for p; that for y follows simply using the Phillips curve.

Clearly the method of solution is a matter purely of convenience. We have discussed four, all of which have been extensively used according to the problem and tastes of the problem-solver. All have their advantages and disadvantages and are worth the reader's while to understand. We now turn to an important problem which may arise in the solution of REFV models.

THE UNIQUENESS PROBLEM

We may illustrate this problem by supposing that for some reason α in our model is negative and < -0.5. Suppose for example that there is a rigid relationship of money to average transactions in a period; and that precautionary transactions demand is positively related to the rate of inflation, because of the irregularity of price changes and the correlation between the size of these changes when they occur and the inflation rate (e.g. I go to the doctor and find he has *just* put up his price by 30 per cent). This is implausible but not impossible. Otherwise, the model is as on p. 21.

Using our basic adjusted method we obtain the solution for p^e_{+i} in (2.28):

$$p^e_{+i} = \bar{m} - y^* + [p^e_0 - (m - y^*)]\left(\frac{1 + \alpha}{\alpha}\right)^i \quad (i \geqslant 0) \quad (2.28)$$

Previously we used the stability condition to choose the unique stable path. However, now all the paths in (2.28) are stable because we have rigged it so that $|(1 + \alpha)/\alpha| < 1$. The stability condition is incapable of selecting a unique solution, therefore. This problem was first pointed out by Taylor (1977); and so far as we know there is nothing to rule out the possibility that REFV macroeconomic models will have an infinity of stable paths.

There is no generally agreed procedure among those using REFV models for this problem, other than to avoid using the ones with this property. One solution has, however, been suggested by Minford, Matthews and Marwaha (1979). Suppose that, instead of the stability condition, the original terminal condition (2.29) is imposed:

$$p^e_{+i} - p^e_{+i-1} = 0 \quad (i \geqslant N + 1) \tag{2.29}$$

This implies, as we saw earlier:

$$p^e_0 = \bar{m} - y^* \tag{2.32}$$

This selects, out of the infinity of the stable paths, the unique path closest to equilibrium (in this case this path is always at equilibrium) – a result much in the spirit of a suggestion by Taylor (1977) that the least variance path will be selected by 'collective rationality'.

We argued earlier that the stability condition was justified by the terminal conditions imposed by forces outside the model (whether social or governmental or competitive or whatever); these forces were argued to be unleashed if the model got off track in some way. If the model is unstable, then it is not hard to see why such forces would come into play. It may perhaps appear harder to justify that they would do so if the model is globally stable and merely has a non-unique solution.

Yet upon consideration it is equally justifiable. Non-uniqueness must cause quite as serious problems as instability. For the endogenous variables may in each period jump by unpredictably large (unbounded) amounts; even though they will subsequently be expected to return to equilibrium, in all subsequent periods there will be shocks with infinite variance. Such uncertainty would be likely to provoke changes in behaviour sufficient to create an incentive for the money-issuer to make a commitment such as is set out in the terminal condition. This commitment would then limit the uncertainty, as we have seen, to that associated with the 'most stable' path.[2]

THE TECHNIQUES IN APPLICATION — A MORE
COMPLICATED EXAMPLE[3]

We now cease to develop the argument. Instead we use a slightly more elaborate REFV model (with a unique stable solution) to illustrate further the *application* of these solution methods.

We retain our Cagan-type money demand equation but date the expectations at t for convenience in the money market. We retain too our simple money supply equation (2.9); but we allow for adjustment costs in the response of output to unexpected price changes (our Phillips curve).

So now we have a new model:

$$m = p + y - \alpha(\mathsf{E}p_{+1} - p) \quad (\alpha > 0) \tag{2.48}$$

$$y - y^* = \frac{1}{\delta}\left(p - \underset{-1}{\mathsf{E}}\, p\right) + \lambda(y - y^*)_{-1}$$

$$= \frac{1}{\delta}\frac{\left(p - \underset{-1}{\mathsf{E}}\, p\right)}{1 - \lambda L} \tag{2.49}$$

$$m = \bar{m} + \varepsilon \tag{2.9}$$

where we have used the backward lag operator, L, in the second expression of (2.49) to facilitate our subsequent operations.

Basic Method

Let us apply our basic method, focusing on the solution for p. Step (1) gives, substituting for (2.49) and (2.9) into (2.48):

$$\bar{m} + \varepsilon = (1 + \alpha)p + y^* + \frac{1}{\delta}\frac{\left(p - \underset{-1}{\mathsf{E}}\, p\right)}{1 - \lambda L} - \alpha\, \mathsf{E}p_{+1} \tag{2.50}$$

Rearranging and multiplying through by $(1 - \lambda L)$ yields:

$$(\bar{m} - y^*)(1 - \lambda) + \varepsilon - \lambda\varepsilon_{-1} = -\alpha \, \mathrm{E}p_{+1} + \left(1 + \alpha + \frac{1}{\delta}\right)p$$

$$+ \left(\alpha\lambda - \frac{1}{\delta}\right) \mathop{\mathrm{E}}_{-1} p - (\lambda + \alpha\lambda)p_{-1} \quad (2.51)$$

Notice that the lag of $\mathrm{E}p_{+1}$ is $\mathop{\mathrm{E}}\limits_{-1} p$ $\Big($not, for example, p or

$\mathop{\mathrm{E}}\limits_{-1} p_{+1}\Big)$.

We now move to step $(2')$, where we must find $\mathrm{E}p_{+1}$ and $\mathop{\mathrm{E}}\limits_{-1} p$. Accordingly, first we take expectations at $t - 1$ to obtain:

$$(\bar{m} - y^*)(1 - \lambda) - \lambda\varepsilon_{-1} = -\alpha \mathop{\mathrm{E}}_{-1} p_{+1}$$

$$+ (1 + \alpha + \alpha\lambda) \mathop{\mathrm{E}}_{-1} p - (\lambda + \alpha\lambda)p_{-1} \quad (2.52)$$

and

$$(\bar{m} - y^*)(1 - \lambda) = -\alpha \mathop{\mathrm{E}}_{-1} p_{+i+1} + (1 + \alpha + \alpha\lambda) \mathop{\mathrm{E}}_{-1} p_{+i}$$

$$- (\lambda + \alpha\lambda) \mathop{\mathrm{E}}_{-1} p_{+i-1} \quad (i \geqslant 1) \quad (2.53)$$

The solution of (2.53) is:

$$\mathop{\mathrm{E}}_{-1} p_{+i} = (\bar{m} - y^*) + A\left(\frac{1 + \alpha}{\alpha}\right)^i + B\lambda^i \quad (i \geqslant 1) \quad (2.54)$$

where A and B are determined by the initial values $\mathop{\mathrm{E}}\limits_{-1} p_{+1}$, $\mathop{\mathrm{E}}\limits_{-1} p$. However, we have only one equation, (2.52), to determine both $\mathop{\mathrm{E}}\limits_{-1} p_{+1}$ and $\mathop{\mathrm{E}}\limits_{-1} p$, so that there is an infinity of paths, all but one unstable. This model therefore has the saddlepath property. Imposing the stability condition then sets $A = 0$, with the result that $B = \mathop{\mathrm{E}}\limits_{-1} p - (\bar{m} - y^*)$ so defining $\mathop{\mathrm{E}}\limits_{-1} p_{+1} = \bar{m} - y^* + \left[\mathop{\mathrm{E}}\limits_{-1} p - (m - y^*)\right]\lambda$. We can now use

(2.52) to solve for $\underset{-1}{\mathsf{E}}\, p$ as:

$$\underset{-1}{\mathsf{E}}\, p = (m - y^*)(1 - \lambda) - \frac{\lambda}{1 + \alpha}\, \varepsilon_{-1} + \lambda p_{-1} \qquad (2.55)$$

We can infer immediately from (2.55) that:

$$\mathsf{E}p_{+1} = (\bar{m} - y^*)(1 - \lambda) - \frac{\lambda}{1 + \alpha}\, \varepsilon + \lambda p \qquad (2.56)$$

This can be verified by leading (2.51) one period, taking expectations at t, and repeating the operations in (2.52)–(2.55) but advanced one period.

We have now completed step (2') and proceed to step (3), substituting $\underset{-1}{\mathsf{E}}\, p$ and $\mathsf{E}p_{+1}$ from (2.55) and (2.56) into (2.51), to obtain after collecting terms:

$$p = (\bar{m} - y^*)(1 - \lambda) - \frac{\lambda}{1 + \alpha}\, \varepsilon_{-1} + \lambda p_{-1}$$

$$+ \left[\frac{1 + \alpha - \alpha\lambda}{(1 + \alpha)\left(1 + \alpha - \alpha\lambda + \dfrac{1}{\delta}\right)} \right] \varepsilon \qquad (2.57)$$

Sargent Method

This parallels the basic method up to (2.53). Sargent now rewrites (2.53) as:

$$-\frac{1}{\alpha}(\bar{m} - y^*)(1 - \lambda) = \left[L^{-1} - \left(\frac{1 + \alpha}{\alpha} + \lambda \right) \right.$$

$$\left. + \left(\frac{1 + \alpha}{\alpha}\lambda \right) L \right] p^e_{+i}$$

$$= \left[1 - \left(\frac{1 + \alpha}{\alpha} + \lambda \right) L \right.$$

$$\left. + \frac{1 + \alpha}{\alpha}\lambda L^2 \right] L^{-1} p^e_{+i}$$

$$= \left(1 - \frac{1 + \alpha}{\alpha} L \right)(1 - \lambda L) L^{-1} p^e_{+i} \quad (i \geqslant 1)$$

$$(2.58)$$

where p^e_{+i} is defined as on p. 23 (i.e. p_{+i} as expected from $t-1$, where this expectation date is *not* altered by the lag operator). Now note that there is an expansion of

$$\left(\frac{1}{1-\gamma L}\right) = \left[\frac{-(\gamma L)^{-1}}{1-(\gamma L)^{-1}}\right]$$

$$= \frac{-1}{\gamma L}\left[1 + \frac{1}{\gamma}L^{-1} + \left(\frac{1}{\gamma}\right)^2 L^{-2} + \cdots\right]$$

(2.58) as it stands implies that p^e_{+i} will be unstable. However, we can conveniently use the alternative forward expansion of:

$$\frac{1}{1 - \frac{1+\alpha}{\alpha}L} = -\left[\left(\frac{1+\alpha}{\alpha}\right)L\right]^{-1}\bigg/1 - \left(\frac{1+\alpha}{\alpha}L\right)^{-1}$$

and write (2.58) as:

$$\frac{-1/\alpha(\bar{m} - y^*)(1 - \lambda)}{1 - \left(\frac{1+\alpha}{\alpha}L\right)^{-1}} = \frac{(1 - \lambda L)L^{-1}}{-\left(\frac{1+\alpha}{\alpha}L\right)^{-1}}p^e_{+i} \quad (i \geqslant 1)$$

$$(2.59)$$

Notice that if we impose stability, the left-hand side generates an infinite forward expansion

$$-\frac{1}{\alpha}(\bar{m} - y^*)(1 - \lambda)\left[1 + \frac{\alpha}{1+\alpha} + \left(\frac{\alpha}{1+\alpha}\right)^2 + \cdots\right],$$

which cancelling and re-arranging terms yields:

$$\mathop{E}_{-1} p_{+i} = p^e_{+i} = \lambda p^e_{+i-1} + (\bar{m} - y^*)(1 - \lambda) \quad (i \geqslant 1) \quad (2.60)$$

which yields the rest of our solution as before. In this infinite forward expansion there was a remainder term $[\alpha/(1+\alpha)]^N$ $\left(\mathop{E}_{-1} p_{+N+1} - \lambda \mathop{E}_{-1} p_{+N} \quad (N \to \infty)\right)$ which the stability condition forced to zero as $N \to \infty$.

The Sargent method thus represents a convenient extension of operator techniques to REFV models. Stable roots are projected backwards, i.e. kept in the form $1/(1 - \gamma L)$, unstable roots are projected forwards, i.e. transformed to $[-(\gamma L)^{-1}]/[1 - (\gamma L)^{-1}]$; this procedure, under the stability condition, gives us the same result as before, but in a very compact manner.

Muth Method

The Muth method is probably the easiest to apply for this model.

The general solution for p will be as before:

$$p = \bar{p} + \sum_{i=0}^{\infty} \pi_i \varepsilon_{-i} \qquad (2.61)$$

and it remains that:

$$\bar{p} = \bar{m} - y^*$$

We now substitute into (2.51) dropping constants to obtain the identities in the ε_{-i} from:

$$\varepsilon - \lambda \varepsilon_{-1} = -\alpha \sum_{i=0}^{\infty} \pi_{i+1} \varepsilon_{-i} + \left(1 + \alpha + \frac{1}{\delta}\right) \sum_{i=0}^{\infty} \pi_i \varepsilon_{-i}$$
$$+ \left(\alpha \lambda - \frac{1}{\delta}\right) \sum_{i=1}^{\infty} \pi_i \varepsilon_{-i} - (\lambda + \alpha \lambda) \sum_{i=1}^{\infty} \pi_{i-1} \varepsilon_{-i} \qquad (2.62)$$

The identities emerge as:

$$(\varepsilon)1 = -\alpha \pi_1 + \left(1 + \alpha + \frac{1}{\delta}\right) \pi_0 \qquad (2.63)$$

$$(\varepsilon_{-1}) - \lambda = -\alpha \pi_2 + (1 + \alpha + \alpha \lambda) \pi_1$$
$$- (\lambda + \alpha \lambda) \pi_0 \qquad (2.64)$$

$$(\varepsilon_{-i, \, i \geqslant 2})0 = -\alpha \pi_{i+1} + (1 + \alpha + \alpha \lambda) \pi_i$$
$$- (\lambda + \alpha \lambda) \pi_{i-1} \qquad (2.65)$$

Applying the stability condition to the solution of (2.65)

$$\pi_i = A \left(\frac{1 + \alpha}{\alpha}\right)^{i-1} + B \lambda^{i-1} \quad (i \geqslant 2) \qquad (2.66)$$

sets $A = 0$, so that:

$$\pi_i = \pi_1 \lambda^{i-1} \quad (i \geqslant 2) \tag{2.67}$$

Substituting this into (2.63) and (2.64) gives:

$$\pi_0 = \frac{1 + \alpha - \alpha\lambda}{(1 + \alpha)\left(1 + \alpha + \dfrac{1}{\delta} - \alpha\lambda\right)} \tag{2.68}$$

$$\pi_1 = \frac{-\lambda}{\delta(1 + \alpha)\left(1 + \alpha + \dfrac{1}{\delta} - \alpha\lambda\right)} \tag{2.69}$$

We can verify by expanding (2.57) that this is the solution arrived at previously.

In this model, non-uniqueness under the stability condition will occur if both $(1 + \alpha)/\alpha$ and λ are stable roots, i.e. if $\alpha < -0.5$. Here again, the terminal condition (2.29) will select the 'most stable' solution by, in effect, ruling out the root with the largest modulus.

If we insert (2.29) into (2.54), we obtain:

$$\frac{A}{B} = \left\{ \alpha(1 - \lambda)\left[\frac{\lambda}{\left(\dfrac{1 + \alpha}{\alpha}\right)} \right]^N \right\} \tag{2.70}$$

For larger N, then if $\lambda < |(1 + \alpha)/\alpha|$, A will be negligible and if $\lambda > |(1 + \alpha)/\alpha|$, B will be negligible. Hence powers of the root with the largest modulus will be multiplied by a negligible number.

In the case where the roots are stable and a complex pair, the terminal condition selects the *phase* of the oscillation in such a way that the cycle is at a stationary point at the terminal condition. It does not alter the damping factor or the amplitude of the oscillation. In this case the stable modulus is unique, the non-uniqueness merely applies to the phase: not perhaps so serious a problem.

OTHER ISSUES

The Case of Too Many Unstable Roots

We have set up the REFV models so far so that they have had a stable solution, whether unique or not. However, it is possible for an REFV model to have no stable solution. For example, in our original model, instead of placing the adjustment parameter in the Phillips curve, place it in the demand for money function, so that our model is:

$$m - p = (1 - \lambda)y - \alpha \left(\mathop{E}_{-1} p_{+1} - \mathop{E}_{-1} p \right)$$
$$+ \lambda(m - p)_{-1} \tag{2.71}$$

$$y = y^* + \frac{1}{\delta}\left(p - \mathop{E}_{-1} p \right) \tag{2.72}$$

$$m = \bar{m} + \varepsilon \tag{2.73}$$

This gives as an equation for p:

$$(\bar{m} - y^*)(1 - \lambda) + \varepsilon - \lambda\varepsilon_{-1} = p + \frac{1}{\delta}\left(p - \mathop{E}_{-1} p \right)$$
$$- \alpha\left(\mathop{E}_{-1} p_{+1} - \mathop{E}_{-1} p \right) - \lambda p_{-1} \tag{2.74}$$

Using the basic method, we take expectations at $t - 1$ to obtain:

$$(\bar{m} - y^*)(1 - \lambda) - \lambda\varepsilon_{-1} = -\alpha \mathop{E}_{-1} p_{+1} + (1 + \alpha) \mathop{E}_{-1} p$$
$$- \lambda p_{-1} \tag{2.75}$$

$$(\bar{m} - y^*)(1 - \lambda) = -\alpha \mathop{E}_{-1} p_{+i+1}$$
$$+ (1 + \alpha) \mathop{E}_{-1} p_{+i}$$
$$- \lambda \mathop{E}_{-1} p_{+i-1} \quad (i \geqslant 1) \tag{2.76}$$

The roots of (2.76) are

$$(\rho_1, \rho_2) = \frac{1 + \alpha}{2\alpha} \pm \sqrt{\left[\left(\frac{1 + \alpha}{2\alpha} \right)^2 - \frac{\lambda}{\alpha} \right]}$$

both of which may be unstable (e.g. $\alpha = -0.1$, $\lambda = -0.9$) in the general solution:

$$\underset{-1}{E} p_{+i} = \bar{m} - y^* + A\rho_1^i + B\rho_2^i \quad (i \geqslant 1) \qquad (2.77)$$

Suppose they are both unstable. The initial values are $\underset{-1}{E} p$, Ep_{+1}. If by the stability condition we set, say, $B = 0$, we have $A = \underset{-1}{E} p - (\bar{m} - y^*)$; but we must also set $A = 0$, hence $\underset{-1}{E} p = \bar{m} - y^*$. It follows that:

$$\underset{-1}{E} p_{+i} = \bar{m} - y^* \quad (i \geqslant 0) \qquad (2.78)$$

But this is impossible within this model. For substituting from (2.78) into (2.74) and into (2.75) yields respectively two incompatible solutions for p. Substituting into (2.74) we obtain:

$$p = \frac{\delta\lambda}{1 + \delta} p_{-1} + \frac{\delta}{1 + \delta} (\varepsilon - \lambda\varepsilon_{-1}) + \frac{\delta(1 - \lambda + 1/\delta)}{1 + \delta} (\bar{m} - y^*)$$

$$(2.79)$$

Substituting into (2.75) gives:

$$p_{-1} = \varepsilon_{-1} + (\bar{m} - y^*) \qquad (2.80)$$

and so (leading 2.80):

$$p = \varepsilon + (\bar{m} - y^*) \qquad (2.81)$$

which contradicts (2.79). There is therefore no feasible stable solution for the model when ρ_1 and ρ_2 are both unstable. The stability condition over-determines the model, by placing two restrictions on it ($A = B = 0$) when only one is required.

Does this imply then that REFV models cannot generate unstable behaviour? It might appear so. For, it seems, either we supply the stability condition – in which case only stable solutions are admitted or we do not – in which case there will not be a unique solution.

This again, like the uniqueness issue, is a question on which there is no agreed answer within the profession (other than to avoid REFV models which pose it). However, as Minford, Matthews and Marwaha (1981) have pointed out, if the original terminal condition (2.29) is used in place of the stability condition, then for an REFV model without a stable condition, a unique solution will exist. It will of course be unstable, but this does give content to the idea of an unstable REFV model.

For example, in this model insert (2.29) into (2.77), to obtain:

$$\frac{A}{B} = \left(\frac{\rho_2}{\rho_1}\right)^N \left(\frac{1 - \rho_2}{1 - \rho_1}\right) \tag{2.82}$$

For large N this will set A or B to a negligible value according to which root has largest modulus, in effect ruling out the one with the largest. Hence this condition selects the solution path which is the 'least unstable' in this sense. (If the unstable roots are complex the terminal condition selects the phase uniquely; the unique modulus of course remains unstable.)

One can visualize a world represented by this model and the terminal condition as one in which there is 'controlled instability'. The authorities (or other source of the terminal condition) intervene periodically to 'stop' the process; when it 'restarts', the instability resumes until the next stop. Whether such a world would continue for long without modifications that produced stability must be open to doubt. But it seems hard to assert its impossibility.

'Will o' the Wisp' Variables

It is possible to add arbitrary variables to the solutions of REFV models, provided they obey certain processes dictated by the coefficients in the model's future expectations (see, e.g., Canzoneri, 1981, and Gourieroux *et al.*, 1982).

For example, take the model of (2.22), (2.8), and (2.9) on page 21, our simplest Cagan model without lags. Suppose people believed at $t-1$, for no good reason, that prices would be affected by $(1 + \alpha/\alpha)^i \underset{-1}{\mathsf{E}} \, \xi_{+i}$ where:

$$\underset{-1}{\mathsf{E}} \, \xi_{+i} = \xi_{-1} \qquad (2.83)$$

(i.e. ξ is a martingale). Their belief, though 'irrational', would formally be validated by the model for:

$$p_{+i} = (\bar{m} - y^*) + \frac{\delta}{1+\delta} \, \varepsilon_{+i} + \left(\frac{1+\alpha}{\alpha}\right)^i \underset{-1}{\mathsf{E}} \, \xi_{+i} \qquad (2.84)$$

is a solution to the model, as can be verified by substituting (2.84) and (2.83) into (2.23). Any 'will o' the wisp' variable, ξ, could therefore produce an irrational solution to an REFV model by this self-validating process.

This is simply an implication of the indeterminacy of p_0^e we noted earlier; so we can write $p_0^e - (\bar{m} - y^*) = \xi_{-1}$ where ξ_{-1} is *anything*. However, the solution to this 'will o' the wisp' problem is one and the same as that of the indeterminacy problem: we have to impose an additional restriction on the model to ensure determinacy.

Hence in this model we notice that $[(1 + \alpha)/\alpha]^i \underset{-1}{\mathsf{E}} \, \xi_{+i}$ is an unstable process. So the stability condition rules it out. This objection does not rule it out in the generality of models. For example, suppose in the above $\alpha < -0.5$ then $[(1 + \alpha)/\alpha]^i \underset{-1}{\mathsf{E}} \, \xi_{+i}$ would be stable. However, the terminal condition in this non-uniqueness case does rule out ξ_{-1}, though as we have seen this remains a controversial solution. Alternatively, some other restriction (such as that suggested by Peel, 1981; Taylor, 1977; or McCallum, 1983) would do the job.

CONCLUSIONS

This has been a chapter designed to equip the reader with the technique to solve rational expectations models in a manner useful for applied work.[4] We have shown how to use four main methods of solution: a 'basic' method, the Sargent forward operator method, and the Muth and Lucas undetermined coefficients methods. We have also discussed the criterion for choosing a unique solution in these models, free of extraneous or 'will o' the wisp' variables. The criterion we propose, namely that terminal conditions are imposed on the model either by the authorities or some other outside force, is not fully accepted by all practitioners. Nevertheless, whatever criterion is used, the practical effect in the macroeconomic models likely to be encountered by applied macroeconomists will usually be the same as that of our criterion, namely to select the 'most stable' path (i.e. the roots with smallest modulus) and one free of extraneous variables; in practice, too, most computer-based solution methods use terminal conditions (this is discussed further in Chapter 11). In many models to be encountered, there will be a unique stable path, which will in principle be the one selected on any of the criteria that have been proposed. The practitioner therefore will be almost invariably on safe ground if he uses the methodology described here.

NOTES

1. For example, in the competitive equilibrium model of the labour market of Lucas and Sargent, as set out e.g. in Sargent (1979a, Ch. 16) the transversality conditions of households and firms supply the necessary terminal conditions. These conditions are necessary for optimality; in other words, explosive paths for labour supply and demand are not followed by households or firms because they are sub-optimal.
2. There have been other suggestions, like Taylor's, as to how society would select such a path. Peel (1981) argues that the monetary authorities will select a feedback rule generating uniqueness; however, it is not clear they do select such rules in practice. McCallum (1983) argues that the solution chosen, when framed according to the Lucas undetermined coefficients method, will contain only the minimum set of state variables; the rationale for this apparently arbitrary procedure, however, is obscure.
3. This section contains advanced material which may be skipped.
4. There are a number of descriptions of solution methods available in the literature; see, e.g., Shiller (1978) and, perhaps the most useful, Aoki and Canzoneri (1979).

3

Stabilization Policy

In this chapter we will outline the implications for stabilization policy if agents in an economy form their expectations rationally. It is of course necessary to define stabilization policies. Typically these are defined as policies which are aimed at reducing deviations (the variance usually) of output and employment from their full-employment ('natural or equilibrium') levels. We will initially use this definition.

Stabilization policies are usefully classified into two groups, namely fixed or flexible rules. Fixed rules are rules without feedback. These rules are more technically called open-loop rules. Flexible rules are rules with feedback or rules which are contingent on certain outcomes in the economy. These types of stabilization policies are called closed-loop rules (for the obvious reason that the additional 'loop' from events back to policy is 'closed'). With open-loop policies the future paths of a government's policy instruments are specified at the beginning of the policy planning period, and are invariant to any information which becomes available in future periods. Perhaps the best known example of an open-loop policy is Milton Friedman's proposal that the authorities should adopt a policy of a fixed rate of expansion of the nominal money stock (Friedman, 1968). In contrast, closed-loop policies are policies in which government policy instruments, such as the money stock, will respond over the planning period, perhaps in a pre-specified manner, to information that accrues to the policy maker over the planning period. One simple example of a closed-loop policy would be one in which the money stock deviates around some target

44

level as the rate of unemployment, U, deviates from the equilibrium or natural rate, U^N:

$$m = \bar{m} + \lambda(U_{-1} - U^N) \qquad (3.1)$$

There is clearly an interesting academic debate as to the relative merits of closed-loop rules *versus* open-loop rules or what is more often called the 'rules versus discretion' debate. We will return to this issue in Chapter 5. However, first it is necessary to outline the impact of stabilization policies in models which incorporate rational expectations.

MODELS WITH THE SARGENT–WALLACE SUPPLY CURVE

An early viewpoint, derived principally from the work of Lucas (1972b) and Sargent and Wallace (1975), is that stabilization policy has no impact on either real output or unemployment in classical equilibrium models if they embody a supply function relating deviations of output to surprise movements in the price level, and further that (a) both private and public agents have identical information sets and (b) are able to act on these information sets. It is worthwhile to illustrate these points formally; they were discussed briefly in Chapter 2 in the context of a simple monetary model, which we now extend somewhat.

Consider the following simple model:

$$y = -\alpha\left(R - \underset{-1}{E}\, p_{+1} + \underset{-1}{E}\, p\right) + \rho_f(y_{-1} - y^*) \qquad (3.2)$$

$$y = y^* + \beta\left(p - \underset{-1}{E}\, p\right) \qquad (3.3)$$

$$m = p + y - cR + v \qquad (3.4)$$

$$m = \bar{m} + \rho_\mu(y_{-1} - y^*) + u \qquad (3.5)$$

α, β, ρ_f, ρ_μ and c are constants (ρ_f, ρ_μ would typically be negative in Keynesian policy rules), u and v are random errors, R is the nominal interest rate.

Equation (3.2) is the aggregate demand schedule; it includes a fiscal feedback response, $\rho_f(y_{-1} - y^*)$, representing government counter-cyclical variations in spending or tax rates.

Equation (3.3) is the Sargent–Wallace supply curve. In this hypothesis supply decisions are taken on the basis of relative prices. The supplier's decision to increase or decrease production relative to normal levels is taken on the basis of the extent to which the price he receives has risen (or fallen) relative to the extent to which prices in general have risen (or fallen). Whilst the supplier is aware of the current value of his own price, it is assumed that information about the general level of prices is not available in the current period. Consequently the supplier has to form an estimate of the current aggregate price level on the basis of prior information (in this case assumed to be last period's data). On aggregating over firms we obtain an aggregate supply curve of the form (3.3).

It is of interest to note that rearrangement of (3.3) gives us:

$$p - p_{-1} = \frac{1}{\beta}(y - y^*) + \mathop{E}_{-1} p - p_{-1} \qquad (3.6)$$

which has of course the form of an 'augmented Phillips curve'. While it is the usual practice – which we follow – to call, (3.3) or (3.6) interchangeably, either a Sargent–Wallace supply curve or a Phillips curve, there is a sense in which this is misleading. We show in Chapter 6 that the standard Phillips curve, as derived from a disequilibrium framework, needs careful reinterpretation under rational expectations and will generally not have the form (3.6).

Equation (3.5) is a money supply rule with a feedback response, $\rho_\mu(y_{-1} - y^*)$. Clearly, putting $\rho_\mu = 0$, it becomes an open-loop policy. On substituting (3.2) for R into (3.4) and equating (3.5) to the result, we obtain:

$$\bar{m} + \rho(y_{-1} - y^*) + w = p + (1 + c/\alpha)y - c\left(\mathop{E}_{-1} p_{+1} - \mathop{E}_{-1} p \right)$$

$$(3.7)$$

where $w = u - v$ and $\rho = [\rho_f(c/\alpha) + \rho_\mu]$. Substitution of (3.3) into (3.7) for y and y_{-1} yields:

$$\bar{m} + \beta\rho\left(p_{-1} - \underset{-2}{\mathrm{E}}\, p_{-1}\right) + w = p + (1 + c/\alpha)\beta\left(p - \underset{-1}{\mathrm{E}}\, p\right)$$

$$- c\left(\underset{-1}{\mathrm{E}}\, p_{+1} - \underset{-1}{\mathrm{E}}\, p\right) + (1 + c/\alpha)y^* \quad (3.8)$$

To solve (3.8) for prices, we use the Muth solution method discussed in Chapter 2, writing:

$$p = \bar{p} + \sum_{i=0}^{\infty} \pi_i w_{-i} \quad (3.9)$$

We find that the identities yield:

$$\bar{p} = \bar{m} - (1 + c/\alpha)y^* \quad (3.10)$$

(terms in w) $\qquad 1 = (\pi_0)[1 + \beta(1 + c/\alpha)] \quad (3.11)$

The identities in the other errors are irrelevant for our purposes here. Since

$$p - \underset{-1}{\mathrm{E}}\, p = \pi_0 w \quad (3.12)$$

substitution in (3.3) yields

$$y = y^* + \beta\pi_0 w \quad (3.13)$$

From (3.11) we see that π_0 does not depend on either ρ_μ or ρ_f and consequently we see from (3.13) that systematic monetary policy does not influence the variance of output in this model. Unanticipated monetary change is of course equal to $m - \underset{-1}{\mathrm{E}}\, m$. Since $\underset{-1}{\mathrm{E}}\, m = \bar{m} + \rho_\mu(y_{-1} - y^*)$

$$m - \underset{-1}{\mathrm{E}}\, m = u \quad (3.14)$$

which is a component of w. Consequently *unanticipated* monetary policy does influence output in the Sargent–Wallace model but not anticipated monetary policy.

This result stems from the nature of the supply curve. Output is set by supply considerations (relative prices, technology, producers' preferences, etc.) and is only influenced by macroeconomic events if these cause surprise movements in absolute prices which in turn are partially (mis)interpreted as relative price movements. Government by definition cannot plan surprises; its feedback responses are *planned* variations in net spending or money supply.

A basic extension of the result occurs if there are adjustment costs in supply; allowance for these in a standard way (e.g. a quadratic cost function) adds a term $+\lambda(y_{-1} - y^*)$ to (3.3) $(0 < \lambda < 1)$. A shock to output now persists, and in principle the business cycle in output can be accounted for by the interaction of a variety of shocks with such a 'persistence mechanism'. (Various forms of it have been suggested by Lucas, 1975; Sargent, 1976a; Fischer, 1980a; and Barro, 1980.)

However, even though a macroeconomic shock now affects output for the indefinite future, it is still impossible for fiscal or monetary feedback rules to affect its variance because they can neither affect the impact of the shock itself, being a surprise, nor alter the adjustment parameter(s) which determine the lagged effects, these parameters being fixed by technology, etc. We leave the demonstration of this – by substituting for y and y_{-1} in (3.8) from the new supply curve in (3.3) – as an exercise for the reader.

DIFFERENT INFORMATION SETS

It is crucial for this neutrality proposition that, even in a model embodying a Sargent–Wallace supply curve, both private and public agents have the same information set.

If, for example, the government has an information superiority, then it can use this to modify the 'surprise' faced by the private sector. For suppose private agents have access only to last period's data in the current period, but the government knows the true price level (assume it collects price statistics over the period and waits before releasing them). Then it may in principle let its net spending or the money supply react to this information; its reaction will modify the price surprises to suppliers. Formally, add $-a_f\left(p - \underset{-1}{E} p\right)$ into (3.2) and $-a_\mu\left(p - \underset{-1}{E} p\right)$ into (3.5) where a_f, a_μ (both positive) are fiscal and monetary responses respectively. To simplify matters set $\rho_\mu = \rho_f = 0$. (3.9) now becomes:

$$\bar{m} - \left(a_\mu + \frac{ca_f}{\alpha}\right)\left(p - \underset{-1}{\text{E}}\, p\right) + w = p + (1 + c/\alpha)\beta\left(p - \underset{-1}{\text{E}}\, p\right)$$

$$- c\left(\underset{-1}{\text{E}}\, p_{+1} - \underset{-1}{\text{E}}\, p\right) + (1 + c/\alpha)y^* \quad (3.15)$$

so that from the terms in w we have:

$$\pi_0 = [1 + (1 + c/\alpha)\beta + a_\mu + ca_f/\alpha]^{-1} \quad (3.16)$$

from which is apparent that the higher a_μ, a_f the smaller the price surprise and hence the output variance.

One may ask, however, why a government in possession of macro information should not release it rapidly as an alternative to implementing such (presumably costly) rules. If it did so, private agents would be able to make better informed judgments about current macroeconomic events. The result is discussed in the next chapter, where it is shown that such government responses then become ineffective.

A further information asymmetry, which may violate neutrality and has had some attention (Turnovsky, 1980; Weiss, 1980; and King, 1982) is that where one group of private agents has superior information to that possessed both by suppliers and by the government.

The simplest method of illustrating this possibility is to modify the aggregate demand schedule (3.2) in the above model to:

$$y = -\alpha(R - \text{E}p_{+1} + p) \quad (3.17)$$

The interpretation of this aggregate demand schedule (3.17) is that investors have instantaneous access to current information on all relevant macro data while other agents such as the government or suppliers of goods receive this information with a one-period lag.

This is the example used by Turnovsky (1980). While the particular example used by Turnovsky is perhaps somewhat strained, the salient point he makes regarding the efficacy of stabilization policy is applicable in any macro model embodying a Sargent–Wallace supply curve in which the expectation of any future variable, such as the exchange rate or interest rate, is conditioned by an information set dated at time t. In defence of this, it is argued that agents in regular contact with asset markets receive global information (such as interest rates and asset prices) almost instantaneously, by contrast with those in the labour market.

Substitution of (3.17) into our model in place of (3.2) yields the following reduced form:

$$\bar{m} + \rho\beta\left(p_{-1} - \underset{-2}{\mathrm{E}}\, p_{-1}\right) + w = (1 + c)p$$

$$+ (1 + c/\alpha)\beta\left(p - \underset{-1}{\mathrm{E}}\, p\right) - c\mathrm{E}p_{+1} + (1 + c/\alpha)y^* \quad (3.18)$$

where $\rho = (\rho_\mu + \rho_f\, c/\alpha)$ as before.

Using the Muth solution the identities are given by:

$$\bar{p} = \bar{m} - (1 + c/\alpha)y^* \qquad (3.19)$$

(terms in w)

$$1 = \pi_0(1 + c + \beta(1 + c/\alpha)) - c\pi_1 \qquad (3.20)$$

(terms in w_{-1})

$$\rho\beta\pi_0 = \pi_1(1 + c) - c\pi_2 \qquad (3.21)$$

(terms in $w_{-i}, i \geqslant 2$)

$$0 = \pi_i(1 + c) - c\pi_{i+1} \qquad (3.22)$$

Equation (3.22) defines an unstable process. Consequently applying the stability condition, we set $\pi_i = 0$ ($i \geqslant 2$). Therefore we can simultaneously solve (3.19) and (3.20) to obtain π_0 and π_1. The important point is that π_0, the coefficient on the current innovation, will depend on ρ. Consequently the variance of output depends on the feedback rules.

The basis of this result is that the agents in the goods market with superior information demand goods this period in reaction to expected future prices because these affect the real interest rate they expect to pay. Even though expected future *output* is invariant to the feedback rule, expected future prices are not in these models – clearly not, since the *demand* for output is affected by feedback and this in turn has to be equated with given output supply by prices and interest rates. So current demand for goods is affected by the feedback parameters via their effect on expected future prices; and the response of goods demand, so of prices and so of output, to shocks is correspondingly modified. The government can thus exploit these agents' information without itself having access to it. The model just used makes the stronger assumption that they know *all* current macro data (this is implicit in taking expectations based on current period data), which is clearly implausible. Nevertheless, the same non-neutrality result occurs when these agents have superior *partial* information (King, 1982). The essential point in the result is the information superiority of one group of agents whose actions depend on expected future prices.

This second asymmetry result is, however, subject to questioning of a similar type: namely, the basis for the restriction of such macroeconomic information to one set of agents. The case for microeconomic information on individual markets being so restricted seems more secure, though this is communicable through asset prices. But macroeconomic information, once available, is a public good which, first, it is usual for the government to insist be made available at low cost; second, even if not so provided, it would pay the possessors to divulge it for a fee to other agents, since this maximizes the overall possibilities for its exploitation; third, asset prices themselves will communicate this information indirectly to other agents. In short, the set-up is highly implausible.

AUTOMATIC STABILIZERS

The next question we consider is whether automatic stabilizers influence the variance of output in models embodying a Sargent–Wallace supply hypothesis and with identical information sets for public and private agents. By automatic stabilizer we mean a mechanism in which, for instance, tax liabilities respond to current income levels, and therefore provide automatic and immediate adjustments to current disturbances.

This is to be distinguished from policy actions in response to global information, such as we have been considering hitherto; 'automatic' implies that the response is effected at the microeconomic level, without recourse to macroeconomic information or to higher political authority. Tax liabilities, when tax rates are set, are of this sort; only the taxpayer, his income and the tax man are involved. In the monetary area, certain open market procedures – such as pegging Central Bank liabilities by Treasury bill sales – also fall into this category. The work of Poole (1970) on monetary policy in a closed economy and of Parkin (1978) on monetary and exchange rate intervention in an open economy can be regarded as dealing with these types of stabilizer.

McCallum and Whittaker (1979) have recently considered the properties of automatic tax stabilizers and show that they do influence the variance of output. Their point can most easily be demonstrated by writing the aggregate demand schedule as:

$$y = \alpha'\left(R - \underset{-1}{E} \, p_{+1} + p \right) - \gamma t y \qquad (3.23)$$

where t is the direct tax elasticity[1] and γ is the elasticity of spending to temporary variations in tax liabilities.

If we define

$$\alpha = \alpha'/(1 + \gamma t) \qquad (3.24)$$

then the solution of the model (3.23), (3.3), (3.4) and (3.5) is the same as (3.9) and (3.10), but where α is defined as in (3.24). Consequently the solution for output is not independent of the automatic stabilizer, given this orthodox aggregate demand function[2]; a higher tax elasticity reduces the variance of output.

MODELS WITH LONG-TERM NON-CONTINGENT CONTRACTS

One of the assumptions required for anticipated monetary policy to have no effect on output in the Sargent–Wallace model is that agents are able to act on their information sets. If we have a situation where, for instance, private agents cannot respond to new information by changing their consumption, wage-price decision, etc, as quickly as the public sector can change any (at least one) of its controls, then scope once again emerges for systematic stabilization policy to have real effects. This insight was developed principally by Fischer (1977) and Phelps and Taylor (1977) in the context of multi-period non-contingent wage or price contracts.

Suppose we have a situation where all wage contracts run for two periods and the contract drawn in period t specifies nominal wages for periods $t + 1$ and $t + 2$. At each period of time, half the labour force is covered by a pre-existing contract. As long as the contracts are not contingent on new information that accrues during the contract period, this raises the possibility of stabilization policy. Firms respond to changes in their environment (say, unpredictable changes in demand which were unanticipated at the time of pre-existing contracts) by altering output and employment at the precontracted wage; only contracts which are up for renewal can reflect prevailing information. If the monetary authorities can respond to new information (new to the wage contractors) that has accrued between the time the two-period contract is drawn up and the last period of the operation of the contract, then systematic stabilization policy is possible. In other words, while there are no information differences between public and private agents, the speed of response to the new information is different.

The essentials of this argument involve replacing the Sargent–Wallace supply equation (3.3) with one based on overlapping contracts. Suppose, following Fischer (1977), that wages are set for two periods so as to maintain expected real wages constant at a 'normal' level. Denote (the log of nominal) wages set in period $t - i$ for period t as $_{t-i}W_t$. Then

$$_{t-i}W_t = \mathop{\mathrm{E}}_{-i} p \qquad (3.25)$$

(where the log of normal wages is set to zero) and current nominal wages are

$$W = 0.5(_{t-2}W_t + {}_{t-1}W_t) = 0.5\left(\mathop{\mathrm{E}}_{-2} p + \mathop{\mathrm{E}}_{-1} p \right) \qquad (3.26)$$

Now let output supply be a declining function of the real wage (from firms maximizing profits subject to a production function with labour input and some fixed overheads):

$$y = -q(W - p) + y^* \qquad (3.27)$$

We derive from these the new supply equation:

$$y = 0.5q\left(\left(p - \underset{-2}{\mathsf{E}}\ p\right) + \left(p - \underset{-1}{\mathsf{E}}\ p\right)\right) + y^* \qquad (3.28)$$

Using it in place of (3.3) with (3.2), (3.4), and (3.5), (3.28) can conveniently be written in terms of the Muth solution as:

$$y = q(\pi_0 w + 0.5\pi_1 w_{-1}) + y^* \qquad (3.29)$$

The model solution equation can now be written:

$$\bar{m} + q\rho(\pi_0 w_{-1} + 0.5\pi_1 w_{-2}) + w$$
$$= p + q(1 + c/\alpha)(\pi_0 w + 0.5\pi_1 w_{-1})$$
$$- c\left(\underset{-1}{\mathsf{E}}\ p_{+1} - \underset{-1}{\mathsf{E}}\ p\right) + (1 + c/\alpha)y^* \qquad (3.30)$$

The identities in the w_{-i} are now:

(terms in w)

$$1 = \pi_0[1 + q(1 + c/\alpha)] \qquad (3.31)$$

(terms in w_{-1})

$$\rho q\pi_0 = \pi_1 + 0.5q(1 + c/\alpha)\pi_1 - c(\pi_2 - \pi_1) \qquad (3.32)$$

(terms in w_{-2})

$$0.5q\rho\pi_1 = \pi_2 - c(\pi_3 - \pi_2) \qquad (3.33)$$

(terms in $w_{-i}, i \geqslant 3$)

$$0 = (1 + c)\pi_i - c\pi_{i+1} \qquad (3.34)$$

Equation (3.34) gives $\pi_i = 0$ $(i \geqslant 3)$, applying the stability condition, whence we can solve the other three equations for π_2, π_1, π_0. ρ enters the solution for π_1 and π_2, and, since π_1 enters the output supply equation, so influences the variance of output. In fact in this particular example, it will raise the variance; minimum variance occurs where $\rho = 0$, since this sets $\pi_1 = \pi_2 = 0$. This illustrates the obvious point that the case for stabilization policy does not rest with showing effectiveness; it is also necessary to show optimality. Nevertheless it is easy to construct examples where $\rho \neq 0$ minimizes output variance; the reader should investigate one such as an exercise, namely when an adjustment term $+\lambda(y_{-1} - y^*)$ is added to (3.27). He should find that, while π_0 is unaltered, the expression for π_1 becomes:

$$\pi_1 = [q\pi_0 + \lambda(\pi_0 - 1)] \bigg/ \left[1 + c(1 - \lambda) \right.$$
$$\left. + 0.5q\left(1 + c/\alpha - \frac{c}{1 + c} \right) \right] \quad (3.35)$$

Since $\lambda(\pi_0 - 1) < 0$, the optimal value of ρ is positive, such that $q\rho\pi_0 + \lambda(\pi_0 - 1) = 0 = \pi_1$; this is the opposite in fact of the normal counter-cyclical response.

Models with overlapping contracts have been developed by Taylor (1979a,b, 1980) in a series of papers in order to show that important features of the business cycle can be captured by integrating this type of supply curve into standard macroeconomic analysis, and to exhibit examples of optimal policy design in such an economy.

Three points of weakness nevertheless remain in this approach. First, the theoretical basis of non-contingent contracts, in which the nominal wage or price is fixed and quantity is set by demand, has not been established. Secondly, while superficially it may appear that money contracts of this sort exist, closer inspection reveals that actual contracts are exceedingly complex once implicit elements are taken into account; for example, they will typically include bonus, discount and lay-off elements for quantity variation, and indexation (whether formal or informal via shop-floor renegotiation) is frequently found. Thirdly, if the authorities were systematically to exploit these contracts in a way that was not envisaged at the time the contracts were set, then this would presumably lead to differences in the way contracts were written (contract length and indexation clauses are clearly endogenous). In the limit, if the government systematically exploited them in a way that altered agents' outcomes excessively from what they wished, then long-run contracts would be written in such a way that they were equivalent to a succession of single-period contracts so that the scope for stabilization policy would disappear. For all these reasons, there remains considerable doubt as to whether non-contingent contracts can be regarded as a firm basis for modelling and policy formulation.

SUPPLY FUNCTIONS WITH 'CLASSICAL' INTERTEMPORAL SUBSTITUTION

The next issue we wish to look at is the potential role for stabilization policy in equilibrium models typified by rational expectations where the supply function is not of the Sargent–Wallace form. The most interesting 'stylized' alternative to the Sargent–Wallace supply function which we consider is that proposed by Lucas (1972a) and reproduced in, for example, Barro (1976) and Barro and Fischer (1976), namely:

$$y - y^* = a\left(p - \mathop{\mathrm{E}}_{-1} p_{+1}\right) + \lambda(y_{-1} - y^*) \qquad (3.36)$$

In this model, supply differs from normal supply (y^*) as the price the supplier receives differs from his prior expectation of future prices. For simplicity we consider only the price level one period ahead, though in principle it should be all future prices. The positive resonse of supply to this price term is thus one of speculative activity over time. Suppliers of goods and services allocate goods between periods in response to anticipated returns. The essential underpinnings of (3.36) are based on the original work of Lucas and Rapping (1969).

In their model, suppliers of labour are assumed to maximize a utility function which is dependent upon both current and future expected values of consumption and leisure respectively. This function is maximized subject to the lifetime budget constraint. The maximization procedure yields the result that labour supply depends, *ceteris paribus*, on the current real wage and also expected future real wages. It is assumed that this labour supply function is transmitted to goods markets via a production function yielding a stylized supply function of the form (3.36) – this is elaborated below. The lagged dependent variable $(y_{-1} - y^*)$ as before captures costs of adjustment.

For simplicity the rest of this model's structure is given by:

$$m = p + y \tag{3.37}$$

and

$$m = \bar{m} + \rho_\mu(y_{-1} - y^*) + u \tag{3.38}$$

Equating (3.37) and (3.38) we obtain:

$$p = \bar{m} - y - \rho_\mu(y_{-1} - y^*) + u \tag{3.39}$$

and:

$$\underset{-1}{E} \, p_{+1} = \bar{m} + \rho_\mu \left(\underset{-1}{E} \, y - y^* \right) - \underset{-1}{E} \, y_{+1} \tag{3.40}$$

Substitution of (3.39) and (3.40) into (3.36) yields:

$$y - y^* = a \left[\rho_\mu(y_{-1} - y^*) - y + u - \rho_\mu \left(\underset{-1}{E} \, y - y^* \right) \right.$$
$$\left. + \underset{-1}{E} \, y_{+1} \right] + \lambda(y_{-1} - y^*) \tag{3.41}$$

or:

$$(1 + a)y = (1 - \lambda)y^* + (a\rho_\mu + \lambda)y_{-1}$$
$$- a\rho_\mu \underset{-1}{E} \, y + a \underset{-1}{E} \, y_{+1} + au \tag{3.42}$$

We look for a solution for y of the form:

$$y = \bar{y} + \sum_{i=0}^{\infty} \pi_i u_{-i} \tag{3.43}$$

The following identities are obtained:

$$\bar{y} = y^*$$

(u)
$$(1 + a)\pi_0 = a \tag{3.44}$$

$(u_{-i}, i \geqslant 1)$
$$a\pi_{i+1} - (1 + a + a\rho_\mu)\pi_i + (a\rho_\mu + \lambda)\pi_{i-1} = 0 \tag{3.45}$$

(3.45) defines an unstable difference equation. Defining the stable root as μ, we have then:

$$\pi_i = \pi_0 \mu^i \quad \text{for} \quad i \geqslant 1$$

and from (3.44):

$$\pi_0 = \frac{a}{1 + a}$$

Consequently we can express y in terms of observables:

$$y = y^* + \pi_0 u + \pi_0 \mu u_{-1} + \pi_0 \mu^2 u_{-2} + \cdots$$

Therefore

$$\mu y_{-1} = \mu y^* + \pi_0 \mu u_{-1} + \pi_0 \mu^2 u_{-2} + \cdots$$

Therefore

$$y - \mu y_{-1} = y^*(1 - \mu) + \frac{a}{1 + a} u \tag{3.46}$$

Since μ depends on ρ_μ from (3.45) we have shown that systematic monetary policy can influence the variance of output in models typified by a Lucas supply function and rational expectations. The reader might like to find the rule which generates the minimum variance of output. In this model, stabilization was possible without having to assume the existence of contracts or different information sets.

McCallum (1978) has suggested that if future prices in the Lucas supply function are appropriately discounted, then the Sargent–Wallace proposition of strict neutrality of anticipated monetary policy will once again reappear.

McCallum's point is illustrated as follows. Let the supply function be written as:

$$y - y^* = a\left(p - \underset{-1}{E} p_{+1} + \underset{-1}{E} R\right) + \lambda(y_{-1} - y^*) \tag{3.47}$$

where R is to be regarded as the aggregate of the discount rates observed at the micro level. Write the inverse of an aggregate demand schedule as:

$$R = -\frac{1}{\alpha} y + \underset{-1}{E} p_{+1} - \underset{-1}{E} p \tag{3.48}$$

Substitute $\underset{-1}{\mathsf{E}}\,R$ from (3.48) into (3.47) to obtain:

$$y - y^* = a\left(p - \underset{-1}{\mathsf{E}}\,p - \frac{1}{\alpha}\,y \right) + \lambda(y_{-1} - y^*) \qquad (3.49)$$

Since $p - \underset{-1}{\mathsf{E}}\,p$ is a function of the current disturbance which, because of the dating of expectations, must be independent of ρ_μ, the monetary feedback parameter, there is no scope for systematic stabilization policy to influence output from (3.49).

One modification, however, of the McCallum model which negates his results is the introduction of wealth effects into the IS schedule – Minford and Peel (1981). This yields the following form for output:

$$y - y^* = a\left[p - \underset{-1}{\mathsf{E}}\,p - \frac{1}{\alpha}(y - y^*) \right] + e\,\underset{-1}{\mathsf{E}}\,(\bar{b} - p)$$
$$+ \lambda(y_{-1} - y^*) \qquad (3.50)$$

where $\bar{b}$ is the log of the stock of bonds (a fixed stock of nominal, variable interest rate, perpetuities, whose value therefore is unaffected by R: a convenient simplification)[3] and high powered money – i.e. the 'outside' financial assets of the public. It turns out that for this model, the solution for output is not necessarily independent of the systematic component of the monetary rule; this is because expected prices enter the output equation (3.50) and these are of course dependent on expected money. We leave the demonstration of this as an exercise.

For wealth effects to occur, we require that government bonds be net wealth, and, since this is an issue central to the behaviour of RE macroeconomic models, we review it separately below (Chapter 9). Before this, however, we explore somewhat more formally the classical supply function from which the Lucas and McCallum illustrations derive, and set out the conditions under which stabilization policy is feasible when the function is fully specified.

THE FULL CLASSICAL SUPPLY FUNCTION

The full classical supply function is derived from worker/consumers maximizing expected utility subject to a lifetime budget constraint (a nicely tractable set-up, which has been explored by Sargent, e.g. 1979a, Chapter 16, is the quadratic utility function with quadratic adjustment costs). From such a framework one can obtain a supply of labour equation of the form:

$$n = f\left(\overset{+}{w^e}, \ \overset{-}{w^e_{+1} - w^e - r}, \ \overset{+}{n_{-1}} \right) \tag{3.51}$$

where w = real wage, n = labour supply (both logarithms), r = real interest rate. The e superscript denotes expected at time t; and the signs of the partial derivatives are given over the arguments of the function.

The information set assumed available to suppliers of labour is last period's macroeconomic information and this period's micro labour market data (i.e. nominal wages). So $w^e = W - \underset{-1}{E} p = w + p - \underset{-1}{E} p$ where W is nominal wages (in logs). The first term represents the long-term effect of rising wages on supply, while the second represents intertemporal substitution with a single-period 'future' for simplicity; the third represents costs of adjustment. w^e_{+1} is standing for the whole future path of real wages and it will be helpful for our purpose here to treat it as a constant, 'the future normal real wage'.

Let us write the equation in (log) linear form as:

$$n = \sigma_0 + \sigma_1\left(w + p - \underset{-1}{E} p \right) + \sigma_2 r + \lambda n_{-1} \quad (0 < \lambda < 1) \tag{3.52}$$

Now juxtapose this with a demand for labour function (3.53) derived from a simple Cobb–Douglas production function (3.54) with a fixed overhead element k:

$$n = y - w \tag{3.53}$$

$$y = \delta k + (1 - \delta)n \tag{3.54}$$

From these last two we have:

$$n = k - \delta^{-1}w \qquad (3.55)$$

or

$$w = -\delta n + \delta k$$

Substituting for w from this into (3.52) yields:

$$n = \frac{(1 + a)^{-1}\left[ak + \sigma_0 + \sigma_2 r + \sigma_1\left(p - \underset{-1}{\text{E}} p\right)\right]}{1 - \gamma L} \qquad (3.56)$$

where

$$\gamma = \frac{\lambda}{1 + a}, \quad a = (\delta\sigma_1)$$

Substituting this into (3.54) gives:

$$y = (1 - \gamma)\delta k + (1 - \delta)(1 + a)^{-1}$$
$$\times \left[ak + \sigma_0 + \sigma_2 r + \sigma_1\left(p - \underset{-1}{\text{E}} p\right)\right] + \gamma y_{-1} \qquad (3.57)$$

The equilibrium values of r and y will depend on the whole model; for simplicity we will normalize them at zero in what follows, since we do not focus on them.

Now write the full model as:

$$y = -\alpha r + \rho_f(y_{-1}) \qquad (3.58)$$

$$y = dr + \beta\left(p - \underset{-1}{\text{E}} p\right) + \gamma y_{-1} \qquad (3.59)$$

$$m = p + y - cR + v \qquad (3.60)$$

$$m = \bar{m} + \rho_\mu y_{-1} + u \qquad (3.61)$$

$$R = r + \underset{-1}{\text{E}} p_{+1} - \underset{-1}{\text{E}} p \qquad (3.62)$$

Equation (3.58) is the IS curve with the fiscal feedback parameter, ρ_f. (3.59) is the supply curve with d, β, γ taken from (3.57) (e.g. $d = (1 - \delta)(1 + a)^{-1}\sigma_2$). (3.60) is money demand, (3.61) money supply with feedback parameter ρ_μ, (3.62) the Fisher identity.

We can immediately establish by equations (3.58) and (3.59) that fiscal feedback is effective, but monetary feedback is not. We obtain:

$$r = \frac{-\beta(1 - \rho_f L)\left(p - \underset{-1}{\text{E}}\, p\right)}{(\alpha + d)\left[1 - \dfrac{\gamma\alpha + \rho_f d}{\alpha + d}\, L\right]} \qquad (3.63)$$

This expression for r then can be substituted into (3.58) to obtain y: clearly the reaction of y to unanticipated prices depends importantly on ρ_f, but not on ρ_μ. As for $p - \underset{-1}{\text{E}}\, p$, this is quickly found as:

$$p - \underset{-1}{\text{E}}\, p = \left[1 + \frac{\beta(\alpha + c)}{\alpha + d}\right]^{-1}(u - v) \qquad (3.64)$$

The intuition behind this result is that fiscal policy is causing *intertemporal substitution* of supply, in order to offset the 'cyclical' effects of shocks. Incidentally, this effect of fiscal feedback is quite independent of wealth effects (i.e. government bonds need not be net wealth). For example, even if private consumption depends only on permanent income and not on transitory income, the government expenditure pattern over time could be altered without affecting the present value of the tax stream, so altering the pattern of total demands over time. Of course, if private consumption depends also on transitory income, then alteration of the temporal pattern of taxes, present value of the tax stream constant, would also have this effect. Such alteration of the patterns of aggregate demand over time then sets off the movement in real interest rates which creates intertemporal substitution in supply.

As with the McCallum result above, however, the ineffectiveness of monetary feedback policy is negated by the introduction of wealth effects into the IS curve (or the supply curve). This can be seen by adding the term, $f(\bar{b} - p)$ into (3.58). We set $\rho_f = 0$ since fiscal policy will remain effective as before, also to simplify the algebra here we set $\gamma = 0$.

Using (3.58) and (3.59) we now obtain:

$$r = -f'p - \beta'\left(p - \underset{-1}{\text{E}}\ p\right) \tag{3.65}$$

where $f' = f/(\alpha + d)$, $\beta' = \beta/(\alpha + d)$. Equating (3.60) and (3.61), and substituting into the result (3.65) for r and (3.59) for y, we obtain the following equation in p:

$$(1 - f'd + f'c)p + f'\rho_\mu dp_{-1} - c\ \underset{-1}{\text{E}}\ p_{+1}$$

$$+ c\ \underset{-1}{\text{E}}\ p + (\beta - \beta'd + \beta'c)\left(p - \underset{-1}{\text{E}}\ p\right)$$

$$- \rho_\mu(\beta - \beta'd)\left(p_{-1} - \underset{-2}{\text{E}}\ p_{-1}\right) = \bar{m} + u - v \tag{3.66}$$

If $p = \sum_{i=0}^{\infty} \pi_i w_{-i} + \bar{p}$, where $w = u - v$, then the identities in the w_{-i} are:

$$(w)[(1 - f'd + f'c) + (\beta - \beta'd + \beta'c)]\pi_0 = 1 \tag{3.67}$$

$$(w_{-1})(1 - f'd + f'c)\pi_1 + f'\rho_\mu d\pi_0$$

$$- c\pi_2 + c\pi_1 - \rho_\mu(\beta - \beta'd)\pi_0 = 0 \tag{3.68}$$

$$(w_{-i}, i \geqslant 2)\pi_{i+1} - \left(\frac{1 - f'd}{c} + 1 + f'\right)\pi_i - \frac{f'\rho_\mu d}{c}\ \pi_{i-1} = 0 \tag{3.69}$$

Suppose (3.69) has a unique stable root, δ: then $\pi_2 = \delta\pi_1$, where δ depends on ρ_μ. π_1 also depends on ρ_μ from (3.68). Now output is given by (3.59) using (3.65), as:

$$y = -df'p + \alpha\beta'\left(p - \underset{-1}{\text{E}}\ p\right) \tag{3.70}$$

from which it is apparent that ρ_μ enters the solution for output also. Wealth effects make monetary feedback policy effective.

The full classical model of labour supply therefore yields two interesting propositions. First, without wealth effects fiscal feedback is effective but monetary feedback is not (this is noted by Sargent, 1979a, Chapter 16). Secondly, *with* wealth effects *both* are effective. Again, this by no means

Stabilization Policy

establishes that feedback rules are beneficial. (Sargent, *ibid*, for example, shows that if welfare is measured by the sum of identical consumers' expected utility, then with no wealth effects zero fiscal feedback is optimal in the case of quadratic utility and production functions.) That issue we defer. As for the existence of wealth effects, on which the effectiveness of monetary policy turns, that too is an issue requiring separate discussion; theoretically and empirically it is at this point an open question. Nevertheless, as a minimum it is of some interest that new classical models in general give scope for fiscal feedback and across a *potentially* broad class also give scope for monetary feedback. This is contrary to the impression given (no doubt unintentionally) by much of the early literature, though subsequently corrected by Lucas and Sargent (1978).

CONCLUSIONS

We have shown, in the context of RE macro linear models, that the conditions required for stabilization of output to be feasible are, first, that the supply hypothesis is not of the Sargent–Wallace form, but rather of a 'classical' form that includes forward expectations; second, that there are wealth effects. *Both* conditions are required for monetary policy stabilization to be feasible; only the first is required for fiscal policy stabilization to be feasible. We have also explained that the presence of either information asymmetries or multi-period contracts will also generate stabilization possibilities; but these are not logically necessary and not, perhaps, natural assumptions for equilibrium models. The general proposition then in this chapter is that *rational expectations as such do not rule out counter-cyclical policy*, but rather they alter its impact,[4] leaving it as an empirical matter whether they do or do not reduce the variance of relevant macro-economic variables, and as a further issue whether they do or do not improve welfare.

NOTES

1. t is MRT/ART, where MRT(ART) = marginal (average) rate of tax, since y is a logarithm.
2. In fact to obtain such a function we require a situation of incomplete debt neutrality – see Chapter 9. In brief, if taxpayers completely capitalize future tax liabilities, and consumption depends on permanent income, then these tax changes will exert no influence on total spending.
3. Such a perpetuity would be, for example, a bond issue at £100 face value which promises to pay £100 × R_i each ith period $i = 1, 2, \ldots, \infty$; its present value will always be £100. The point made here goes through for all types of *nominal* bonds; only if bonds are indexed will it not do so, for the obvious reason that the path of prices becomes irrelevant to the value of net wealth.
4. This viewpoint is to some extent reinforced by more recent work (e.g. Dickinson, Driscoll and Ford, 1982) which has taken up a suggestion of Shiller (1978) and shown that if a non-linear version of the Sargent–Wallace supply function replaces their original linear version then even retaining all other assumptions stabilization policy is feasible. Clearly non-linearity will be a typical feature of models of national economies; nevertheless, we doubt whether this source of stabilization leverage is of much practical importance.

4

The Effects of Partial Information[1]

We showed in the previous chapter (equations 3.17–3.22) that if the expectation of the future value of a variable in a macroeconomic model is conditioned by an information set dated at time t, then even in a model embodying a Sargent–Wallace (1975) supply curve (in which agents otherwise use information dated at $t - 1$) systematic monetary policy will, in general, influence the variance of output.

The question arises as to the circumstances in which it is appropriate to date expectations at time t in macroeconomic models. The usual rationale for such a procedure is based on the view that *some* agents have current knowledge of *some* aggregate variables such as the exchange rate or interest rates (or in the case of Turnovsky, prices). It is indeed clear that, in many economies, due to the presence of capital markets some aggregate information such as exchange rates or interest rates is available essentially instantaneously. Consequently it might appear correct to date expectations of such variables at time $t + 1$ on an information set dated at time t. However this procedure will in general be incorrect.

To date, any expectation at time t in a rational expectations model carries the *analytic* property that it implies that the model can be solved as if these agents know *all* current disturbances. For instance, in the model discussed in Chapter 3 the *analytic* solution of the model required that all real and nominal disturbances are known at time t. However, *partial* knowledge of some macroeconomic variables does not in general confer on agents knowledge of all shocks in the complete model. Rather agents face a statistical inference problem. Observation of the current values of macroeconomic variables, given knowledge of the variance of disturbances in the economy, allows agents to form an optimal expectation of the currently unobserved random variables using Kalman filter methods. (See, e.g. Kalman, 1960.) In particular, if a variable z is observed which is the sum of two random variables (u, ε), i.e.:

$$z = u + \varepsilon \tag{4.1}$$

then the current expectation of u and ε are respectively given by:

$$E(u) = \frac{\sigma_u^2}{\sigma_u^2 + \sigma_\varepsilon^2} \, z \tag{4.2}$$

$$E(\varepsilon) = \frac{\sigma_\varepsilon^2}{\sigma_u^2 + \sigma_\varepsilon^2} \, z \tag{4.3}$$

where σ_u^2, σ_ε^2 are the known variances of the disturbances. (See Graybill, 1961, for a fuller discussion.) The coefficient on z in (4.2) or (4.3) can be thought of as that of a simple Ordinary Least Squares regression of u on z (carried out by agents over an infinite sample).

The purpose in this chapter is to consider what occurs in a simple macroeconomic model, if agents' information sets include observations of current macroeconomic variables, as occurs in models where there is an economy-wide or global capital market. Since the asset price (exchange rate or interest rate) will depend on aggregate variables, so its value will convey to agents some information about currently unobserved variables. The model we consider is a model embodying a Sargent–Wallace supply curve in which all agents can observe the current interest rate. Some alternative models in which the implications of partial global information are considered are Barro (1980), Saidi (1980), Lucas (1973).

THE SARGENT–WALLACE MODEL WITH PARTIAL GLOBAL INFORMATION

Our model embodying a Sargent–Wallace supply function is given by:

$$y = a(p - \mathsf{E}p) + u \tag{4.4}$$

$$m = p + y - cR \tag{4.5}$$

$$m = \rho m_{-1} + \varepsilon \tag{4.6}$$

$$y = -\alpha R - \alpha E p_{+1} - \alpha E p + v \tag{4.7}$$

c, α, a, ρ are constants; u, v and ε are random shocks with known variances σ_u^2, σ_v^2 and σ_ε^2; (4.4) is aggregate output supply; (4.5) money demand; (4.6) money supply; (4.7) is demand for aggregate output. The information set that conditions the expectations operator E in this model consists of all variables at time $t - 1$ (and before), and the current aggregate interest rate, R. Clearly, without current observation of the interest rate R, the model would exhibit the well-known features analysed by Sargent and Wallace (1975)[2] and discussed in the previous chapter.

Notice that, unlike Turnovsky (1980), we assume that *all* agents possess the same information sets. This appears a more natural assumption initially under which to analyse the efficiency of monetary stabilization policy, since alternative information structures lead to natural questions, discussed in Chapter 3, about how they occurred and what would enable their continuation.

To solve this model, we first obtain a basic equation in the errors as deviations from their expected values. Taking expectations of (4.4) and subtracting from (4.4) yields:

$$y - Ey = a(p - Ep) + u - Eu \tag{4.8}$$

Equating (4.5) with (4.6) and following the same procedure as with (4.4) yields:

$$\varepsilon - E\varepsilon = p - Ep + y - Ey - c(R - ER) \tag{4.9}$$

(4.7) analogously gives:

$$y - Ey = -\alpha(R - ER) + v - Ev = v - Ev \tag{4.10}$$

since $R = ER$, R being known.

Simple manipulation then yields our basic equation in the errors:

$$(1 + a)(v - Ev) = a(\varepsilon - E\varepsilon) + u - Eu \tag{4.11}$$

We may also note in passing that, given that $Ey = Eu$ from (4.4):

$$y = Eu + v - Ev \tag{4.12}$$

and that

$$p - Ep = \varepsilon - E\varepsilon - (v - Ev) \tag{4.13}$$

This linear model has a solution for R of the form

$$R = Zm_{-1} + Au + Bv + D\varepsilon \tag{4.14}$$

(i.e. a linear function of the lagged information and the current shocks), where Z, A, B and D are constants known to agents, and that we shall determine from the model (4.4)–(4.7).

Consequently, using the Graybill formula, the best estimates of u, v, ε, given $R - Zm_{-1}$ are:

$$Eu = \frac{1}{A}\,\phi_u(Au + Bv + D\varepsilon) \tag{4.15}$$

$$Ev = \frac{1}{B}\,\phi_v(Au + Bv + D\varepsilon) \tag{4.16}$$

$$E\varepsilon = \frac{1}{D}\,\phi_\varepsilon(Au + Bv + D\varepsilon) \tag{4.17}$$

where

$$\phi_u = \frac{A^2\sigma_u^2}{X}\,; \quad \phi_v = \frac{B^2\sigma_v^2}{X}\,; \quad \phi_\varepsilon = \frac{D^2\sigma_\varepsilon^2}{X} \tag{4.18}$$

and

$$X = A^2\sigma_u^2 + B^2\sigma_v^2 + D^2\sigma_\varepsilon^2$$

Substituting (4.15), (4.16) and (4.17) into (4.11) we obtain:

$$(1 + a)v - a\varepsilon - u = \left[(1 + a)\frac{\phi_v}{B} - \frac{a\phi_\varepsilon}{D} - \frac{\phi_u}{A}\right](Au + Bv + D\varepsilon) \tag{4.19}$$

Since v, ε, and u may each be any real number, (4.19) is only satisfied if the coefficients on each alone add up to zero, that is if:

$$1 = \phi_v - \frac{a}{1+a}\frac{B}{D}\phi_\varepsilon - \frac{1}{1+a}\frac{B}{A}\phi_u \text{ (coefficients on } v\text{)} \quad (4.20)$$

$$1 = \frac{-(1+a)}{a}\frac{D}{B}\phi_v + \phi_\varepsilon + \frac{1}{a}\frac{D}{A}\phi_u \text{ (on } \varepsilon\text{)} \quad (4.21)$$

$$1 = -(1+a)\frac{A}{B}\phi_v + a\frac{A}{D}\phi_\varepsilon + \phi_u \text{ (on } u\text{)} \quad (4.22)$$

Further since we know that $\phi_v + \phi_\varepsilon + \phi_u = 1$ while each may range over any number between 0 and 1, it follows at once that:

$$\frac{D}{A} = a; \quad \frac{D}{B} = \frac{-a}{1+a}; \quad \frac{A}{B} = \frac{-1}{1+a} \quad (4.23)$$

Consequently

$$\phi_u = \frac{\sigma_u^2}{X'}, \quad \phi_v = \frac{\sigma_v^2(1+a)^2}{X'}, \quad \phi_\varepsilon = \frac{a^2\sigma_\varepsilon^2}{X'} \quad (4.24)$$

where

$$X' = \sigma_u^2 + (1+a)^2\sigma_v^2 + a^2\sigma_\varepsilon^2$$

The full solution of this model can now be found. From (4.4), (4.5) and (4.6) we have:

$$p + a(p - \mathsf{E}p) + u - cR = \rho m_{-1} + \varepsilon \quad (4.25)$$

from which we obtain, taking expectations and using $R = \mathsf{E}R$:

$$R = \frac{1}{c}(\mathsf{E}p + \mathsf{E}u - \mathsf{E}\varepsilon - \rho m_{-1}) \quad (4.26)$$

Equating (4.4) with (4.5), taking expectations and substituting for R from (4.26), we get:

$$\mathsf{E}u - \mathsf{E}v = -\frac{\alpha}{c}(\mathsf{E}p + \mathsf{E}u - \mathsf{E}\varepsilon - \rho m_{-1}) + \alpha\mathsf{E}p_{+1} - \alpha\mathsf{E}p$$

or rearranging:

$$\mathrm{E}p_{+1} - \frac{(1+c)}{c} \mathrm{E}p = \frac{\alpha+c}{\alpha c} \mathrm{E}u - \frac{1}{\alpha} \mathrm{E}v - \frac{1}{c} \mathrm{E}\varepsilon - \frac{\rho}{c} m_{-1}$$

$$(4.27)$$

Following Sargent's procedure (see Chapter 2), we write the left hand side of (4.27) as:

$$B^{-1} \left[\frac{1 - \left\{ \frac{1+c}{c} \right\}^{-1} B^{-1}}{- \left\{ \frac{1+c}{c} \right\}^{-1} B^{-1}} \right] \mathrm{E}p$$

$$= - \left\{ \frac{1+c}{c} \right\} \left[1 - \left\{ \frac{c}{1+c} \right\} B^{-1} \right] \mathrm{E}p \quad (4.28)$$

where B is the backward operator instructing one to lag variables but not the expectations date (e.g. $BEP = EP_{-1}$). (4.28) can now be written as:

$$\mathrm{E}p = - \left\{ \frac{c}{1+c} \right\} \frac{1}{\left[1 - \left(\frac{c}{1+c} \right) B^{-1} \right]}$$

$$\times \left(\frac{\alpha+c}{\alpha c} \mathrm{E}u - \frac{1}{\alpha} \mathrm{E}v - \frac{1}{c} \mathrm{E}\varepsilon - \frac{\rho}{c} m_{-1} \right)$$

$$= - \frac{\alpha+c}{\alpha(1+c)} \mathrm{E}u + \frac{c}{\alpha(1+c)} \mathrm{E}v + \left\{ \frac{1}{1+c} \right\} \mathrm{E}\varepsilon$$

$$+ \frac{\rho}{1+c} \sum_{i=0}^{\infty} \left\{ \frac{c}{1+c} \right\}^i \mathrm{E}m_{-1+i} \quad (4.29)$$

Since $\mathrm{E}m_{-1+i} = m_{-1}, \ \rho m_{-1} + \mathrm{E}\varepsilon, \ \rho^2 m_{-1} + \rho \mathrm{E}\varepsilon, \ \ldots$, for $i = 0, 1, 2, \ldots$. (4.29) becomes:

$$\mathrm{E}p = \frac{-(\alpha+c)}{\alpha(1+c)} \mathrm{E}u + \frac{c}{\alpha(1+c)} \mathrm{E}v$$

$$+ \frac{1}{1+c(1-\rho)} \mathrm{E}\varepsilon + \frac{\rho}{1+c(1-\rho)} m_{-1} \quad (4.30)$$

whence:

$$Ep_{+1} = \frac{\rho}{1 + c(1 - \rho)} \quad Em = \frac{\rho^2 m_{-1} + \rho E\varepsilon}{1 + c(1 - \rho)} \quad (4.31)$$

To find R, substitute from (4.30) into (4.26), to obtain:

$$R = \frac{-(1 - \alpha)}{\alpha(1 + c)} Eu + \frac{1}{\alpha(1 + c)} Ev$$

$$- \frac{1 - \rho}{1 + c(1 - \rho)} E\varepsilon - \frac{\rho(1 - \rho)}{1 + c(1 - \rho)} m_{-1} \quad (4.32)$$

We can write

$$Eu = \phi_u Q; \quad Ev = \frac{-\phi_v}{1 + a} Q; \quad E\varepsilon = \frac{\phi_\varepsilon}{a} Q$$

where

$$Q = u - (1 + a)v + a\varepsilon \quad (4.33)$$

Hence

$$A = -[\alpha(1 + c)]^{-1}[(1 - \alpha)\phi_u + (1 + a)^{-1}\phi_v]$$

$$- \{a[1 + c(1 - \rho)]\}^{-1}(1 - \rho)\phi_\varepsilon$$

$$B = -(1 + a)A; \quad D = aA; \quad Z = \frac{-\rho(1 - \rho)}{1 + c(1 - \rho)} \quad (4.34)$$

'PARADOXICAL' RESPONSES TO SHOCKS

It is of some interest to compare the reaction of this 'economy' when R is known with that when R is not known. Table 4.1 shows the reactions of output to the three shocks. When R is not known, all shocks have 'normal' positive effects on output. Clearly the sizes of the coefficients are quite different when R is known. This is hardly surprising since now output only responds (4.12) to expected supply shocks (Eu) and the *difference* of demand shocks, v, from their expected level. However, furthermore the sign of effect can be different for the various shocks. We can understand this as follows. Suppose the noise in ε dominates; then $\phi_\varepsilon \to 1$, $(\phi_u, \phi_v) \to 0$ and u has no effect because $Eu \to 0$, $Ev \to 0$.

Table 4.1 *Output reactions to shocks*

	u	v	ε
y (R not known)	W	$a\dfrac{c}{\alpha}W$	aW
y (R known)	$\phi_u + (1+a)^{-1}\phi_v$	$\phi_\varepsilon - a\phi_u$	$a\phi_u + a(1+a)^{-1}\phi_v$

where $W = \left[1 + a\left(1 + \dfrac{c}{\alpha}\right)\right]^{-1}$

Suppose noise in v dominates; then $(\phi_\varepsilon, \phi_u) \to 0$ and v has no effect. But suppose noise in u dominates; then $Ev \to 0$, $\phi_u \to 1$, so that $\partial(v + Eu)/\partial v = -a$. Hence a demand shock has a *negative* effect on output if supply shocks predominate, because agents misinterpret the effect of the positive demand shock on interest rates as that of a *negative* supply shock; expected prices consequently rise, more than actual prices, and supply of output is reduced.

Similar 'peculiarities' can occur in the reactions of p and R; Table 4.2 documents them. It is worth stressing therefore that the economy's behaviour in response to shocks can be 'paradoxical' if the shocks are 'misinterpreted'. Such effects are well-known at the level of everyday comment (*cf.* the

Table 4.2
Price and interest rate reaction to shocks

	u	v	ε
p (R not known)	$-\left(1 + \dfrac{c}{\alpha}\right)W$	$\dfrac{c}{\alpha}W$	W
p (R known)	$-S$	$(1+a)S - 1$	$1 - aS$
R (R not known)	$-\dfrac{a}{\alpha}W$	$\left(1 + \dfrac{ac}{\alpha}\right)\dfrac{W}{\alpha}$	$-\dfrac{a}{\alpha}W$
R (R known)	A	B	D

where

$$S = \frac{\alpha + c}{\alpha(1+c)}\phi_u + \frac{[c + \alpha(1+c)]}{\alpha(1+c)(1+a)}\phi_v + \frac{c(1-\rho)}{a(1 + c(1-\rho))}\phi_\varepsilon$$

behaviour of the UK economy in 1980, when the interest rates were interpreted as responding to 'overshooting' of its target by the money supply; subsequently it turned out that the money supply, truly measured, had contracted substantially). It is of interest that they can be rationalized within a stylized framework.

MONETARY STABILIZATION POLICY

We now turn to issues of 'monetary stabilization policy' within this model. It is of course apparent from the solution for y (given in Table 4.2) that feedback policy will not affect the variance of output, as in the usual Sargent–Wallace case without any current information; ρ does not enter the solution for y.

The same is true of an 'automatic response' to the current interest rate, as discussed by Poole (1970). Suppose we rewrite the money supply function $m = \rho m_{-1} + \eta R + \varepsilon$ when R is not known; assume that the monetary authorities can respond at a micro level (e.g. in the Treasury bill market) to a market interest rate, with the effect aggregated over the whole security market of ηR. Then the effect is to augment c, whenever it occurs in the solution, to $c' = c + \eta$. This will, as Poole suggested, dampen the effect on output of money shocks, ε, and exaggerate the effect of demand shocks, v, as can be verified from Table 4.1 first line. However, now suppose R to be known to all; then the same policy (now no longer a response to micro data, but one to macroeconomic information) has no effect on output at all, as can be seen from the second line of Table 4.1 where c does not enter.

We therefore have the result that interest rate stabilization is rendered ineffective (on output) in a Sargent–Wallace framework when the interest rate is universally observed. The reason is that any such response is impounded into Ep (because people can work out the money change due to ηR) and cannot affect the surprise element $p - Ep$.

This would not be true of any variable to which the monetary authorities could respond at a micro level and which was not universally observed. In this case people could not work out the money change due to this response, and it could affect the surprise element, $p - Ep$. However, plausible candidates for such a variable are hard to think of.

Nevertheless, the interesting possibility is introduced by global information, that the authorities can reduce the variance of output by raising the variance of the money supply shock, ε, i.e. by deliberately making larger rather than smaller mistakes.[3] Previously this was impossible; higher var ε necessarily implied higher var y since ε entered y additively. But now var ε affects the coefficients of the y expression via $\phi_u, \phi_v, \phi_\varepsilon$.

Consider the asymptotic variance of y, σ_y^2. Substituting for $\phi_u, \phi_v, \phi_\varepsilon$ from (4.24) in the y expression (Table 4.1, line 2) we obtain:

$$\sigma_y^2 = \sigma_v^2 \left[\frac{a^2\sigma_\varepsilon^2 - a\sigma_u^2}{X'} \right]^2 + \left[\frac{\sigma_u^2 + (1 + a)\sigma_v^2}{X'} \right]^2 [\sigma_u^2 + a^2\sigma_\varepsilon^2]$$

$$(4.35)$$

Now we find that as $\sigma_\varepsilon^2 \to \infty$, $\sigma_y^2 \to \sigma_v^2$, the variance of the demand shock. In this case, the variance of output is dominated by the variance of demand shocks because suppliers' price errors reflect solely u, v shocks, the former exactly cancelling the supply shock itself. It is clear that this may reduce the variance of output compared to the no monetary noise model; thus, as $\sigma_\varepsilon^2 \to 0$,

$$\sigma_y^2 \to \frac{a^2\sigma_v^2(\sigma_u^2)^2 + [\sigma_u^2 + (1 + a)\sigma_v^2]^2\sigma_u^2}{[\sigma_u^2 + (1 + a)^2\sigma_v^2]^2}$$

$$(4.36)$$

which, depending on σ_u^2 and a, can exceed σ_v^2.

Yet it can be shown that σ_y^2 is an inappropriate indicator of welfare and that the optimal policy is, commonsensically, to minimize σ_ε^2 (i.e. for the central bank cashiers to make as few and as small mistakes as possible).

Abstracting from the usual problems (public goods, externalities, incomplete markets, etc.) the Pareto-optimal situation under certainty is one of Walrasian equilibrium when all the shocks are known to all agents (this is discussed at greater length in Chapter 5). In the context of our model, output would in this situation be simply $y = u$, because

$Ep = p$ and u, the supply shock, would shift our vertical supply curve fully along the quantity axis.

The optimal outcome under uncertainty, under normal assumptions for social welfare, is one which minimizes the variance of output from this outcome, as well as ensuring that this is the expected outcome: i.e. such that $Ey = Eu$ and $\sigma_{yu}^2 = E(y - u)^2$ is a minimum. All rational expectations outcomes, whatever the information set, guarantee that $Ey = Eu$. The problem therefore reduces to choosing σ_ε^2 to minimize σ_{yu}^2. However $\sigma_{yu}^2 = a^2 E(p - Ep)^2$, so that the optimal policy is equivalently to minimize the variance of unanticipated price changes, σ_{pe}^2.

Using our earlier expression for y (Table 4.1, line 2), we find that:

$$(p - Ep) = \frac{y - u}{a} = [a(1 + a)]^{-1}\{-[\phi_\varepsilon + a(1 - \phi_u)]u$$

$$+ ((1 + a)\phi_u + \phi_v)a\varepsilon + [(1 + a)\phi_\varepsilon - a(1 + a)\phi_v]v\} \quad (4.37)$$

Hence

$$\sigma_{pe}^2 = [a(1 + a)]^{-2}\{[\phi_\varepsilon^2 + a^2(1 - \phi_u)^2 + 2a\phi_\varepsilon(1 - \phi_u)]\sigma_u^2$$

$$+ [(1 + a)^2\phi_u^2 + \phi_v^2 + 2(1 + a)\phi_u\phi_v]a^2\sigma_\varepsilon^2$$

$$+ [(1 + a)^2\phi_\varepsilon^2 + a^2(1 + a)^2\phi_u^2$$

$$- 2a(1 + a)^2\phi_\varepsilon\phi_u]\sigma_v^2\} \quad (4.38)$$

As $\sigma_\varepsilon^2 \to 0$, we find that

$$\sigma_{pe}^2 \to \frac{\sigma_v^2\sigma_u^2}{\sigma_u^2 + (1 + a)^2\sigma_v^2} \quad (4.39)$$

and that as $\sigma_\varepsilon^2 \to \infty$

$$\sigma_{pe}^2 \to \frac{\sigma_v^2 + \sigma_u^2}{a^2} \quad (4.40)$$

The ratio of (4.40) to (4.39), K, is given by

$$K = \left(\frac{\sigma_v^2 + \sigma_u^2}{a^2}\right)\frac{[\sigma_u^2 + (1 + a)^2\sigma_v^2]}{\sigma_v^2\sigma_u^2} > 1 \quad (4.41)$$

so that the low extreme dominates the high extreme.

We can also show that minimizing σ_ε^2 minimizes σ_{pe}^2; for $\partial\sigma_{pe}^2/\partial\sigma_\varepsilon^2 > 0$ throughout the range of σ_ε^2. Thus using x' to mean $\partial x/\partial\sigma_\varepsilon^2$, in what follows:

$$
\begin{aligned}
\partial\sigma_{pe}^2/\partial\sigma_\varepsilon^2 = [a(1+a)]^{-2}\{&\sigma_u^2[2\phi_\varepsilon\,\phi_\varepsilon' - a^2 2(1-\phi_u)\phi_u' \\
&+ 2a(1-\phi_u)\phi_\varepsilon' - 2a\phi_\varepsilon(1-\phi_u)\phi_u'] \\
&+ a^2\sigma_\varepsilon^2[(1+a)^2 2\phi_u\,\phi_u' + 2\phi_v\,\phi_v' \\
&+ 2(1+a)\phi_u\,\phi_v' + 2(1+a)\phi_v\,\phi_u'] \\
&+ a^2[(1+a)^2\phi_u^2 + \phi_v^2 + 2(1+a)\phi_u\,\phi_v] \\
&+ \sigma_v^2[(1+a)^2 2\phi_\varepsilon\,\phi_\varepsilon' + 2a^2(1+a)^2\phi_u\,\phi_\varepsilon' \\
&- 2a(1+a)^2\phi_\varepsilon\,\phi_u' - 2a(1+a)^2\phi_u\,\phi_\varepsilon']\}
\end{aligned} \tag{4.42}
$$

Now

$$
\phi_\varepsilon' = \frac{a^2}{X'}(1-\phi_\varepsilon); \quad \phi_u' = \frac{-a^2}{X'}\phi_u; \quad \phi_v' = \frac{-a^2}{X'}\phi_v;
$$

while $1 - \phi_\varepsilon = \phi_u + \phi_v$, $1 - \phi_u = \phi_\varepsilon + \phi_v$. Substituting these into (4.42) and collecting terms yields:

$$
\begin{aligned}
\frac{\partial\sigma_{pe}^2}{\partial\sigma_\varepsilon^2} = (1+a)^{-2}\{&\phi_u^2\phi_\varepsilon[1 + a^2 + 2a(\phi_\varepsilon + \phi_v)] \\
&+ 4a^2\phi_u^2\phi_v + \phi_v^2\phi_\varepsilon + 4a\phi_\varepsilon\,\phi_u\,\phi_v \\
&+ (\phi_u + \phi_v)[(1+a)\phi_u + \phi_v]^2\} > 0
\end{aligned} \tag{4.43}
$$

Hence welfare is unambiguously maximized by minimizing the variance of the money supply, as we would instinctively expect to be the case.

CONCLUSIONS

The procedure of solving rational expectations models on an information set dated at time t because agents observe *some* current global information is incorrect. We have implemented the correct procedure for an illustrative model of a closed economy, one with a Sargent–Wallace supply function in which all agents possess some current global information.

This model may exhibit 'perverse' responses to shocks, depending on the relative size of their variances. It is no longer possible to predict these responses without taking into account where people think the shocks are coming *from.*

In this model, neither the feedback component of monetary policy, nor any automatic response to interest rates will influence the variance of output; this represents an extension of the previous Sargent–Wallace result to automatic responses to the piece of global information.

In a curious further extension, the variance of the monetary policy rule *will* influence and may well reduce the asymptotic variance of output around its mean. However, the appropriate measure of social loss is, in this model, the variance of output around its full information level or equivalently the variance of price prediction errors; this is minimized, as commonsense would indicate, by minimizing the variance of money supply errors.

It should be apparent from the model studied in this chapter that proper allowance for partial information has wide-ranging, important and paradoxical effects on the properties of rational expectations models which, while awkward to implement, cannot be neglected.

NOTES

1. The material of this chapter is based on Minford and Peel (1983c).
2. The current aggregate price level, p, is *not* observed by agents. They only observe local prices which, in this model, are not assumed to convey information about aggregate current shocks. The actual current price level in (4.4) and (4.5) is obtained by way of aggregation. See Lucas (1973) for a model where a is not independent of variances.
3. This curious idea – which as will be seen is indeed suboptimal – can be implemented easily enough in principle by instructing the central bank cashiers to inject randomly chosen amounts of monetary base periodically into the system.

5

Problems in Choosing
Optimal Policies

In the last two chapters we discussed the potential *effec-tiveness* (for output) of stabilization policy. We have shown that in general such policy can be effective. The question then arises of whether any such policy is optimal and, if so, how it should be designed. We will discuss three issues that bear on this: the welfare *criterion*, the *evaluation* of policy effects, and finally, how optimal policies might be *designed* (given a welfare criterion and a model appropriate for evaluation). We will find that this discussion will carry us far away from the conventional post-war ideas of 'optimal control' in economic policy; indeed, we will have few conclusions other than that 'optimal' policies are hard to identify except as a broad class and that changeable policies which undermine government credibility should be ruled out. In our present state of knowledge, a modest aim would be to choose simple rules of government behaviour that minimize private sector uncertainty about the things that government controls: tax rates, money supply, government spending, and deficits. No doubt better (and optimal) ones exist; but we cannot pin them down and the attempt to do so with wrong parameter estimates[1] could be very costly.

THE WELFARE CRITERION

The yardstick of welfare that is most widely used by econo-mists is the Pareto criterion. Pareto-optimality is the condi-tion in which no-one can be made better off without someone else being made worse off; it can be illustrated for a two-person world by an Edgeworth box diagram (Figure

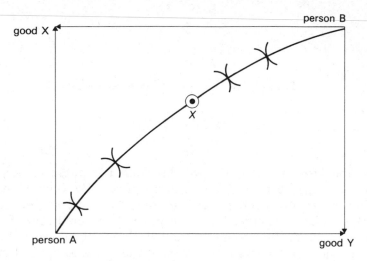

Figure 5.1 *Edgeworth box*

5.1), in which the 'contract curve' joins the points of tangency of the two sets of indifference curves, these points being all Pareto-optimal. If it is then assumed that distributional considerations are absent, either because they do not matter or because the government achieves the socially desired distribution at all times, there can be a unique Pareto-optimum for the specified distribution, illustrated as point X in Figure 5.1.

The proof that, for a given distribution function there exists a unique Pareto-optimum, has been established for an economy with well-behaved preferences and technology in Walrasian equilibrium when markets are competitive, complete and there are no distortions (discrepancies between private social costs due, for example, to externalities); the proof is due to Arrow, Debreu and Hahn (see Arrow and Hahn, 1971). In an economy of this type, the steady state level of output at the Pareto-optimum would be the y^* in our models.

Of course in actual economies, with incomplete and some monopolistic markets and with distortions, y^*, the equilibrium level of output, will not be at a Pareto-optimum. However, it is usual in macroeconomics to assume that these problems are the province of 'micro' policies, and that there should be no attempt by macroeconomic policy to push y systematically away from y^*; indeed we have already seen that any such attempt in an adaptive expectations model would cause ever-accelerating or -decelerating prices and in a rational expectations model would be completely frustrated. Instead y^* is taken, from the viewpoint of macroeconomic policy, to be the optimum output level in a steady state.

Supposing this to be so, the question arises of what is the optimum short-run output level. In Keynesian disequilibrium models with adaptive (or other backward-looking) expectations, if output is less (or more) than y^*, this is involuntary and suboptimal, the result of 'market failure', hence Var($y - y^*$) is a natural criterion for minimization.[2] This is the one on which we focused in the last chapter's discussion of effectiveness.

Sometimes, in these models, other measures also have been included in the minimand to represent the costs due to loss of consumer surplus not included in GDP – for example, the variance of inflation or interest rates as proxies for consumer and financial uncertainty. However, it is usually assumed in the context of the stabilization policy that the variations in these costs from alternative policies are small in relation to those from output fluctuations; this would also be our assumption.

In equilibrium models with adaptive expectations (such as that implicit in Milton Friedman's AEA address, 1968), output deviations from y^* arise because of expectations errors which could have been avoided by efficient use of available information. Again, Var($y - y^*$) is a natural minimand because agents would wish they had made output decisions on the basis of good forecasts.

In equilibrium models with rational expectations, however, $y \neq y^*$ because of the current or lagged effects of expectations errors which were unavoidable, given available information. Output is always at its 'desired' level in the sense that, given available information, agents are maximizing their welfare subject to their private constraints. Then, provided the level of distortion in the economy does not increase with $(y - y^*)^2$, government cannot improve and may reduce

welfare by reducing $\text{Var}(y - y^*)$ for the simple reason that it
was already being maximized; an example of this is given by
Sargent (1979, Ch. 16) in a classical labour supply model
where fiscal policy is effective because of intertemporal substitution, as discussed in Chapter 3, and the same point has
been stressed by Beenstock (1980).[3]

The proviso that the level of distortion does not increase
with $(y - y^*)^2$ will be violated in practice when unemployment benefits do not vary with wages; for when depres-
sive shocks reduce output and employment, the integral of
the gap between the private and the social cost of unemployment will increase. This is illustrated in Figure 5.2 where
b is the fixed real benefit level, SS is the 'undistorted' supply
curve of labour, $S_b S_b$ is the supply curve in the presence of
the fixed benefit level, DD the demand curve ($D'D'$ the curve
after the shock). The shaded areas, a and a', are respectively
the distortion from benefits before and after the shock; a' is
clearly greater than a. It follows that $\text{Var}(y - y^*)$ should be a
minimand even in equilibrium RE models, if distortions
behave in this way.[4]

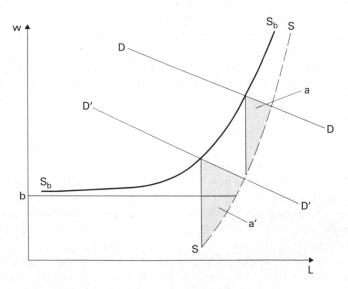

Figure 5.2 *Benefit distortions and stabilization*

We are left with the rational expectations models of a 'disequilibrium' variety, i.e. models in which non-contingent wage/price contracts are signed (e.g. Fischer, 1977; Phelps and Taylor, 1977, see Chapter 3). Here it is usual to assume that, if $y \neq y^*$, agents are involuntarily out of equilibrium, and to argue hence for $\text{Var}(y - y^*)$ as the minimand. Yet since the contracts were signed voluntarily, presumably they represent agents' optimal response to potential shocks. In these circumstances – at least in the current absence of a theory as to why these contracts might be involuntary – the arguments applied to equilibrium RE models must apply equally to 'disequilibrium' RE models. The use of $\text{Var}(y - y^*)$ accordingly again turns on the behaviour of distortions over the business cycle.

To sum up, in rational expectations models, there are *prima facie* reasons to believe that in general stabilization policy, even if effective, will not improve welfare, the main exception being where distortions are positively correlated with the cycle; the importance of this exception will vary with the nature of the benefit system. One may note finally that such an argument for stabilization policy is in principle also an argument for a change in the benefit system.

THE LUCAS CRITIQUE OF POLICY EVALUATION

It was Lucas (1976) who first pointed out that if expectations are formed rationally, then unless the estimated equations used by model builders to evaluate the consequences of alternative government policies are genuinely structural or behavioural, the implications of such simulations or evaluations may be seriously flawed. The essential insight of Lucas is that, when expectations are formed rationally, agents react to the behaviour of government, consequently unless the equations estimated by the model builder are structural, the coefficients in equations which are estimated over one policy regime will implicitly depend on the parameters of the government policy rule in operation. It follows that when alternative policy rules are simulated, not only will the government policy rule change, but so also will the par-

ameters in the equations which are not structural. Consequently, the evaluations of alternative policy can be quite
misleading.

Lucas gives a number of different examples of this theme,
but we can clarify the argument by consideration of the following simple open economy model based on Dornbusch
(1976). The structural equations of the model or hypothetical
economy are given by:

$$m = \bar{m} + u \qquad (5.1)$$

$$m = p - \lambda(\mathrm{E}e_{+1} - e) \qquad (5.2)$$

$$p - p_{-1} = \delta(e_{-1} - p_{-1}) \qquad (5.3)$$

where e is the exchange rate (rise = depreciation).

Equation (5.1) is the money supply equation ($\bar{m}$ is fixed, u
is a random error). (5.2) is the money demand equation in a
simple open economy version; $\mathrm{E}e_{+1} - e$, the expected
exchange rate change, is assumed equal to the interest rate
differential because of foreign speculation and, foreign interest rates being set to zero for convenience, so replaces the
interest rate in the function. (5.3) is a 'sticky-price' adjustment
mechanism, whereby, should purchasing power parity be disturbed by shocks, prices adjust back towards parity. Output
in this model is held fixed for simplicity. (This type of model
will be discussed more fully in Chapter 6.) Expectations,
$\mathrm{E}e_{+1}$, are assumed to be conditional on the full information
set at t. The rational expectations of the future exchange rate
is for this model given by the regressive expectations mechanism (see Chapter 7):

$$\mathrm{E}e_{+1} - e = (1 - \mu)(\bar{e} - e) + \pi u \qquad (5.4)$$

where $\bar{e} = \bar{m}$,

$$\pi = \frac{1 - \delta}{\lambda(\mu - 1) - \lambda(1 - \delta)},$$

and μ is the stable root of the equation

$$\lambda\mu^2 - [\lambda + \lambda(1 - \delta)]\mu + [\lambda(1 - \delta) - \delta] = 0 \qquad (5.5)$$

After substituting (5.4) into (5.2), equating (5.1) and (5.2) we obtain:

$$u + \bar{m} = p - \lambda((1 - \mu)(\bar{e} - e) + \pi u) \tag{5.6}$$

Using (5.3) and (5.6) and rearranging gives:

$$e = \alpha_0 \bar{m} + \alpha_1 e_{-1} + \alpha_2 p_{-1} + \alpha_3 u \tag{5.7}$$

where

$$\alpha_0 = (1 + \lambda(1 - \mu))J^{-1}$$
$$\alpha_1 = -\delta J^{-1}$$
$$\alpha_2 = -(1 - \delta)J^{-1}$$
$$\alpha_3 = (1 + \lambda\pi)J^{-1}$$
$$J = \lambda(1 - \mu)$$

or

$$e = \alpha_0 m + \alpha_1 e_{-1} + \alpha_2 p_{-1} + \alpha_3' u \tag{5.8}$$

where

$$\alpha_3' = \alpha_3 - \alpha_0$$

(5.7) is the rational expectations solution for the nominal exchange rate e in this economy. Given a data sample in which the fixed level of money stock ($\bar{m}$) has been maintained, (5.8) will predict the behaviour of the exchange rate contingent on the previous behaviour of prices and the exchange rate and the current behaviour of the money stock.

Suppose that instead of the behavioural equations (5.1), (5.2) and (5.3), our macroeconomic model consisted of an equation such as (5.8). We now suppose that the macro model builder simulates an alternative monetary rule in which, instead of a fixed level of money stock ($\bar{m}$), the authorities endeavour to stabilize the economy by the fixed feedback rule:

$$m = \bar{m}^0 + g(e - \bar{m}^0) + u \tag{5.9}$$

where g is a constant parameter.

Instead of (5.4) being the appropriate reduced form for the

rational expectation of the exchange rate, the new appropriate regressive reduced form is:

$$E e_{+1} - e = (1 - h)(\bar{m}^0 - e) + \pi_1 u$$

where

$$\pi_1 = \frac{1 - \delta}{g + \lambda(h - 1) - \lambda(1 - \delta)} \tag{5.10}$$

and h is the stable root of the equation

$$\lambda h^2 + (g - \lambda - \lambda(1 - \delta))h + (\lambda(1 - \delta) - \delta - (1 - \delta)g) = 0 \tag{5.11}$$

Consequently instead of (5.7) and (5.8) we obtain:

$$e = \beta_0 \bar{m}^0 + \beta_1 e_{-1} + \beta_2 p_{-1} + \beta_3 u \tag{5.12}$$

where

$$\beta_0 = 1 - g + \lambda(1 - h)$$
$$\beta_1 = -\delta k^{-1}$$
$$\beta_2 = -(1 - \delta)k^{-1}$$
$$\beta_3 = (1 + \lambda \pi_1)k^{-1}$$
$$k = \lambda(1 - h) - g$$

or

$$e = \beta_0 m + \beta_1 e_{-1} + \beta_2 p_{-1} + \beta_3' u \tag{5.13}$$
$$\beta_3' = \beta_3 - \beta_0$$

Quite clearly (5.12) and (5.13) are different from either (5.7) or (5.8); their parameters have changed because of the new policy rule. Consequently if the macro model builder simply changed the money supply rule in equation (5.8) to the new rule (5.9) and continued to use (5.8), the consequences of the policy change will be simulated in an inappropriate manner. Clearly the appropriate procedure for the model builder is to ensure that the estimated equations in his model are behavioural equations whose predictions are stable across regime changes and that expectations are explicitly modelled.

Unfortunately this problem is easier to solve in principle

than in practice. Earlier work by Lucas (1973) has exemplified the strong possibility that many parameters in what were normally regarded as structural equations in macro models may be related to the particular policy regime in operation. The particular model considered by Lucas (1973) is one in which, due to signal extraction problems (as discussed in Chapter 4) faced by the individual supplier, the slope of the aggregate supply curve (i.e. the parameter on unanticipated inflation, p^{ue}) is related to the variance of real and nominal shocks; the essential point being that if the supplier thinks that p^{ue} is dominated by *nominal* shocks he will respond little to it, if by *real* shocks he will respond a lot. Quite clearly in this solution the move from a stable monetary policy regime with a low variance of nominal shocks to another high variance policy will lead to a change in the parameter in the supply curve. Yet there are no instances to date of successful estimation of Phillips curves allowing for this problem. (Lawrence, 1983, does however report some interesting attempts.) This illustrates the practical difficulties of estimating truly structural parameters (i.e. invariant to relevant regime change) in macroeconomic models.

One reaction to this problem has been to assert that only the parameters of preferences and technology ('deep structure') will be regime-invariant and that macroeconomists should therefore estimate these. Recently a number of authors (see Hansen and Sargent (1980), Sargent (1978, 1981)) have begun to pursue a research methodology along these lines. This work models agents at the microeconomic level as intertemporal optimizers subject to the constraints of budget and technology, and attempts to retrieve the parameters of the (aggregated) utility and production functions. These attempts have met with little empirical success so far to date, and have been too restricted in scope to be usable for macroeconomic policy evaluation. However it is early days.

Another reaction has been to model expectations explicitly, but to continue to treat as structural the parameters of such macroeconomic model equations as the consumption and investment functions; this approach has been adopted for example in the Liverpool Model (Chapter 11) and other examples are Blanchard and Wyplosz (1981), Taylor (1979a), and Holly and Zarrop (1983). It is recognized by these authors that the parameters of these equations will change as regimes change, but it is argued that the major impact of regime change will be felt in the expectations variables, while that on the parameters themselves, except for quite violent regime change, may be of second order importance. Again it is too early to pronounce on the relative success of this approach.

It remains possible that a third school of thought referred to in Chapter 1, of which a major proponent is Sims (1979), is correct in asserting that there is no practical possibility of policy evaluation and the best we can achieve is the estimation of time-series models whose parameters will shift in an unpredictable way with regime change.

We end this section therefore in a cautious vein: policy evaluation is certainly difficult and may even be impossible, but various researches are in hand which may offer scope for better evaluation in the future.

OPTIMAL ECONOMIC POLICIES AND TIME INCONSISTENCY

A crucial feature of an economy in which agents form their expectations of the future value of variables in a rational manner is that current outcomes and the movement of the system's state depend in part upon anticipated future policy decisions. This will obviously not be the case when expectations are formed in a backward-looking manner, since in these circumstances current outcomes and the movement of the system's state depend only upon current and past policy decisions and upon the current state. Kydland and Prescott (1977) showed how, in a dynamic economic system in which agents possess rational expectations, the optimal policy at time $t = 0$, which sets future paths for the control variables (taxes, subsidies, monetary growth), implies values of the control variables at some later time $t + i$, that will not be optimal when policy is re-examined at $t + i$, even though the preferences of agents are unchanged. This possibility is known as the time inconsistency of optimal plans.

Two illustrative examples of time inconsistency taken from

Kydland and Prescott (1977) and from Fischer (1980b) relate to examinations and patent policy. Optimal policy at the beginning of a course is to plan to have a mid-session exam. However, on the morning of the exam when all student preparation is complete, the optimal policy is to cancel the exam, saving the students the trouble of writing and the lecturer the trouble of marking. Optimal policy may analogously be to withdraw patent protection after resources have been allocated to successful inventive activity on the basis of continued patent protection.

Both these examples illustrate how the optimal policy is dynamically inconsistent. A method of ensuring a consistent economic policy does in fact exist in backward-looking models. This can be found by using the method of dynamic optimization known as Bellman's Principle of Optimality. (See Chow (1975) for an excellent discussion.) While the precise mathematics of such a procedure need not detain us here, the essential idea of the procedure is as follows. A policy should have the property that it is optimal in the last period (T), given any initial conditions in the previous period $(T - 1)$. Similarly choice of policy at time $T - 1$ should be optimal, given the initial conditions in the previous period $(T - 2)$ and so on until the last policy is chosen on the basis of information available at the beginning of the period. In other words, the optimal policy is chosen on the basis of *backward* optimization. However, this is impossible with forward-looking expectations, since the policy chosen for T will influence events *before* it, from $t = 1$ onwards. Hence policy in each period has to be chosen simultaneously at $t = 0$,[5] and this set of policies will in general be time-inconsistent (i.e. the policy-maker will find it optimal to change them once he has carried through part of his plans).

These points can be easily demonstrated by consideration of a simple two-period problem presented in Kydland and Prescott (1977).

Let $\Pi = (\Pi_1, \Pi_2)$ be a sequence of policies for periods 1 and 2 and $X = (X_1, X_2)$ be the corresponding sequence for economic agents' decisions. The social objective function is given by:

$$S(X_1, X_2, \Pi_1, \Pi_2) \qquad (5.14)$$

Agents' decisions in period t depend upon all policy decisions and their past decisions as follows:

$$X_1 = X_1(\Pi_1, \Pi_2) \qquad (5.15)$$

$$X_2 = X_2(X_1, \Pi_1, \Pi_2) \qquad (5.16)$$

Consider first the consistent policy. Π_2 must be chosen to maximize (5.14) given the past decision Π_1 and X_1 and the constraint (5.16). Assuming the usual conditions for a maximum to exist, we obtain the first-order condition for a backward-looking model by Bellman's principle as:

$$\left(\frac{\partial S}{\partial X_2}\right)\left(\frac{\partial X_2}{\partial \Pi_2}\right) + \frac{\partial S}{\partial \Pi_2} = 0 \qquad (5.17)$$

The consistent policy in a backward-looking model can ignore the effects of Π_2 upon X_1. However, here for the optimal decision rule, the first-order condition is given by:

$$\left(\frac{\partial S}{\partial X_2}\right)\left(\frac{\partial X_2}{\partial \Pi_2}\right) + \frac{\partial S}{\partial \Pi_2} + \frac{\partial X_1}{\partial \Pi_2}\left[\frac{\partial S}{\partial X_1} + \left(\frac{\partial S}{\partial X_2}\frac{\partial X_2}{\partial X_1}\right)\right] = 0$$

$$(5.18)$$

It follows from inspection of (5.18) that, only if either the effect of Π_2 upon X_1 is zero (i.e. $\partial X_1/\partial \Pi_2 = 0$), or the effect of changes in X_1 upon S both directly and indirectly though X_2 is zero [i.e. $\partial S/\partial X_1 + \partial S/\partial X_2(\partial X_2/\partial X_1) = 0$], does Bellman's principle give the optimal policy.[6]

It is possible to draw up an 'optimal' policy for each period that *is* time consistent i.e. has the property that there is no incentive to change it in subsequent periods.[7] In the above two examples, the time-consistent policy would recognize that exams would not be held and that patents would be withdrawn; in effect, mid-term exams and patents respectively would not be in the feasible set of policies. In general, however, such time-consistent policies will be unattractive as compared with time-inconsistent policies chosen at $t = 0$ and carried through.

This poses an unhappy dilemma. Either policy-makers choose bad policies which they have no incentive to deviate from, or they choose good policies which they probably will not stick to; if they do the latter, severe problems of future credibility and therefore later policy effectiveness are likely to arise.

Quite clearly, time inconsistency of policy choice by the authorities may be appropriate if it has no longer-run consequences. In some circumstances it may appear to be correct to deceive agents for their own good. However, it is clear that if agents are repeatedly deceived, then at some point agents will endogenize against such a possibility and then in a sense the time-inconsistent policy becomes consistent, with the consequent possibility of producing an inferior outcome to that which would have occurred had the original policy been stuck to. The essence of the problem revolves around the amount of credibility which agents place in the policy-makers' announced policy. It is for this reason that interest in constitutional limitations on the power of politicians to change course has been widely aroused. If a constitution prevents back-sliding at least for a sensibly long period, then politicians can choose optimal plans, safe in the knowledge that, though these are time-inconsistent, this no longer matters because they are protected from temptation.[8]

This type of solution has been advocated by Kydland and Prescott, who suggest that the authorities should be limited to the choice of a policy rule which has the most attractive operating characteristics (i.e. performs best on average over a period) and that this rule will most likely be of the open-loop type, i.e. without feedback from events to future actions (see Chapter 3). However, this is not necessarily the case; as Chapter 3 made clear, there are models in which closed-loop (i.e. feedback) policies are effective and whether they are optimal will then depend upon the welfare function and existing distortions (e.g. Buiter, 1981).

There is the final problem that the constitution itself will be subject to time inconsistency. There will typically always remain incentives to break the rules. Times of war or emergencies in general are times when expediency rules. Nevertheless, there are and probably should be strong pressures to avoid constitutional override, even though it is clear that the constitution cannot itself be immune to change. The issue of optimal constitutions and parallel social arrangements to facilitate optimal private and public decision making has therefore been thrust into the forefront of the rational expectations research programme.

CONCLUSIONS

'Optimal control' methods of varying sophistication have been used on Keynesian models for much of the post-war period; these have given rise to closed-loop, feedback policies, the so-called 'fine-tuning' 'demand-management' policies of the Keynesian era. One firm conclusion of this chapter is that such methods are dangerously misconceived, both because they do not allow for effects on private behaviour through expectations and because they take a naive view of the social welfare function.

Where conclusions are less firm is what policies *are* optimal. Two things, however, do stand out. Government policy should be as *predictable* as possible; higher variance, whether of money supply or fiscal policy, has been shown uniformly to reduce welfare.

Secondly, government policy should be as *credible* as possible (i.e. be expected to remain in place as promised for a long period into the future); lack of credibility causes private behaviour to insure against backsliding which in turn limits policy options, and the overall result is likely to be inferior to that of consistent policies, even if these were suboptimal.

Within these guidelines, the present state of knowledge does not enable policy-makers to choose sophisticated feedback rules with any confidence, even though we would grant that there is likely to be scope in theory for them to be effective and even beneficial in the institutional circumstances of some economies. The choice, however, between simple closed- and open-loop rules is not one that can be made on general grounds, even if the burden of proof seems to lie in a rational expectations framework on those urging feedback.

NOTES

1. In case it is not already clear, rational expectations implies that agents act at the micro level as if they know the probability distributions over future events (and hence the parameters of the true model); it does *not* imply that governments or other observers of the aggregates, including econometricians, have this knowledge. This distinction is based first on incentive structures. The 'micro-agent' is assumed to face significant costs of expectations errors and the threat of these costs is assumed to force him close enough to 'full knowledge' for this to be a reasonable approximation for aggregate modelling purposes. This is not true in general of government employees or econometricians when dealing with aggregate data; considerations of power in the first case and of academic prestige in the second are as important, if not more so, than the need to be *right*. There is more to the distinction. An individual micro-agent may well not know the true model (in fact is unlikely to do so even on an 'as if' basis); but misconceptions of the model across micro-agents should, because of commercial pressures operating symmetrically to weed out poor agents, be randomly distributed around the true model, and on the average the misconceptions will cancel out for a large number of agents. A government too may get the model wrong; unfortunately there is only one government at any one time and, if it relies on being right in computing sophisticated policies, it risks egregious error.

2. If output, however, changes for *supply* reasons (e.g. crop failure), this would naturally be added into y^* and the variance taken round this adjusted figure, as in Chapter 4.

3. This situation is not one of full Pareto-optimality, as markets are incomplete and distortions assumed to exist; however, it is a situation of restricted Pareto-optimality, under the provisos given.

4. This has particular relevance in the UK as argued in Chapter 11, pp. 206–14.

5. Recent procedures as exemplified by Chow (1980) or Holly and Zarrop (1983) have modified the optimality principle to allow for the dependence of current states on future states and policy instruments. If the policy-maker now *implements* this policy, then expectations will be confirmed. However, the policy will not generally be optimal in future states. Rather such methods can give the best plans possible on the *assumption* that they are pre-announced, believed and carried through.

6. We should recognize as implicit in Kydland and Prescott and demonstrated formally by Calvo (1978) that the dynamic inconsistency problem can still occur in models in which the private sector behavioural functions are derived from optimization of the same utility function as the government is maximizing.

7. This is a problem like that of drawing up incentive-compatible contracts (Hart, 1983), The best contracts may be ruled out because the party with the power to cheat has an incentive to do so. Provided a cheap method of policing is available, the best outcome in these problems can be achieved by outlawing cheating.

8. Human affairs are full of such arrangements, of which perhaps the sacred marriage vow used to be the prize example.

6

The Nature of the 'Phillips Curve' Under Rational Expectations[1]

We have already made frequent reference to 'Phillips curves', meaning some partial relationship between output deviations from equilibrium, $y - y^*$, and unanticipated inflation, p^{ue}; we have also referred synonymously to 'aggregate supply curves' and identified a number of variants in Chapter 3 – Sargent–Wallace, Lucas, classical and so on. In this chapter, we pause to clarify the different routes by which these relationships can be obtained, since the nature of the supply curve is so central to macroeconomics under rational expectations.

Both Lucas (e.g. 1972b) and Sargent and Wallace (e.g. 1975) have argued that a supply or Phillips curve relating output (and unemployment) to unexpected inflation can be derived from a set-up in which there are rational expectations, full market-clearing, and information asymmetries. In this chapter we reconstruct their derivation within a stylized macro framework, and subject it to certain criticisms. We then suggest an alternative contract-based derivation of the Phillips curve, in which wages are set by contract but prices adjust flexibly; in the process we draw attention to the need for care in the specification of wage equations under rational expectations, explicitly rejecting one standard specification of the (wage) Phillips curve following Lipsey (1960).

THE LUCAS–SARGENT–WALLACE SUPPLY HYPOTHESIS
The Direct Route via Goods Markets

One way to underpin the supply hypothesis is to ignore the labour market altogether and simply deal with the goods market. This is the way some presentations proceed (Lucas, 1972b; Sargent and Wallace, 1975).

We seek a supply function of the form

$$y = y^* + \phi(p - p^*) + \cdots \tag{6.1}$$

where p^* is the expected price level defined as either Ep_{+1} or $\underset{-1}{E}\,p$ and E is the expectations operator, y is real output, p is the price level, ϕ is a positive constant, and other arguments may enter; it is a partial relationship therefore.

In the direct story, y^* is 'normal' output, that is that output which would prevail if $p = p^*$. Now if $p^* = Ep_{+1}$, (6.1) implies that output will react positively to an incentive to produce now rather than later. Notice that following the normal conventions, stock-holding demand is placed in the 'IS' curve so that (6.1) cannot be regarded as a *sales* function (i.e. production minus net stock change); rather it is a pure production relationship. It therefore must state that factor use is shifted between periods according to relative real *profit* in the two periods, suitably discounted by the real rate of interest. So we must write in full:[2]

$$y = y^* + \phi\left[(p - C) - \left(\underset{-1}{E}\,p_{+1} - \underset{-1}{E}\,C_{+1} - r\right)\right] + \varepsilon_1$$

$$(6.2)$$

where C is the (logarithm of) factor costs, ε_1 is a random error and r is the real rate of interest as expected currently, i.e.:

$$r = R - \underset{-1}{E}\,p_{+1} + \underset{-1}{E}\,p$$

Unfortunately (6.2) is crucially incomplete as a theory of supply since C is unexplained. It may, however, serve as a basis for a goods-supply equation in conjunction with a labour-supply equation and as such we will return to it.

Notice that y^* is interpreted as the output that would be produced if profits were expected to be at their permanent future level, i.e. zero in a competitive economy.

If $p^* = \underset{-1}{\text{E}}\ p$, then output responds positively to an unanticipated price rise. The idea, explained in Lucas (1972b), is that agents do not have sufficient information at time t to know whether the price rises they perceive for their own goods are relative or general; an implication explored by Lucas (1973) is that the more 'monetary noise' in the system, i.e. the greater the disturbances to the price level are relative to real disturbances, the lower the supply elasticity to price rises (i.e. the lower ϕ). In other words, agents do not know prices in *general* at time t; they only have their previous period's expectations of these prices to go on. What about costs? Presumably, just as output responds positively to higher than expected prices, so also it does to lower than expected costs, assuming as one must that the producer has current information on his own costs. We can now write this supply equation in full as:

$$y = y^{*\prime} - \phi\left(p - \underset{-1}{\text{E}}\ p - C + \underset{-1}{\text{E}}\ C \right) \qquad (6.3)$$

Notice that in (6.3) $y^{*\prime}$ is no longer the zero-profit output of (6.2) (an acceptable enough definition of normal output). It is now simply the output that would occur if expectations were realized. In other words, it is simply expected output. Hence, if profits were high in period t relative to the future, this would not cause an 'abnormally' high output according to (6.3); any effect would be included in $y^{*\prime}$. An easy way to see what this limitation implies is to expand (6.2) as:

$$y = y^* + \phi\left(p - \underset{-1}{\text{E}}\ p - C + \underset{-1}{\text{E}}\ C \right)$$
$$+ \phi\left[\underset{-1}{\text{E}}\ p - \underset{-1}{\text{E}}\ C - \left(\underset{-1}{\text{E}}\ p_{+1} - \underset{-1}{\text{E}}\ C_{+1} - r \right) \right] \qquad (6.4)$$

It follows that $y^{*\prime}$ consists of not only y^* but also the expected (at $t-1$) value of the change in profit minus r.

Now it is usual to treat y^* in practice as a constant or a trend. Yet clearly there would be no basis for treating $y^{*\prime}$ in such a way, at least without considerably more argument based on the behaviour of the model as a whole.

There is a further deficiency with (6.3), namely that, as in the case of (6.2), it leaves C unexplained. If we were to suppose – attractively – that C is totally predictable for the next period, this would allow us to eliminate $\left(C - \underset{-1}{\text{E}} \, C\right)$ from (6.3) leaving simply $y = y^{*\prime} + \phi\left(p - \underset{-1}{\text{E}} \, p\right)$. But as we have seen, $y^{*\prime}$ itself contains values of $\underset{-1}{\text{E}} \, C$, $\underset{-1}{\text{E}} \, C_{+1}$; so there remains the problem of determining expected costs to determine $y^{*\prime}$.

Our conclusion is that the 'direct' route to justifying an equation of type (6.2) or (6.3) is not adequate because it is open-ended, in that it leaves costs unexplained. Version (6.3) appears to by-pass this problem, but only at the expense of shifting it to $y^{*\prime}$; it is in any case unacceptable, because $y^{*\prime}$ (or expected output) is not a satisfactory equivalent of normal output (at least without a full solution of the model). We therefore proceed to examine total theories that underpin equation (6.2), total in the sense that they incorporate the labour market and so costs.

The Indirect Route via Goods and Labour Markets

The natural starting point for a total theory is, following Lucas (1972a), the Fisherian labour supply hypothesis of Lucas and Rapping (1969). This hypothesis is common to all proponents of the 'supply hypothesis'. It states that:

$$L_s = \left(\overset{+}{w'}, \, \underset{-1}{\text{E}} \, \overset{-}{w_{+1} - w'}, \, \overset{+}{r}, \, \varepsilon_3 \right) \qquad (6.5)$$

which we write conveniently as:

$$L_s = \beta_0 + \beta_1 w' + \beta_2 \left(r - \underset{-1}{\text{E}} \, w_{+1} + w' \right) + \varepsilon_3 \qquad (6.6)$$

where L = labour units supplied, $w = W - p$, the actual real wage, and $w' = W - \underset{-1}{\text{E}} \, p$, or the 'observed' real wage, all in natural logarithms. It is normally assumed that $\beta_1 > 0$ so that, if wages rise equally in all time periods, labour supply rises (implying gross substitution between money and leisure); $\beta_2 > 0$ reflects the substitution between current and future effort.

In getting from this to a theory of *un*employment there are, however, differences. Equilibrium is assumed to prevail in the labour market $(L_s = L_D)$ so unemployment is 'voluntary'. However, measured unemployment which is one major indicator of the 'economic cycle' has to be explained.

Minford and Peel (1980) showed that, if Lucas and Rapping's theory is reconstructed using rational expectations, we can obtain the following relationship in the spirit of their model:

$$U = L_s^{*\prime} - L_s = (\beta_1 + \beta_2)\left(\underset{-1}{\mathsf{E}}\ W - W \right) \qquad (6.7)$$

where W is the nominal wage and U is the fraction of the labour force unemployed. This says that unemployment figures reflect search, and that this search occurs because workers react to the wage offers they obtain in the light of their most recent expectations (we assume last period's) of what the going wage is. $L_s^{*\prime}$ is what they would supply if the wage offer were equal to that expectation (notice the parallel with $y^{*\prime}$ above). Hence, the lower the wage offer is relative to their expectation, the longer the unemployed search, and *vice versa*.

This account of unemployment fits naturally with the US unemployment concept derived as it is from the Bureau of Labour Statistics survey (this records as unemployed those who state that they are 'actively seeking work'), and we call it the 'US' model.

However, another theory from the same supply curve can be put forward which would be more appropriate to European unemployment measures, based as these are more or less (and in the UK now totally, since end-1982) on registration for unemployment pay. This theory accepts that people will be considered unemployed if they are members of the insured labour force and not working, regardless of whether they are genuinely 'searching' or not. This would include especially those who regard themselves as 'laid off' (and returning to the same job in due course) and those who prefer to wait for better future wage offers (but who see no point in searching because such offers are not expected to be currently available). It can be written as

$$U = \bar{L} - L_s \tag{6.8}$$

where $\bar{L}$ is the insured labour force and hence is a socially determined variable with at most a very long-term relationship to the labour supply. We regard it as a constant in what follows and this implies that U is nothing other than the labour supply function with sign reversed and an altered constant term. We call it the 'European' model.

To complete the model we require additional functions. These we take to be, in standard fashion, a demand-for-labour function, our output supply equation (6.2), a costs equation (to relate these two), a demand for output ('IS' curve), and a demand for money ('LM' curve).

We take the simplest approach to costs and labour demand:

$$L = \gamma_0 + \gamma_1 y \quad (\gamma_1 > 1) \quad \text{(demand for labour)} \tag{6.9}$$

$$C = W \quad \text{(costs)} \tag{6.10}$$

We disregard productivity growth for convenience and adopt a labour-only production function as indicated above. (6.9) is our production function inverted as a log-linear approximation to quadratic technology ($\gamma_1 > 1$ reflects diminishing marginal productivity). It follows from (6.10) that:

$$p - C = -w \tag{6.11}$$

The demand for output we write as:

$$y - y^* = -\alpha(r - r^*) + \varepsilon_2 \tag{6.12}$$

an IS curve in which random variations in demand, ε_2, and the response of savings and investment to the real interest rate affect output demand.

The LM curve reads:

$$\bar{m} + \varepsilon_4 = y + P - \mu R \tag{6.13}$$

where $\bar{m} + \varepsilon_4$ is the nominal money supply with fixed and random components and R is the nominal interest rate.

The model in full can now be written as Model A:

$$y = y^* + \phi\left(\underset{-1}{E}\ w_{+1} - w + r\right) + \varepsilon_1 \qquad (6.14)$$

$$y - y^* = -\alpha(r - r^*) + \varepsilon_2 \qquad (6.15)$$

$$L = \beta_0 + \beta_1\left(w + p - \underset{-1}{E}\ p\right)$$

$$+ \beta_2\left(r - \underset{-1}{E}\ w_{+1} + w + p - \underset{-1}{E}\ p\right) + \varepsilon_3 \qquad (6.16)$$

$$L = \gamma_0 + \gamma_1 y \qquad (6.17)$$

$$U = (\beta_1 + \beta_2)\left(\underset{-1}{E}\ W - W\right) \qquad \text{(6.18a–US)}$$

$$U = \bar{L} - \beta_0 - \beta_1\left(w + p - \underset{-1}{E}\ p\right)$$

$$- \beta_2\left(r - \underset{-1}{E}\ w_{+1} + w + p - \underset{-1}{E}\ p\right) - \varepsilon_3 \qquad \begin{array}{c}\text{(6.18b–}\\\text{European)}\end{array}$$

$$\bar{m} + \varepsilon_4 = y + p - \mu R \qquad (6.19)$$

$$R = r + \underset{-1}{E}\ p_{+1} - \underset{-1}{E}\ p \qquad (6.20)$$

(6.14) is obtained by substitution of (6.11) into (6.2). Notice that equations (6.14–6.17) form a 'real sector' which solves for y, w, L, r in terms of ε_1 to ε_3 and $p - \underset{-1}{E}\ p$; (6.19) and (6.20) (the nominal sector) then solve for p and R given y, r and ε_4, the money supply shock, and (6.18) solves for U given these solutions. The link between the real and nominal sectors is through $p - \underset{-1}{E}\ p$ which reflects both real and nominal shocks.

y^*, 'normal' output, from equation (6.2) is treated as equilibrium output as given by the model. We may also derive equilibrium values w^*, r^*, and L^*, and p^*, C^*, W^*; but we do not focus on these here. Notice that U^* will be 0 in the US version (because there is no search) but will generally be positive in the European version (until $\bar{L}$ eventually is pushed by social pressures towards L^*).[3]

To gauge the responses of the model to shocks, we treat all variables as deviations from equilibrium values. Hence dropping constants and exogenous variables, we obtain the following final form for w:

$$\underset{-1}{\mathrm{E}}\, w_{+1} - \delta w = \eta \tag{6.21}$$

where:

$$\eta = \left[-(\beta_2 + \alpha\gamma_1)\varepsilon_1 + (\beta_2 - \gamma_1\phi)\varepsilon_2 + (\phi + \alpha)\varepsilon_3 \right.$$

$$\left. + (\beta_1 + \beta_2)(\phi + \alpha)\left(p - \underset{-1}{\mathrm{E}}\, p \right) \right] \Big/ (\phi\gamma_1\alpha + 2\phi\beta_2 + \alpha\beta_2)$$

$$\delta = (\phi\gamma_1\alpha + 2\phi\beta_2 + \alpha\beta_2 + \alpha\beta_1)/(\phi\gamma_1\alpha + 2\phi\beta_2 + \alpha\beta_2)$$

The general solution of (6.21) is some linear function of current and past η; we therefore use the Muth method and postulate that:

$$w = \sum_{i=0}^{\infty} q_i \eta_{-i} \tag{6.22}$$

The identities in the η_{-i} are then derived from:

$$\sum_{i=1}^{\infty} q_{i+1}\eta_{-i} - \delta \sum_{i=0}^{\infty} q_i \eta_{-i} = \eta \tag{6.23}$$

and are:

$$(\eta_0) - \delta q_0 = 1 \tag{6.24}$$

$$(\eta_{-i}, i \geqslant 1)q_{i+1} = \delta q_i \tag{6.25}$$

Since $\delta > 1$, the solution for w is:

$$w = -(\eta/\delta) \tag{6.26}$$

by appeal to the stability condition.

The solutions for the other real variables follow from this and (6.14–6.17) as:

$$r = -\frac{(\beta_1 + \beta_2)w}{\beta_2 + \alpha\gamma_1} + \frac{\gamma_1\varepsilon_2 - \varepsilon_3 - (\beta_1 + \beta_2)\left(p - \underset{-1}{E}\ p\right)}{\beta_2 + \alpha\gamma_1} \qquad (6.27)$$

$$y = -\phi(w - r) + \varepsilon_1 \qquad (6.28)$$

$$L = -\gamma_1\phi(w - r) + \gamma_1\varepsilon_1 \qquad (6.29)$$

Notice that

$$\underset{-1}{E}\ w_{+1} = \underset{-1}{E}\ r_{+1} = \underset{-1}{E}\ y_{+1} = \underset{-1}{E}\ L_{+1} = 0$$

The final form for p and R, given y and r as derived above, is from (6.19) and (6.20):

$$\underset{-1}{E}\ p_{+1} - \mu^{-1}p - \underset{-1}{E}\ p = (\mu^{-1}y - r) \qquad (6.30)$$

Here $(1 + \mu)/\mu > 1$, so that the solution is, by the same argument as for $\delta > 1$ above:

$$p = -y + \mu r; \quad \underset{-1}{E}\ p = \underset{-1}{E}\ p_{+1} = 0 \qquad (6.31)$$

The solution for R follows from this and (6.20) as:

$$R = r \qquad (6.32)$$

The unemployment solutions are:

$$U(\text{Eur}) = -(\beta_1 + \beta_2)w - \beta_2 r - (\beta_1 + \beta_2)\left(p - \underset{-1}{E}\ p\right) - \varepsilon_3 \qquad (6.33)$$

and $\left(\text{remembering that }\underset{-1}{E}\ W = \underset{-1}{E}\ p + \underset{-1}{E}\ w = 0\right)$

$$U(\text{US}) = -(\beta_1 + \beta_2)(w + p) \qquad (6.34)$$

The 'Phillips curve' we seek is a *partial* relationship derived from the supply side of the model, namely equations (6.14), and (6.16–6.18) of the form[4]:

$$y - y^* = f\left(\overset{+}{p - \underset{-1}{E}\ p}, \ldots\right)$$

and in parallel:

$$U - U^* = f\left(p - \overset{+}{\underset{-1}{E}} p, \dots\right)$$

The general point is that unanticipated inflation should, *ceteris paribus*, induce an increase in output supply and a reduction in unemployment through an increase in labour supply. Such relationships can then be set beside the demand side of the model (equations (6.15), (6.19) and (6.20)) to derive the full equilibrium. They can readily be found as we see from (6.14), (6.16) and (6.17):

$$(y - y^*) = (\phi\gamma_1 + \beta_1 + \beta_2)^{-1}\left[\phi(\beta_1 + \beta_2)\left(p - \underset{-1}{E} p\right)\right.$$
$$\left. + \phi(\beta_1 + 2\beta_2)(r - r^*) + (\beta_1 + \beta_2)\varepsilon_1 + \phi\varepsilon_3\right] \quad (6.35)$$

The positive coefficient on r is the result of intertemporal substitution by both firms and labour to present production. (6.18a) yields:

$$U - U^* = -(\beta_1 + \beta_2)\left(w - \underset{-1}{E} w + p - \underset{-1}{E} p\right)$$
$$= [-(\beta_1 + \beta_2)(\phi\gamma_1 + \beta_1 + \beta_2)^{-1}]$$
$$\times \left[\phi\gamma_1\left(p - \underset{-1}{E} p\right) + (\phi\gamma_1 - \beta_2)(r - r^*) + \gamma_1\varepsilon_1 - \varepsilon_3\right]$$
$$(6.36)$$

(6.18b) yields:

$$U - U^* = (\bar{L} - L) - (\bar{L} - L)^* = L^* - L = \gamma_1(y^* - y)$$
$$(6.37)$$

which is at once derivable from (6.35).

The solution of (6.35), our supply (PP or Phillips) curve, interacting with the demand side of the model, already derived above, can be illustrated in a two-quadrant diagram. Figure 6.1 shows the equilibrium and the effects of a temporary monetary expansion. The LM curve shifts rightwards

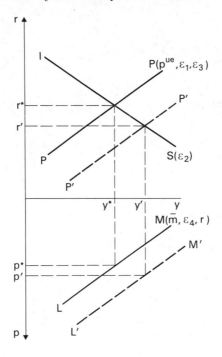

Figure 6.1 *Effects of temporary rise in money supply* (ε_4). $p^{ue} = p - \underset{-1}{E} p$.

raising prices unexpectedly, which in turn shifts the PP to the right. The consequential fall in interest rates raises money demand and moderates the rightward shift of the LM curve; obviously, the higher the interest-elasticity of demand for money, the greater the dampening effect.

Figure 6.2 illustrates the two possible effects of a temporary bond-financed fiscal expansion shifting the IS curve to the right along the PP curve. In case (a) with a high interest-elasticity of money, the LM shifts out (as interest rates rise) sufficiently to *raise* prices, so that the PP shifts to the right, reinforcing the rise in output. In case (b) with a low interest-elasticity of money, the LM shifts insufficiently to prevent prices *falling*, so that the PP shifts leftwards, dampening the rise in output. The model therefore has the standard property

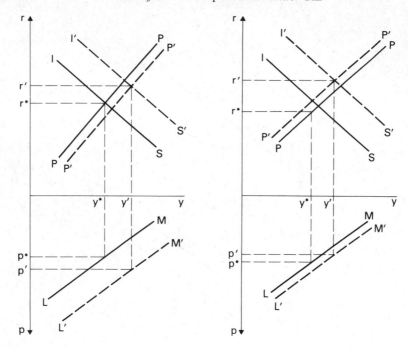

Figure 6.2 *Effects of temporary bond-financed fiscal expansion* (ε_2)

    (a) *high interest-elasticity*   (b) *low interest-elasticity*
       of money   *of money*

that a higher interest-elasticity of money dampens the effect of monetary policy on output, but reinforces the effects of fiscal policy on output.

Nevertheless, the Phillips curve of this model is extraordinarily vulnerable to plausible changes in the information set-up. The model assumes that firms have perfect current access at the micro level to all costs and prices relevant to them. Thus they know their own W and p. Workers on the other hand know their own W but not their p, because it is assumed they spread their purchases over a long time period and cannot sample the prices of all the goods they are interested in each time they offer their labour.

Yet these are arbitrary assumptions; 'ad hoc' in the sense

that this information set-up is not derived from the optimizing behaviour of agents, whether individual or collective.

Moreover, other assumptions are as plausible (i.e. apparently consistent with the facts). Firms also spread their input purchases and output sales over a long time period; each time they make a production decision, they cannot necessarily sample all their input and output prices. The decision, for example, how much to produce of a motor car (even once the capital is installed), requires assessment of the likely market state at home and abroad at the time of delivery, of how one's wages may change and of how wages of other producers delivering inputs may change, over the production period. The point in general is that it may well be as costly for a firm to take decisions in such a way that it can always avoid using expectations about current data, as it would be for a worker/consumer to do so.

The model's Phillips curve collapses if any of the following is true:

(1) Firms know their input prices but not their output prices; in this case output reacts *negatively* to unanticipated inflation.
(2) Firms know *neither* their input *nor* their output prices; here output does not respond at all.
(3) Equation (6.14) holds for firms (i.e. they know *both*), and workers know *both* their wages and the prices of the goods they buy (zero output response).
(4) Equation (6.14) holds and workers know *neither* their wages *nor* their prices (zero output response).
(5) Equation (6.14) holds and workers know their prices but not their wages (negative output response).

The Phillips curve is, however, strengthened if firms know their prices but not their wages, while workers know their wages but not their prices. The reason is obvious: *every* agent in this case thinks that rising prices means a better relative price for him.[5]

We now proceed to develop an alternative structural model which, it could be argued, is more in conformity with how labour and goods markets work at the micro level. It assumes that prices and wages are set for some period and that supplies are offered on these terms for the duration of this (contract) period. The choice of contract period we suppose to be determined by some decision weighing transaction costs of price changes against the desirability of being in constant equilibrium. This contract period will be inversely related to the expected long-run rate of inflation (see Minford and Hilliard, 1977). For our purposes we hold the period fixed, since we are primarily concerned in this chapter with deviations around the equilibrium. Nevertheless, the long-run equilibrium solution must of course take into account the variation in contract period.

A CONTRACT FRAMEWORK

We move now into a different world where, instead of 'supply' equations for goods and labour, we look for wage- or price-setting equations by suppliers and assume that quantities are determined by demand. To avoid getting involved in problems of overlapping contracts or of time-aggregation, we assume that the contract period and the period of observation used in the model are the same.

The world is the familiar world of the 'Phillips curve' and its underpinnings are familiar from the work of Lipsey (1960), Phelps (1970) and others. However, it is not possible – as some have seemed to assume – to incorporate rational expectations straightforwardly into the Phillips curve or its pricing equivalent.

Wage Setting

Consider the usual 'story' given for the inflation-augmented wage equation:

$$\Delta W = \left(\underset{-1}{E} \, p - p_{-1} \right) - \phi(U) \qquad (6.38)$$

Workers and firms are involved in guessing the equilibrium nominal wage and a *tâtonnement* process occurs whereby it is gradually bid up or down by excess demand or supply. However, in our case they bid it up immediately by the full amount of the expected inflation rate because agents do not have money illusion; it is assumed that this is the general inflation expectation and that they mentally convert nominal wages into expected real wages. Thus it is expected real wages, w^E, that adjust in response to unemployment. We are to picture a dynamic system where L, labour quantity, is on the demand curve and w^E is shifted over a series of periods towards equilibrium (w^*, L^*).

Why does w^E reach w^* only gradually? The reasoning goes that the individual agent has incomplete information (perhaps virtually none) about the general market situation. His best information is the 'going (expected real) wage'. If a worker finds himself jobless involuntarily (i.e. he does not wish to continue searching), he will offer his services at a rate slightly below the going rate; if he is faced by competing offers, he will offer his services at slightly above the going rate. These new offers by individual workers will be registered by job centres and private agencies and will change the going rate. This process will take some time, implying that in any period there will not necessarily be sufficient movement in the rate to converge.

But this story makes little sense if we assume rational expectations. Implicit in it is that the worker believes that by offering *slightly* below (or above) the existing rate he will place his labour for the best available wage. Yet for the worker to believe this, he must be assumed to be quite unaware of the dimensions of the unemployment situation, locally and generally. For if he were aware, he would wish to use this information in pitching his offer. In this case he would pitch it at what he believes to be the market-clearing rate for his particular area and skill (we could make more complicated assumptions based on expected utility maximization subject to the probability distribution of hires, etc, but this is needless for our purpose).

If we are to reconstruct the Phillips curve under rational expectations, we must allow our workers access to a reasonable information set. It is generally accepted that this will include local and national *price* information, and so it must also include local and national *quantity* information. It follows from our assumption about workers' offers that the wage rate in the market (i.e. the average of offers registered) will equal the expected *equilibrium wage*, in the light of this information.

Hence if the (*ex ante*) supply curve of labour[6] is:

$$L_s = \beta_0 + \beta_1 \left(w + p - \underset{-1}{E}\, p \right)$$

$$+ \beta_2 \left(r - \underset{-1}{E}\, w_{+1} + w + p - \underset{-1}{E}\, p \right) + \varepsilon_3 \qquad (6.16)$$

and the demand curve is:

$$L_d = \gamma_0 + \gamma_1 y \qquad (6.17)$$

then the nominal wage 'set' (by the totality of offers registered) will be the expected real wage solution of $(6.16) = (6.17)$, plus the expected price level, or:

$$W = \underset{-1}{E}\, p + (\beta_1 + \beta_2)^{-1}$$

$$\times \left[\gamma_0 - \beta_0 + \gamma_1 \underset{-1}{E}\, y + \beta_2 \left(\underset{-1}{E}\, w_{+1} - \underset{-1}{E}\, r \right) \right] \qquad (6.39)$$

To compare this with (6.38), difference (6.39) to obtain:

$$\Delta W = \left(\underset{-1}{E}\, p - \underset{-2}{E}\, p_{-1} \right) + (\beta_1 + \beta_2)^{-1}$$

$$\times \left[\gamma_1 \left(\underset{-1}{E}\, y - \underset{-2}{E}\, y_{-1} \right) \right.$$

$$\left. + \beta_2 \left(\underset{-1}{E}\, w_{+1} - \underset{-2}{E}\, w - \underset{-1}{E}\, r + \underset{-2}{E}\, r_{-1} \right) \right]$$

$$(6.40)$$

Equation (6.40) differs from (6.38) in two main respects:

(1) In (6.40),

$$\left(\underset{-1}{E}\, p - \underset{-2}{E}\, p_{-1} \right) = \underset{-1}{E}\, p - p_{-1} + \left(p_{-1} - \underset{-2}{E}\, p_{-1} \right)$$

includes the past period's error in price forecasting, whereas in (6.38) $\left(\underset{-1}{E}\, p - p_{-1} \right)$ does not.

(2) In place of the *actual* unemployment *level* in (6.38), we have the *rate of change* of *expected* output etc. in (6.40).

Price Setting

The arguments we used above for wage equations apply with equal force to price equations. Consider first a competitive industry framework. As for the labour market, so we must assume for the goods market that agents have information on quantities as well as prices. Firms pitch their prices therefore at the expected market-clearing level.

If then the supply and demand curves for output are given by (6.14) and (6.15) where (6.14) has an *ex ante* interpretation (the output that would be supplied in the absence of contracts), we have the expected equilibrium price level given by setting expected (6.14) = (6.15). However, since actual output will by assumption be equal to output demanded, it is convenient to write, using (6.14) only:

$$\mathop{E}_{-1} y = y^* + \phi\left(\mathop{E}_{-1} w_{+1} - \mathop{E}_{-1} w + \mathop{E}_{-1} r\right) \qquad (6.41)$$

Rearranging we have:

$$p = \mathop{E}_{-1} p = \mathop{E}_{-1} W - \left(\mathop{E}_{-1} w_{+1} + \mathop{E}_{-1} r\right) + \phi^{-1}\left(\mathop{E}_{-1} y - y^*\right) \qquad (6.42)$$

Taking first differences we have:

$$\Delta p = \mathop{E}_{-1} W - \mathop{E}_{-2} W_{-1}$$
$$- \left(\mathop{E}_{-1} w_{+1} - \mathop{E}_{-2} w + \mathop{E}_{-1} r - \mathop{E}_{-2} r_{-1}\right)$$
$$+ \phi^{-1}\left(\mathop{E}_{-1} y - \mathop{E}_{-2} y_{-1}\right) - \phi^{-1}\Delta y^* \qquad (6.43)$$

Here inflation depends on the change in expected wages and the change in expected excess output demand, as well as the change in discounted expected real wages.

The Contract Model in Full: Model B

We now propose to show how the model behaves if we substitute our new competitive wage- and price-setting equations, (6.39) and (6.42), for the output and labour supply equations (6.14) and (6.16). We call it Model B.

The equilibrium is unchanged, since the wage- and price-setting equations are geared to give the same equilibrium as the supply equations they replace. In terms of deviations from equilibrium, we now obtain the final equation for w as:

$$\underset{-1}{E} \, w_{+1} - \delta \underset{-1}{E} \, w = 0 \qquad (6.44)$$

This is the same as (6.21) above, except that now current errors do not affect the current real wage since it is set in the previous period. Since $\delta > 1$, we find that the solution is that $w = \underset{-1}{E} \, w = 0$, i.e. that real wages are continuously set at their equilibrium.

We are then left with the rest of the model (remembering that quantities are set by the demand equations), in terms of deviations from equilibrium, as:

$$y = -\alpha r + \varepsilon_2 \qquad (6.15)$$

$$L = \gamma_1 y \qquad (6.17)$$

$$\varepsilon_4 = y + p - \mu R \qquad (6.19)$$

$$R = r + \underset{-1}{E} \, p_{+1} - \underset{-1}{E} \, p \qquad (6.20)$$

Since $p = \underset{-1}{E} \, p$ and $\underset{-1}{E} \, y = 0 = \underset{-1}{E} \, r$ we obtain from (6.19) and (6.20) by taking expectations:

$$0 = \underset{-1}{E} \, p_{+1} - (1 + \mu)\mu^{-1} \underset{-1}{E} \, p \qquad (6.45)$$

and since $(1 + \mu)\mu^{-1} > 1$, this gives $\underset{-1}{E} \, p_{+1} = \underset{-1}{E} \, p = 0$,

It follows from (6.19), (6.20) and the above that:

$$r = (\varepsilon_2 - \varepsilon_4)/(\mu + \alpha) \qquad (6.46)$$

therefore:

$$L = \gamma_1 y = \gamma_1[\mu(\mu + \alpha)^{-1}\varepsilon_2 + \alpha(\mu + \alpha)^{-1}\varepsilon_4] \qquad (6.47)$$

Clearly, in this 'disequilibrium' world (because of contracts) we cannot regard unemployment as voluntary as both (6.18a) and (6.18b) do. Unemployment in the US sense now becomes the difference between the supply of labour and the demand, or:

$$U = \beta_0 + \beta_1 w + \beta_2\left(r - \underset{-1}{\mathrm{E}}\, w_{+1} + w\right) + \varepsilon_3 - L$$

(6.18aa)

(and in deviation form):

$$U = (\beta_2 - \gamma_1\mu)(\mu + \alpha)^{-1}\varepsilon_2 + \varepsilon_3 - [(\beta_2 + \gamma_1\alpha)(\mu + \alpha)^{-1}]\varepsilon_4$$

(6.48)

(Remember that search as such will no longer occur since $W = \underset{-1}{\mathrm{E}}\, W$, i.e. wages contracted are known in advance.) Provided β_2 is not large, the effects of ε_2 will be negative on U which obeys 'Okun's Law'; ε_3 plausibly has a positive sign.

In the European sense unemployment now becomes the difference between $\bar{L}$, those socially insured, and L, those actually employed:

$$U = \bar{L} - L$$

(6.18bb)

(or in deviation form):

$$U = -[\gamma_1\mu(\mu + \alpha)^{-1}]\varepsilon_2 - [\gamma_1\alpha(\mu + \alpha)^{-1}]\varepsilon_4$$

(6.49)

Here too Okun's Law holds.

To summarize, we have taken Phillips curves for goods and labour markets and adapted them for rational expectations. We have found that this give rise to a contract world in which equilibrium is expected to return *next* period, but current shocks disturb output and employment, real interest rates and unemployment: prices and wages are undisturbed because of the contract assumption. The effects of the shocks are in accordance with the stylized facts of Okun's Law. Nevertheless, in contrast to the model we derived earlier from Fisherian supply theory, we have found that simple Lucas-type relationships of the form:

$$y - y^* = \phi\left(p - \underset{-1}{\mathrm{E}}\, p\right) + \cdots$$

or

$$y - y^* = \phi(p - \mathrm{E}p_{+1}) + \cdots$$

do not emerge from this model, because $p = \underset{-1}{\mathrm{E}} \; p = \mathrm{E}p_{+1} = 0$.

A 'MIXED' CONTRACT-FLEXIBLE PRICE MODEL

Though a full contract model cannot therefore obviously underpin a Phillips curve, we now propose to show that a possible underpinning lies in models where wages are fixed by contract but prices are flexible, a set-up which, though quite *ad hoc*, is nevertheless plausibly in line with observation.

Adopt the wage equation (6.39) in place of the labour supply curve (6.16), and otherwise use the model (6.14)–(6.20). This assumes wages are set in accordance with a contract for one period ahead, prices are set by the equilibrium of supply and demand. Since labour is always on its demand curve, the unemployment relationships (6.18aa) and (6.18bb) are the relevant possibilities, in place of (6.18a) and (6.18b).

Again the equilibrium is the same, so using deviations from equilibrium we have Model C:

$$W = \underset{-1}{\mathrm{E}} \; W = \underset{-1}{\mathrm{E}} \; p + (\beta_1 + \beta_2)^{-1}$$

$$\times \left[\gamma_1 \underset{-1}{\mathrm{E}} \; y + \beta_2 \left(\underset{-1}{\mathrm{E}} \; w_{+1} - \underset{-1}{\mathrm{E}} \; r \right) \right] \qquad (6.50)$$

$$y = \phi \left(\underset{-1}{\mathrm{E}} \; w_{+1} - w + r \right) + \varepsilon_1 \qquad (6.51)$$

$$y = -\alpha r + \varepsilon_2 \qquad (6.52)$$

$$L = \gamma_1 y \qquad (6.53)$$

$$\varepsilon_4 = y + p + \mu \underset{-1}{\mathrm{E}} \; p - \mu \underset{-1}{\mathrm{E}} \; p_{+1} - \mu r \qquad (6.54)$$

We can rewrite (6.50) as:

$$(\beta_1 + \beta_2) \underset{-1}{\mathrm{E}} \; w = \gamma_1 \underset{-1}{\mathrm{E}} \; y + \beta_2 \underset{-1}{\mathrm{E}} \; w_{+1} - \beta_2 \underset{-1}{\mathrm{E}} \; r \qquad (6.55)$$

and substituting for $\underset{-1}{\text{E}}\, r$ and $\underset{-1}{\text{E}}\, y$ from the expected values of (6.52) and (6.51), we obtain:

$$\underset{-1}{\text{E}}\, w_{+1} - \delta \underset{-1}{\text{E}}\, w = 0 \qquad (6.56)$$

as before. It follows, as before, that:

$$\underset{-1}{\text{E}}\, w = \underset{-1}{\text{E}}\, w_{+1} = Ew_{+1} = \underset{-1}{\text{E}}\, r = \underset{-1}{\text{E}}\, y = 0$$

We now note that:

$$w = \underset{-1}{\text{E}}\, w + \left(W - \underset{-1}{\text{E}}\, W - p + \underset{-1}{\text{E}}\, p \right) = \underset{-1}{\text{E}}\, p - p \qquad (6.57)$$

since

$$W = \underset{-1}{\text{E}}\, W \quad \text{and} \quad \underset{-1}{\text{E}}\, w = 0$$

It can immediately be seen that (6.51) is a Phillips curve, which we may write:

$$y - y^* = \phi\left(p - \underset{-1}{\text{E}}\, p + r - r^* \right) + \varepsilon_1 \qquad (6.58)$$

Similarly (6.18aa) becomes:

$$U - U^* = -(\beta_1 + \beta_2 + \gamma_1\phi)\left(p - \underset{-1}{\text{E}}\, p \right)$$
$$- (\gamma_1\phi - \beta_2)(r - r^*) + \varepsilon_3 - \gamma_1\varepsilon_1 \qquad (6.59)$$

and (6.18bb) becomes:

$$U - U^* = -\gamma_1(y - y^*) - \gamma_1\varepsilon_1 \qquad (6.60)$$

Notice that all the previous macroeconomic analysis of Figures 6.1 and 6.2 goes through qualitatively unaltered by this change in underpinning. However, (6.58) gives a quantitatively large effect of unanticipated inflation on output than (6.35), our original derivation of the Lucas supply curve; the effect of r in (6.58) may be larger or smaller than in (6.35).

CONCLUSIONS

The purpose of this chapter has been to consider methods of integrating labour and goods markets (or wage and price equations), so as to provide underpinnings for the Phillips curve under rational expectations. We were able to derive a number of interesting results.

First, the 'direct' route to justifying the Lucas–Sargent–Wallace (LSW) equation, namely to ignore the labour market and simply deal with the 'goods' markets, does not provide an underpinning since it leaves costs unexplained. Second, Fisherian supply hypotheses in labour and goods markets, together with assumed equilibrium also can yield the LSW equation, but this result disappears for plausible variations in the information set-up assumed. Third, while a contract framework in which we look for wage- or price-setting equations by suppliers rather than 'supply' equations for goods and labour clearly does not provide underpinnings for the LSW equation, a model in which – plausibly consistent with common observation – wages are set by contract and prices are flexible does yield the LSW supply hypothesis.

Our ability to underpin the LSW hypothesis with a model in which prices are flexible and wages set one period ahead by contract is of some importance. In particular we might note that this type of scenario seems implicit in the work of M. Friedman (1968). He describes a situation in which an unanticipated increase in nominal demand leads to an increase in prices relative to wages 'because selling-prices of products typically respond to an unanticipated rise in nominal demand faster than the prices of factors of production' (*ibid*, p. 10).

In the course of developing the wage- and price-setting equations used in the above analysis, we showed that the original Phillips–Lipsey formulation needs careful modification if there are rational expectations. In particular the early derivations were in error, in that an implicit asymmetry of information between quantity and price information was assumed. Our modification alters in a number of ways the Phillips–Lipsey form. For example, in our reformulation the past period's error in forecasting prices occurs, whereas in the conventional level, we have the rate of change of expected output. Such an equation is quite clearly different from the LSW supply hypothesis which has been the main focus of this chapter.

NOTES

1. The material in this chapter is based on Minford and Peel (1982b).

2. To preserve log-linearity (for simplicity), our measure $p - C$ is more accurately an approximate measure of real profit per unit of output than profit *per se*. Note on timing: we assume firms have access at the micro level to W (nominal wage) and P, workers only to W. Expectations have to be formed by reference to macro data; this is assumed available with a one-period lag. Hence expectations operative on today's decisions are all written E_{-1}. The real interest rate depends on current views about the expected future and current *general* price level (which no-one observes), for which the information set is last period's data in this set-up. In reaching this formulation, we utilize the framework suggested by Sargent (1979, Chapter 16) where firms have a quadratic production function in labour alone with quadratic costs of adjustment. The upshot of this set-up is that the demand for the factor, labour, depends negatively on the expected normal level of real costs and negatively on current real costs relative to expected future real costs. Output is linked to labour use through the production function; normal output, y^*, is identified with the level implied by normal expected real costs. We drop all lagged terms for convenience, since they are inessential to our subsequent argument.

3. We ignore frictional unemployment for convenience.

4. The form $y - y^* = f(p - E p_{+1}, \ldots)$ as, e.g., in Lucas (1972a) is not pursued here any further as a Phillips curve; rather it is to be regarded as a stylized version of the 'classical' supply function (see pp. 56–7).

5. See also B. Friedman (1978) for discussion along similar lines.

6. Note by supply we now mean what would be supplied if contracts were not binding. We have called this *ex ante* as opposed to *ex post* or actual supply.

7

The Behaviour of 'Efficient'
Asset Markets

The purpose of this chapter is to consider the relationship between the concepts of financial market efficiency and rational expectations. A particular feature of financial markets is that trading can occur, in principle, almost continuously, and the market price is free to move to eradicate any imbalance between demand and supply. Furthermore since the assets traded (stocks, bonds, commodities) can be resold or traded in future periods it follows that financial markets are, more obviously than others, speculative in the technical sense that expectations of future asset prices affect current asset prices.

We begin this chapter by defining the concept of an efficient capital market and contrast this with the concept of a perfect capital market. A brief review of the empirical evidence for efficiency in asset markets in general is then presented.

We then go on to consider two important applications of efficiency in macroeconomics and the evidence in these areas. First, we discuss a model of the open economy and the exchange rate based on that of Dornbusch (1976) in which goods and labour markets are typified by sticky prices but financial markets, including the market for foreign exchange, are efficient. The model has the property that the exchange rate in response to permanent change in the money stock will, in the short run, 'overshoot' its long-run value. We extend the discussion to models in which the goods and labour market are in continuous equilibrium; and we find that here too an efficient exchange market will exhibit 'overshooting'.

Secondly, we consider the behaviour of long-run interest rates under market efficiency, and show that they will follow a random walk. We conclude with some general implications of efficiency for macroeconomic model building.

EFFICIENCY, PERFECTION AND ASSET PRICING IN
CAPITAL MARKETS

A capital or asset market is defined to be efficient when prices (e.g. stock prices, bond prices or exchange rates) fully and instantaneously reflect all available relevant information. Fama (1970) has defined three types of market efficiency, according to the extent of the information reflected in the market:

(1) Weak-form efficient: a market is weak-form efficient if it is not possible for a trader to make abnormal returns by developing a trading rule based on the past history of prices or returns.

(2) Semi-strong form efficient: a market where a trader cannot make abnormal returns using a trading rule based on publicly available information. Examples of publicly available information are past money supply data, company financial accounts, or reports in periodicals such as *The Investors Chronicle*.

(3) Strong-form efficient: where a trader cannot make abnormal returns using a trading rule based on any information source, whether public or private.

These three forms of efficiency represent a crude partitioning of all possible information systems into three broad categories, the precise boundaries of which are not easily defined. However they are useful, as we shall see, for classifying empirical research on market efficiency. As their names suggest, strong form efficiency implies semi-strong efficiency which in turn implies weak form efficiency, while of course the reverse implications do not hold.

It is useful to distinguish between the concept of an efficient capital market and that of a perfect capital market. A perfect capital market could be defined as one in which the following conditions hold (see Copeland and Weston, 1979):

(1) Markets are informationally efficient, that is information is costless and it is received simultaneously by individuals.
(2) Markets are frictionless, that is there are no transactions costs or taxes, assets are perfectly divisible and marketable and there are no constraining regulations.
(3) There is perfect competition in product and securities markets, that is agents are price-takers.
(4) All individuals are rational expected-utility maximizers.

If conditions (1) to (4) were met (and assuming no significant distortions elsewhere in the economy), the capital market would be allocationally efficient, in that prices would be set to equate the marginal rates of return for all producers and savers, and of course consequently savings are optimally allocated. The notion of capital market efficiency is therefore much less restrictive. An element of imperfect competition in product markets would imply capital market imperfection; nevertheless, the stock market could determine a security price which fully reflected the present value of the stream of expected future monopoly profits. Consequently the stock market could still be efficient in the presence of imperfection.

Asset prices, in order to give the correct signals to traders, must fully and instantaneously reflect all available information.[1] However as pointed out by, for example, Grossman and Stiglitz (1976, 1980), it cannot be the case that market prices do fully and instantaneously reflect all available information. If this were so, agents would have no incentive for collecting and processing information, since it would already be reflected in the price which each individual is assumed to be able to observe costlessly. It is the possibility of obtaining abnormal profits in the course of arbitraging which provides the incentive to collect and process new information. In the Grossman and Stiglitz model, individuals choose to become informed or uninformed, and in equilibrium each individual is indifferent between remaining uninformed on the one hand, and collecting information (or buying the expertise of brokers), so becoming informed, on the other. This is because after deducting information costs each action offers the same expected utility.

Nevertheless, a reasonable interpretation of empirical tests of the efficient market hypothesis is, given that the data is collected at discrete intervals, that the process of arbitrage has occurred *within* the period. Consequently the implications of different available information can then be analysed without modelling the process of arbitrage itself (Begg, 1982) and this is the usual assumption in empirical work.

Because all definitions of market efficiency invoke the concept of abnormal returns, we are also required for empirical work to have a theory of the equilibrium expected rate of return for assets. This is a central topic in modern portfolio theory and the interested reader is directed to, for example, Copeland and Weston (1979) for a full discussion. The following brief account of the Capital Asset Pricing Model must suffice here.

Only if traders are risk neutral[2] will they be indifferent to the variability of the returns (i.e. the risk) on their portfolio. Risk averse individuals will be concerned about aggregate portfolio risk and will require a risk premium on each asset (or class of assets). By combining assets in a portfolio it is possible to diversify away some of the risk (the 'unsystematic' risk) associated with an asset. However, to the extent that the returns on an asset move with the market, there will be a component of risk (systematic risk) that cannot be diversified away. Assuming optimal portfolio diversification, the risk premium reflects the asset's systematic risk and hence its contribution to the overall variability of returns on the portfolio. This premium will be included in the equilibrium expected rate of return on this asset, in addition to the general rate of return on the portfolio.

Tests of market efficiency are conducted after allowance for the equilibrium rate of return. If the riskiness of an asset does not change over time (or conversely if its risk changes randomly over time) then, for example, weak form efficiency implies that there should be no extrapolative pattern in the time series of returns. If there were a recurring pattern of any type, traders who recognized the pattern would use it to make abnormal profits. The very effort to use such patterns would, under the efficiency hypothesis, lead to their elimination.

Rational Expectations and Market Efficiency

The semi-strong form efficient markets model, i.e. that based on publicly available information, is an application of the concept of rational expectations, though this was not stressed in the early literature on efficiency which goes back much further than the rational expectations literature. If expectations are non-rational, then publicly available information will not be reflected in asset prices and systematic abnormal profit opportunities will be available. This can be seen simply enough by noting that market agents have to know the model governing prices (or act as if they know it) in order to eliminate abnormal expected returns; if the model governing expected prices is different from that governing actual prices, there will be systematic abnormal returns available in the market.

Strong form efficiency also implies that agents have rational expectations, since they must know how to use all sorts of private information as well as public; where strong form efficiency differs from semi-strong is in the effects of private information on the market, but this is a difference of assumptions about behaviour in response to expectations, not about expectations-formation itself.

Not quite the same is true of weak form efficiency. If, as in the weak case, agents make efficient use only of the past history of prices, they must know the time-series model governing prices; this does not strictly imply that they know the structural model, since there will be generally insufficient identifying restrictions. Nevertheless in practice, with limited samples and structural change, recovery of the time-series parameters by market agents from the data can effectively be ruled out. It is therefore natural, if not necessary, to assume in this case too that agents have rational expectations and so know the underlying model, from which they are then able to derive the time-series parameters.

While, therefore, market efficiency can be regarded as implying rational expectations, rational expectations does not imply market efficiency. Market efficiency is a joint hypothesis about expectations and the market behaviour of participants. The main hypothesis about behaviour is the Capital Asset Pricing Model; and in empirical tests more detailed assumptions must also be made about how equilibrium returns will move. Further hypotheses concern the behaviour of the agents with access to different sets of 'available' information. Under weak form efficiency, active market participants are assumed to make effective use only of the past history of prices in their market; one theoretical basis for this has been in the costs of obtaining and processing wider information (Feige and Pierce, 1976). Under semi-strong form efficiency, the assumption made is the usual one in rational expectations macro models that active agents use all publicly available information, presumed to be useable at zero or low cost. Finally in the strong form case, it is assumed that those agents with access to private information deploy, or influence indirectly, funds to eliminate expected returns from this source of information; there are, however, problems with this, since private information cannot be sold at a fair price (once divulged it is valueless, but before divulgence it is impossible for the buyer to assess) and those with access have, by definition, in general only limited funds.

While rational expectations macro models do not always assume market efficiency, it has become increasingly common for them to assume semi-strong efficiency in financial markets. The Capital Asset Pricing Model is widely accepted by macroeconomists, the assumption of costless public information is of course shared and the equilibrium expected rate of return is easily endogenized within the model. We will be examining examples of these macro models later in this chapter.

Tests of Market Efficiency

Numerous tests have been conducted of weak form efficiency (see e.g., Fama and Blume, 1970; Sargent, 1972; 1979b; Taylor 1982). While studies generally find some serial dependence in asset prices, it seems fair to conclude that it is insufficient to imply the possibility of abnormal returns once allowance is made for transactions costs and risk premia (though see Taylor, 1982, for an alternative view). As with weak form tests, there have been numerous tests of semi-strong efficiency, much of it in the accountancy literature where the relationship between company financial statement data and the behaviour of security prices has been considered (see Beaver, 1981, for an excellent summary). Again on balance the available evidence does not appear to be seriously inconsistent with semi-strong efficiency (see also below specifically on the foreign exchange market).

There is not much evidence on strong form efficiency and some of it is somewhat anecdotal, see e.g. Jaffe (1974) and Finnerty (1976) on insider trading. The evidence, such as it is, suggests that insiders are able to 'beat the market' on a risk-adjusted basis both when buying and selling, contrary to the strong form hypothesis.

OPEN ECONOMY MODELS WITH EFFICIENT FINANCIAL MARKETS

We now consider the implications of financial market efficiency in rational expectations models of the open economy under floating exchange rates.

Our first model is based on that outlined by Dornbusch (1976) in his seminal paper. For simplicity it is assumed that there is perfect capital mobility between countries (i.e. transactions costs are negligible and international assets are perfect substitutes). Consider an agent who is faced with the choice between holding a domestic and foreign bond over a particular holding period of say 90 days. The rates of interest in the foreign country and in the domestic country are given by R_F and R respectively. Since the bonds are perfect substitutes, asset market equilibrium requires that the expected rates of return on the two bonds be equal. This expected rate of return has two components. The first component is the interest rate on the bond, which we can assume to be known at t; the second component is the expected capital gain or loss from exchange rate changes during the 90-day period.

It follows that the condition for equilibrium is:

$$R = R_F + Ee_{+1} - e \qquad (7.1)$$

where e is the logarithm of the current exchange rate (the domestic price of foreign currency) and Ee_{+1} is the expectation of the rate in period one. A rise in e in our notation represents a depreciation of the home currency; (7.1) therefore states that the interest rate differential in favour of domestic bonds must be equal to the expected depreciation of the exchange rate.

For example, if the domestic currency pays 12 per cent interest and the foreign currency pays 4 per cent interest, a domestic investor buying foreign currency at the beginning of the period and converting back at the end of the period will, assuming the domestic currency depreciates by 8 per cent expect to finish up with sufficient domestic currency to make him indifferent between holding domestic or foreign bonds.

We may note in passing that there is a forward market for foreign exchange (i.e. traders can at time t contract to trade foreign currency at time $t + 1$), and that the forward rate is a direct measure of the market's expectation of the future exchange rate (since, in the forward market, large transactors are required to put up only very small amounts of money as 'margin requirements', there is no need to discount). Under floating rates, if agents are risk neutral and form rational expectations, the forward rate should be an efficient predictor of future spot rates. This hypothesis has been the subject of much empirical testing to be discussed later in the chapter.

In the Dornbusch model it is assumed that prices in goods or labour markets are in the short term 'sticky' with respect to changes in market conditions. This could be due for instance to the existence of multi-period wage or price contracts. It follows from this assumption that purchasing power parity does not hold in the short run. Purchasing power parity (PPP) or the 'law of one price' states that in the absence of transport costs and other transaction costs, international arbitrage in goods should eliminate differentials between the prices of traded goods in different countries.

Under these circumstances we would have:

$$e = p - p_F \qquad (7.2)$$

where p, p_F are the logarithms of the domestic and foreign price level (and assuming for simplicity that the prices of non-traded and traded goods move proportionally together).

It immediately follows with perfect capital mobility and PPP, that (7.1) and (7.2) imply the equalization of expected real rates of interest:

$$R - \mathsf{E}p_{+1} + p = R_F - \mathsf{E}p_{F+1} + p_F \qquad (7.3)$$

If it is the case that arbitrage in goods is not infinite, then PPP will not hold in the short run. However, we might wish to impose this condition as a long-run feature of any exchange rate model that we build. Absence of PPP in the short run means that we may examine the behaviour of the real exchange rate, x, defined as:

$$x = e - p + p_F \qquad (7.4)$$

Clearly transactions costs, and other features, may result in a non-zero long-run equilibrium real exchange rate, in which case in the long run:

$$x = e - p + p_F = \alpha \qquad (7.5)$$

The numerous tests of PPP that have been carried out (see e.g. Krugman, 1978) indicate clearly that PPP does not hold in the short run.

For simplicity we assume that output (in logs), real interest rates, foreign interest rates and the foreign price level (in logs) are fixed and set at zero; but this does not affect the features of the model on which we focus here. The model is given by:

$$R = \mathsf{E}e_{+1} - e \qquad (7.1)$$

$$m + \bar{m} = p - \lambda R \qquad (7.6)$$

$$p - p_{-1} = k(e_{-1} - p_{-1}) + u \qquad (7.7)$$

where m is a monetary shock (variance σ_m^2), u is a supply shock (variance σ_u^2), λ, k are positive constants, $\bar{m}$ is the constant level of money supply; the exogenous foreign interest rate and price level, as well as domestic output and real interest rates are normalized at zero for simplicity. Equation (7.6) is a conventional demand for money function equated to money supply. Equation (7.7) is a price adjustment mechanism, in which inflation depends upon aggregate demand, this in turn depending on the real exchange rate via its effects on the volume of net trade.

We solve this model under the assumption that agents have full current information. Following the procedure outlined in Chapter 2, the solution for the exchange rate in the full-information case is given by:

$$e = (1 - z)\bar{m} + ze_{-1} + \gamma_0 m + \gamma_1 m_{-1} + \gamma_2 u \qquad (7.8)$$

where z is the stable root of the equation:

$$z^2 + (k - 2)z + 1 - \frac{k(1 + \lambda)}{\lambda} = 0 \qquad (7.9)$$

$$\gamma_0 = \frac{(1 - z)}{\lambda(1 - z) + k} \qquad (7.10)$$

$$\gamma_1 = -(1 - k)\gamma_0 \qquad (7.11)$$

$$\gamma_2 = -\frac{[(1 - z) + (1 - k)]}{\lambda(1 - z) + k} \qquad (7.12)$$

We notice from (7.8) that, in the long run, the elasticity of the exchange rate with respect to an increase in the permanent level of money supply is unity. In other words, in the long run the exchange rate depreciates by the change in $\bar{m}$. Given that $\bar{m}$ is a constant, (7.1) implies that R is zero in the long run, and hence (7.6) that prices have the same response to $\bar{m}$ as the exchange rate. (7.7) implies also that in the long run PPP must hold. Leading (7.8) one period and taking expectations we obtain:

$$Ee_{+1} - e = (1 - z)(\bar{m} - e) + \gamma_1 m \qquad (7.13)$$

(7.13) defines an expectations mechanism known as regressive expectations. It tells us that when the equilibrium exchange rate ($\bar{e} = \bar{m}$) is above the current exchange rate, then expectations are revised upwards and *vice versa*. The fact that regressive expectations can by choice of the regressive parameter $(1 - z)$ be rational is one implication of this Dornbusch model. However we should note that this property can hold in rational expectations models only where there is one stable root; it does not hold generally.[3]

We can substitute (7.13) into (7.1) and (7.6) to obtain:

$$e = \left(\frac{1 + \lambda(1 - z)}{\lambda(1 - z)}\right)\bar{m} + \left(\frac{1 + \lambda\gamma_1}{\lambda(1 - z)}\right)m - \frac{p}{\lambda(1 - z)} \quad (7.14)$$

(7.14) illustrates another key insight of Dornbusch. The impact of a change in the permanent level of money supply $(\bar{m})$ in the short run is greater than unity and consequently greater than the long-run impact. This phenomenon is known as 'overshooting'. The rationale for this effect is that because, in the short run, prices are at a moment in time fixed (or sticky), the only way the money market can remain in equilibrium as the permanent level of money supply is increased is for the interest rate to fall. However, a falling interest rate has to be associated with an expected appreciation of the currency. Consequently the current exchange rate has to depreciate further than its long-run value in order to give rise to anticipations of an appreciation as it moves to its ultimate long-run value.

This mechanism can be illustrated diagrammatically in Figure 7.1. Suppose at time $t = 0$ the pound/dollar rate is $\$1 = \pounds1$. At time $t = N$ the authorities increase the level of

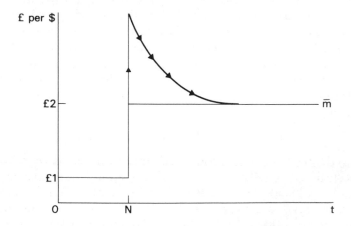

Figure 7.1 *Exchange rate overshooting*

the money supply by 100 per cent. In the long run this causes the pound to depreciate against the dollar to $1 = £2.0. However, in the short run the pound depreciates further, to say $1 = £3.0 and then follows the arrowed path back to long-run equilibrium. We notice that along the arrowed path the pound is appreciating, but has always depreciated relative to $t = 0$. The possibility that efficient asset markets, in conjunction with sticky product prices, could give rise to volatile behaviour of asset prices was a principal insight of Dornbusch and various refinements to the basic model are still an active research area (see e.g. Buiter and Miller, 1981).

We should also note from the solution for the exchange rate that, while a positive monetary shock causes a depreciation of the currency, the impact of the shock can be greater or less than unity (but of course since $\bar{m}$ has not changed, there will always be an 'overshoot' of the *long-run* equilibrium). The Dornbusch result applies to permanent (unanticipated) changes in the money stock ($\bar{m}$).

A number of authors have attempted to test the Dornbusch model (see e.g. Driskill, 1981; Frankel, 1979; Hache and Townend, 1981; and Demery, 1981), by examining the properties of reduced form exchange rate equations derived from structural models of the Dornbusch type. The empirical results the authors report are unfavourable to the model. However there are a number of problems with these tests, the main one being that they all assume the regressive form for expectations, which is in general incorrect (Minford and Peel, 1983a). For example, Hache and Townend (1981) and Frankel (1979, 1982) specify models in which lagged adjustment or wealth effects are introduced into the demand for money function or lagged adjustment is introduced into the interest arbitrage condition (7.1); in these models, expectations will not be regressive.

Testing the Efficiency of the Exchange Market

A standard test of efficiency in the exchange market has been to consider the relationship between the spot and forward rate in relationships of the type:

$$e = \alpha_0 + \alpha_1 f_{-1} + u \qquad (7.15)$$

where α_0, α_1 are constants, u is an error term, where f_{-1}, the forward rate, is the expectation of e formed at time $t - 1$. If traders are risk neutral, α_0 and α_1 should not be significantly different from zero and one respectively and the error term u should be random.

Many empirical studies of this relationship for different countries and different time periods have been carried out (see e.g. Frenkel, 1977; Frenkel and Levich, 1975; Levich, 1978; Frenkel, 1981). The general results have been favourable to the efficiency hypothesis. The coefficient α_1 has typically not been different from unity and the error term has been generally uncorrelated. The constant term α_0, has typically been close to zero, suggesting the market behaves as if traders are risk neutral. However, more recently some authors (e.g. Cornell, 1977; Baillie *et al*, 1983) have rejected the hypothesis of efficiency. Both sets of authors find evidence of serial correlation in the error term. One rationale for their results, as the authors recognize, is that their analysis could capture a variable liquidity premium which, whilst possibly having a mean of zero, could vary over time in such a way as to produce the observed autocorrelations in the error term.

Another possibility, however, is that incomplete current information at the time the forward rate is set (and the future expectation formulated) introduces overlapping information into the error term. The error term could include 'news' which was partially known only at this time, but becomes fully known by the maturity date; it is not clear to us at this stage how far this could explain some of these negative results. (The Appendix to this chapter discusses just how in principle incomplete information can affect efficiency tests.)

Exchange Rate Overshooting in Equilibrium Models

We now turn to the issue of whether exchange rate overshooting, which occurs in the Dornbusch model as a result of disequilibrium in goods or labour markets, must always be regarded in a real economy as occurring as a consequence of such features. We will demonstrate that this is not the case. 'Overshooting' can indeed, and generally will, occur in equilibrium open-economy models. In order to explain this, we adopt the model of the previous section.

In keeping with the equilibrium framework, we assume that all agents form expectations on the basis of the same set of macro information. This we date at $t - 1$, and for simplicity ignore *current* global information (but this does not alter our point). Hence the exchange market equilibrium condition becomes:

$$\underset{-1}{E} e_{+1} - e = R \tag{7.16}$$

and the real interest rate differential, r, is defined as:

$$r = R - \underset{-1}{E} p_{+1} + p \tag{7.17}$$

Demand for money is as before:

$$m = p + \phi y - \lambda R \tag{7.18}$$

Money supply is:

$$\Delta m = \varepsilon + \bar{m} + \Delta v \tag{7.19}$$

where

$$\Delta \bar{m} = u.$$

This money supply function now allows not only for (unanticipated) temporary changes in the level of money (v) and once-for-all changes in the level (ε) but also for once-for-all changes in the steady state rate of increase (u). It will thus permit us to examine the different reactions to these shocks.

From the definition of real interest rates and the real exchange rate, $x = e - p$, and from (7.16) we have:

$$\left(R - \underset{-1}{E} p_{+1} + p \right) = \underset{-1}{E} e_{+1} - \underset{-1}{E} p_{+1} - (e - p)$$

or

$$= \underset{-1}{E} x_{+1} - x \tag{7.20}$$

i.e. the *real* interest differential must equal the expected *real* depreciation.

Now complete the model with an IS and a Phillips curve:

$$y = -\alpha r + \delta x \tag{7.21}$$

$$y = \beta r + \gamma\left(p - \underset{-1}{\text{E}}\ p\right) + \sigma y_{-1} \tag{7.22}$$

(7.22) has the full classical form discussed in Chapter 3. Note that neither α nor β are infinite, so that r *will* vary.[4] The model has been set up so that $y = r = x = 0$ in equilibrium.

Define the superscript 'ue' as 'unanticipated at $t - 1$'; hence for example $p^{ue} = p - \underset{-1}{\text{E}}\ p$. Equations (7.20)–(7.22) can be solved as a recursive block in terms of p^{ue} to give:

$$x = \mu x_{-1} + \pi_0 p^{ue} + (\pi_1 - \mu\pi_0)p^{ue}_{-1} \tag{7.23}$$

where

$$\pi_0 = \gamma/(\alpha + \beta + \delta), \quad \pi_1 = \sigma\pi_0(\alpha + \delta)/[(\alpha + \beta)(1 - \mu) + \delta]$$

and μ is the (assumed unique) stable root of the characteristic equation

$$\mu^2 - \left(1 + \frac{\alpha\sigma + \delta}{\alpha + \beta}\right)\mu + \frac{\sigma(\alpha + \beta)}{\alpha + \beta} = 0.$$

r and y have similar solutions: a first-order moving average in p^{ue} and first order autoregressive coefficient μ. From (7.18) using these, we obtain:

$$p^{ue} = qm^{ue} \tag{7.24}$$

$$x^{ue} = \pi_0 qm^{ue} \tag{7.25}$$

where $q = [1 + \lambda + \lambda\pi_0 + \phi(\alpha + \delta)\pi_0]^{-1}$ is greater than 0 and less than 1. The nominal exchange rate depreciation is:

$$e^{ue} = x^{ue} + p^{ue} = q(1 + \pi_0)m^{ue} \tag{7.26}$$

where

$$m^{ue} = \varepsilon + u + v.$$

We can usefully rewrite $q(1 + \pi_0) = [\alpha + \beta + \delta + \gamma]/(\alpha + \beta + \delta)(1 + \lambda) + \gamma(\lambda + \phi\alpha + \phi\delta)$, which makes it clear that the value is positive and greater or less than unity, depending on all the impact parameters. Notice that 'overshooting' properties occur in the broad sense that both the nominal and the real exchange rate depreciate in a 'volatile' manner in response to positive money shocks.

For the case where the money supply is growing over time, we define overshooting as a reaction of the nominal exchange rate by a greater proportion than the change in the (current) equilibrium nominal exchange rate, i.e. that which would prevail were the present money supply difference to be maintained in perpetuity, apart from elements expected to be reversed (i.e. v).

On this basis, we can determine from (7.26) that:

(1) The exchange rate may respond more than proportionately to a *once-for-all* change in $m(\varepsilon)$, and so the equilibrium exchange rate. This is the overshooting considered by Dornbusch (1976), which deals with surprise shifts in the permanent level of m.

(2) It also may respond more than proportionately to a rise in m which is due to a permanent rise in its *growth rate* (u). However, since there is no way that speculators can distinguish between ε and u shocks *when they occur*, the reactions to both are the same.

(3) It also *responds* to a temporary change in $m(v)$, which on our definition does *not* change the equilibrium exchange rate. This is also a form of overshooting, though not that dealt with by Dornbusch.

All these types of 'overshooting' in response to monetary shocks are qualitatively the same as those in the 'sticky price' models of Dornbusch and Frankel, yet they emerge from an equilibrium model. By altering our assumptions about the availability of current global information, these results could be easily 'enriched' to give a variety of potential overshooting responses; substantial overshooting is exhibited in empirical application by an equilibrium model of the UK economy (Minford, 1980, the Liverpool Model, Chapter 11). To sum up, volatility of the nominal exchange rate ('overshooting'), as well as of the real exchange rate and real interest differentials, is *not prima facie* evidence of 'price stickiness', 'disequilibrium' or 'inefficiency' in goods or labour markets.

*Distinguishing Equilibrium from Disequilibrium Models of
the Exchange Rate*

It is of some interest now to ask whether on the basis of a
reduced form exchange rate equation *on its own* it is possible
to determine whether it comes from an equilibrium or disequilibrium model. For this purpose, we set up two models
identical in all respects except in their 'supply' behaviour.
The first model is the one just dealt with; it consists of the
demand for money function (7.18), money supply function
(7.19), efficient market condition (7.16), IS curve (7.21), and its
supply curve is an equilibrium one (7.22). The second model
consists of the same equations apart from (7.22) where it has
a 'sticky price' Phillips curve as in Frankel (1979), namely:

$$p - p_{-1} = \gamma x_{-1} + \bar{m} \qquad (7.22)^{\mathrm{S}}$$

(We also assume in the spirit of disequilibrium models that
speculators have full current information, and condition the
expectations operator throughout on the basis of current
information.) It turns out that the solution for x in this
model is:

$$x = \mu_2 x_{-1} + \left[\frac{\varepsilon + \lambda u + (1 - \mu_1^{-1})(v - v_{-1})}{(\lambda + \phi\alpha)(1 - \mu_2) - (\lambda\gamma - \phi\delta)} \right] \qquad (7.27)$$

where μ_2 is the stable, μ_1 the unstable root of the characteristic equation:

$$\mu^2 - \left[2 - \left(\frac{\lambda\gamma - \phi\delta}{\lambda + \phi\alpha} \right) \right]\mu + \left[1 - \left(\frac{\gamma(1 + \lambda) + \phi\delta}{\lambda + \phi\alpha} \right) \right] = 0$$

Compare this to the solution for the equilibrium model:

$$x = \mu x_{-1} + \pi_0 q m^{ue} + q(\pi_1 - \mu\pi_0)m^{ue}_{-1} \qquad (7.28)$$

This shows that it is not possible to distinguish between the
equilibrium and disequilibrium models on the basis of the
reduced form (real) exchange rate equations alone. It follows
that the models can only be distinguished, if at all, on the
basis of full structural estimation. This is another example of
'observational equivalence' (see Chapter 10).

   This concludes our discussion of the behaviour of

exchange rates in an economy in which the exchange market is efficient. We have shown that evidence of overshooting does not imply the economy is typified by disequilibrium in goods or labour markets; equilibrium models will make similar predictions under a wide range of parameter values.

We now turn to the implications that market efficiency has for the behaviour of interest rates.

THE BEHAVIOUR OF LONG-RUN INTEREST RATES UNDER RATIONAL EXPECTATIONS

Government bonds can typically be regarded by investors as free of default risk. Bonds do have different coupon rates, but are essentially similar except that the various bonds differ in their term to full maturity. For an individual trader, long-run bonds are substitutable for short-run bonds, since it is possible for him to hold a series of short bonds rather than a long bond over the same holding period, or conversely to hold a long bond for a short period and then sell it rather than hold a short bond to maturity.

More formally, let us assume initially that traders are completely certain of the future and that we can ignore the complication which can occur due to periodic coupon payments; that is we treat all bonds as pure discount bonds, so that the return is simply the discount from par at which the bond is sold at the beginning of the period relative to the redeemed par price at the end of the period. Then the following condition must hold:

$$(1 + R^k)^k = (1 + R)(1 + R_{+1})(1 + R_{+2}) \cdots (1 + R_{+k-1})$$

$$(7.29)$$

The left hand side of (7.29) is simply the rate of return on holding a k period bond until maturity. The right side of (7.29) is the rate of return implied by holding a one-period bond for one period, then reinvesting the proceeds (principal plus interest) in a one-period Treasury bond for the next period and so on.

By taking logarithms and recalling that for small values of Z, $\log(1 + Z)$ can be approximated by Z, we can rewrite (7.29) as:

$$R^k = 1/k(R + R_{+1} + R_{+2} + \cdots + R_{+k-1}) \qquad (7.30)$$

In other words (7.30) tells us that long-run interest rates are simply averages of future interest rates over the time period to maturity. It tells us, for instance, that if short-run interest rates remain constant for the indefinite future, then long rates will be equal to short rates. Conversely, if future short rates are expected to fall, the current long rate will be beneath the short rate. This relationship is known as the expectations theory of the term structure of interest rates.

When we relax the assumption of perfect knowledge of the future and recognize that traders can observe the current long rate R_t^k and the current one-period short rate R_t, it follows if traders are risk neutral that:

$$R^k = 1/k[R + \mathsf{E}R_{+1} + \mathsf{E}R_{+2} + \cdots + \mathsf{E}R_{+k-1}] \qquad (7.31)$$

If traders are risk averse, then we must add a risk premium $\bar{R}$ to the right-hand side of (7.31).[5] Consequently:

$$R^k = 1/k[R + \mathsf{E}R_{+1} + \mathsf{E}R_{+2} + \cdots + \mathsf{E}R_{+k-1}] + \bar{R} \qquad (7.32)$$

Suppose initially that the risk premium does not change over time, then in period $t - 1$ we have:

$$R^k_{-1} = 1/k[R_{-1} + \underset{-1}{\mathsf{E}} R + \underset{-1}{\mathsf{E}} R_{+1} + \cdots + \underset{-1}{\mathsf{E}} R_{+k-2}] + \bar{R}$$

$$(7.33)$$

Subtracting (7.33) from (7.32) we obtain:

$$R^k - R^k_{-1} = 1/k\left[\left(R - \underset{-1}{\mathsf{E}} R\right)\right.$$

$$+ \left(\mathsf{E}R_{+1} - \underset{-1}{\mathsf{E}} R_{+1}\right) + \cdots + \left.\left(\mathsf{E}R_{+k-1} - \underset{-1}{\mathsf{E}} R_{+k-1}\right)\right]$$

$$+ 1/k\left(\underset{-1}{\mathsf{E}} R_{+k-1} - R_{-1}\right) \qquad (7.34)$$

It follows from the assumption of rational expectations that the revision terms in square brackets can occur only as a consequence of news. Thus (7.34) simplifies to:

$$R^k - R^k_{-1} = \varepsilon + 1/k\left(\underset{-1}{E} \; R_{+k-1} - R_{-1} \right) \qquad (7.35)$$

Clearly if k is sufficiently large, as it would be for, say, undated securities ($k \rightarrow \infty$), then since the difference between $\left(\underset{-1}{E} \; R_{+k-1} - R_{-1} \right)$ cannot be infinite (owing to the usual terminal conditions), (7.35) simplifies to:

$$R^k - R^k_{-1} = \varepsilon \qquad (7.36)$$

This striking result tells us that for sufficiently long-dated bonds, assuming that risk premiums are relatively constant, the long-run interest rate should follow a random walk. Consequently, no information available at time $t - 1$ should allow us to predict systematic changes in the long-run interest rate. A number of empirical studies have tested this implication (see e.g. Sargent, 1972, 1976a; Pesando, 1978; Mishkin, 1978a). The empirical results of these studies are favourable to the hypothesis. More recently Shiller (1979) has provided some evidence which is inconsistent with (7.36). However one interpretation of Shiller's analysis is that the risk premia due principally to inflation uncertainty cannot be modelled as a constant over his sample period (see Begg, 1982).

We notice market efficiency does not at all imply that changes in *short-run* nominal rates of interest need be random. Movements in short-run rates will be dependent on the precise model structure. The random walk property only applies to long-term interest rates under the precise assumptions outlined above.

CONCLUSIONS

In this chapter we have discussed some of the implications and evidence for the proposition that financial markets are efficient. As particular applications of the proposition we examined the behaviour of exchange rates and bond markets.

In general the empirical evidence for (approximate) semi-strong efficiency in the capital markets is sufficiently powerful and convincing for it to be regarded as a 'stylized fact'. Consequently macroeconomic model builders cannot in our view legitimately continue to simulate or forecast the impact of changes in government policy within models that assume serious capital market inefficiency. Mishkin (1978a, 1978b) for example shows how the imposition of the assumption of market efficiency radically changes the simulation properties of models without it. The reason is clear. Take for instance an announced permanent increase in monetary growth which, within conventional models would have its effects with long lags: with market efficiency this will cause an immediate jump in very long-run interest rates (to their equilibrium value) and also jumps in the exchange rate (and stock market prices). The transmission mechanism of monetary policy will be radically altered. These properties are illustrated later (Chapter 11) in a discussion of the Liverpool Model which embodies financial market efficiency.

APPENDIX: PARTIAL INFORMATION AND TESTS
OF EFFICIENCY

The purpose of this appendix is to show the manner in which the standard test of efficiency based on (7.15) of the chapter has to be modified if agents have an incomplete current information set. For analytical simplicity (though the argument is quite general), we write a series y as the summation of two infinite moving average error processes in the two white noise errors, ε, and z. Consequently:

$$y = \bar{y} + \sum_{i=0}^{\infty} \pi_i \varepsilon_{-i} + \sum_{i=0}^{\infty} \partial_i z_{-i} \qquad (7.A.1)$$

where $\bar{y}$ is the mean of the series, the π_i and ∂_i are constant coefficients.

Consider the rational expectation of y_{+1} formed at time t. If there is full current information at time t the expectation will be given by:

$$\mathsf{E}\, y_{+1} = \bar{y} + \sum_{i=1}^{\infty} \pi_i \varepsilon_{-i+1} + \sum_{i=1}^{\infty} \partial_i z_{-i+1} \qquad (7.A.2)$$

In this case, given the one-period forceast horizon, the *ex post* forecast error will be given by a white noise error:

$$y_{+1} - \mathsf{E}\, y_{+1} = \pi_0 \varepsilon_{+1} + \partial_0 z_{+1} \qquad (7.A.3)$$

Consequently the standard tests based on (7.15) are correct in these circumstances.

Suppose next that agents have incomplete current information at time t, and instead observe some current global information (for instance via asset markets), but other global information with a one-period lag. In particular we will assume for simplicity (though the argument is easily generalized) that there is one global indicator (say the interest rate) which is given the representation:

$$R = \bar{r} + \sum_{i=0}^{\infty} d_i \varepsilon_{-i} + \sum_{i=0}^{\infty} h_i z_{-i} \qquad (7.A.4)$$

where $\bar{r}$ is the mean of the series and the d_i and h_i are constant coefficients.

In this incomplete current information case the one period expectation of y is given by:

$$\mathsf{E}\, y_{+1} = \bar{y} + \pi_1 \mathsf{E}\varepsilon + \sum_{i=2}^{\infty} \pi_i \varepsilon_{-i+1}$$

$$+ \partial_1 \mathsf{E}z + \sum_{i=2}^{\infty} \partial_i z_{-i+1} \qquad (7.A.5)$$

Consequently the forecast error is given by:

$$y_{+1} - \mathsf{E}\, y_{+1} = \pi_0 \varepsilon_{+1} + \partial_0 z_{+1}$$

$$+ \pi_1 [\varepsilon - \mathsf{E}\varepsilon] + \partial_1 [z - \mathsf{E}z] \qquad (7.A.6)$$

Given current observation of the global indicator R, and using the usual signal extraction formulae (as discussed in Chapter 4) we obtain:

$$\mathsf{E}\varepsilon = \frac{1}{d_0} \phi_\varepsilon (d_0 \varepsilon + h_0 z) \qquad (7.A.7)$$

$$\mathsf{E}z = \frac{1}{h_0} (1 - \phi_\varepsilon)(d_0 \varepsilon + h_0 z) \qquad (7.A.8)$$

where

$$\phi_\varepsilon = \frac{d_0^2 \, \sigma_\varepsilon^2}{d_0^2 \, \sigma_\varepsilon^2 + h_0^2 \, \sigma_z^2}$$

and σ_ε^2 and σ_z^2 are the variances of the two errors, ε and z respectively. Consequently the forecast error (K_{+1}) is given by:

$$K_{+1} = \pi_0 \varepsilon_{+1} + \partial_0 z_{+1} + \pi_1 \left[(1 - \phi_\varepsilon)\varepsilon - \frac{h_0}{d_0} \, \phi_\varepsilon z \right]$$

$$+ \partial_1 \left[\phi_\varepsilon z - \frac{d_0}{h_0} (1 - \phi_\varepsilon)\varepsilon \right] \quad (7.A.9)$$

Serial Correlation of Forecast Errors

If we take expectations of two successive errors we find:

$$\mathsf{E}(K_{+1}, K) = \frac{(\sigma_z^2)(\sigma_\varepsilon^2)}{d_0^2 \, \sigma_\varepsilon^2 + h_0^2 \, \sigma_z^2} \, [\pi_1 h_0 - \partial_1 d_0][\pi_0 h_0 - \partial_0 d_0]$$

$$(7.A.10)$$

Consequently, in general, incomplete current information will give rise to a moving average error process. This will not be the case if, first, we have, implicitly, full current information (for example if there are as many global indicators in the economy as random shocks (see Karni 1980), or second, if we observe the current value of the variable which is to be forecast, which is itself a global indicator for, in this case, $\pi_0 = d_0$, $\partial_0 = h_0$, (also $\pi_1 = d_1$, $\partial_1 = h_1$) and the expected correlation in (7.A.10) is equal to zero.

It would appear from this result that standard tests of efficiency based on (7.15) will have the usual properties for asset prices in particular (which it can be assumed are observed currently), even under incomplete current information. However, the general point remains that variables *not* currently observed (i.e. the majority) will under incomplete information be inappropriately tested for efficiency by these methods. Furthermore, one needs to scrutinize carefully the assumption that the asset prices in question are *contemporaneously* observed. In very high frequency data (e.g. hourly) this will obviously not be so except for a few continuously broadcast asset prices; it will also not be so in lower frequency data for *averages* of variables (e.g. the level of all short-term interest rates), which are often examined in these studies.

In general, in circumstances of incomplete current information the moving average error in equation (7.15) will be given by $s + j - 1$, where s is the time horizon of the forecast and j is the longest lag on global information relevant for forecasting y. Clearly there may be some *a priori* doubt as to the magnitude of j, which may cause some problems in interpretation of tests based on (7.15). As a consequence of the moving average error process, least squares estimates of (7.15) under incomplete current information will give rise to biased estimates of the variances of a and b and inefficient estimates of a and b. However the least squares estimates of a and b will be unbiased since:

$$E(K_{+1}, E(y_{+1})) = 0 \qquad (7.A.11)$$

and least squares estimates have the property of unbiasedness even in the presence of moving error processes. This situation is the same as that of overlapping information in the usually assumed case of full current information; overlapping information here occurs with $s > 1$, familiarly introducing a moving average process with the same effects.

These results have potential implications for a number of empirical studies (see e.g. Holden and Peel, 1977; Turnovsky, 1970) in which an implicit assumption of full current information has been made when studying directly observed consumer price expectations data which cannot readily be assumed part of the current information set. The point here is that *price* data is not currently observable on any reasonable assumptions. Consequently, the 'expectations errors' should be serially correlated, as indeed has often been found in these tests. It is possible that these survey data may well reveal rationality after all. For further implications of partial current information sets for the testing of efficiency, see Minford and Peel (1983b).

NOTES

1. Hellwig (1982) in an interesting paper has challenged the Grossman and Stiglitz proposition that the informativeness of market
prices in equilibrium is bounded away from full informational
efficiency. Hellwig points out that this proposition rests on the
assumption that agents learn from current prices before any
transactions at these prices take place. In contrast, Hellwig
assumes that agents learn from prices at which transactions have
actually been completed. This is a model in which investors
learn from past equilibrium prices but not from the auctioneer's
current price offer. Hellwig is able to show that if the time span
between successive market transactions is short, the market can
approximate full informational efficiency arbitrarily closely and
yet the return to being informed remains bounded away from
zero. This results from the fact that informed agents can utilize
this information before uninformed agents have an opportunity
to infer it from current market prices.

   Hellwig also pursues the implications that arise if one relaxes
the assumption that agents cannot assure themselves of being
informed in a given period, but rather agents choose the frequency on average at which they obtain information. It appears
that relaxing such assumptions leaves unimpaired his salient
result that approximate informational efficiency of market does
not destroy the incentive to acquire resources at cost. Clearly
the issues raised by Grossman, Stiglitz and Hellwig remain an
active research issue. We should also draw attention to the
papers surveyed by Jordan and Radner (1982).

2. Consider an individual faced with a possible gamble; he may
choose either to receive a certain £100, or to toss a coin and
receive £50 if heads occur and £150 if tails occur. The expected
outcome of this latter choice is £100(0.5(50) + 0.5(150)). The
question is will the individual prefer the actuarial value of the
gamble (that is its expected outcome) with certainty or will he
prefer the gamble itself? If he prefers the gamble he is a risk
lover; if he is indifferent he is risk neutral; and if he prefers the
actuarial value with certainty he is risk averse.

   It is also possible to compute the maximum amount of wealth
an individual would be willing to give up in order to avoid the
gamble. This is the notion of a risk premium. (See Pratt, 1964;
Arrow, 1971; Markowitz, 1959).

3. This can be seen by solving any model in which two stable roots

are required for a unique solution. The analogue of Ee_{+1} would then depend not only on e but also on e_{-1}.

4. For the real interest rate differential to be constant, as investigated by Mishkin (1981), an infinitely large intertemporal substitution response is required for either α or β. The evidence does not support such responses; it is therefore not surprising that Mishkin concludes from his reduced form work that the differential varies over time. Similar arguments apply to variation of the real interest rate within a closed economy, as investigated by Fama (1975) for the US; this evidence has now been found (by Nelson and Schwert, 1977) to support non-constancy, which again is not surprising. We may also note that the *size* of variation in both the differential and the closed (e.g. world) economy level of real interest rates cannot be suggested *a priori*; nor can the length of time to convergence (determined by μ in this model, as influenced by all the parameters).

5. For more detailed literature on the risk premium in the term structure context, see e.g. Meiselman (1962), Keynes (1936), Hicks (1939) and Modigliani and Sutch (1966).

8

The Political Economy of Democracy

One of the major developments in the public choice literature over the last few years has been the construction and empirical testing of models that consider the interaction of the preferences of government and electors and the behaviour of the economy.

Important examples of this work are the papers by Nordhaus (1975), MacRae (1977), Frey and Schneider (1978a, 1978b). A key assumption of this work is that expectations are formed in an error learning or adaptive manner. The purpose of this chapter is to consider the implications that the rational expectations hypothesis has for the behaviour or role of the authorities. We shall assume in this context that the authorities, as well as voters, form rational expectations of the outcomes of different policy rules.

This raises the interesting issues of whether there is scope for differences in economic policy between different political parties and of how voters will react to differences in policy and economic performance.

We begin by outlining the recent work in the public choice literature which is based on adaptive expectations. We then consider the rational expectations alternative and discuss the empirical evidence in favour of it. We conclude that voting behaviour is, on the basis of very incomplete research, consistent with rational expectations and that national parties will choose different economic policies and will *not* obey the 'median voter theorem'.

144

THE NORDHAUS MODEL

Perhaps the most interesting model of an adaptive expectations vintage which stresses the interaction of the preferences of the government and the elector is the model of Nordhaus (1975). The Nordhaus model is based on the Downs (1957) hypothesis that governments have an overriding goal of winning the next election. Hence they obey the 'median voter theorem' (namely, that their policies will be designed with maximum appeal to the floating voter who will decide the election) and are consequently concerned to maximize their popularity over their period of office.

Their popularity is assumed to depend on a number of key economic variables, notably the rate of inflation and unemployment. It is further assumed that voters are myopic, which implies that they give highest weight in voting to the current rates of inflation and unemployment, with no consideration of their future values. The government is assumed to maximize its popularity subject to the constraint that the rate of inflation, the rate of unemployment and the expected rate of inflation, are linked via an augmented Phillips curve. Finally it is assumed that price expectations are formed adaptively. The Nordhaus model thus has the following mathematical structure (in continuous time):

$$\text{Maximize } P = \int_0^T F(p, U)(1 + r)^t \, dt \qquad (8.1)$$

subject to the constraints:

$$p = g(U) + p^e \qquad (8.2)$$

$$Dp^e = \phi(p - p^e) \qquad (8.3)$$

where p is the rate of inflation (p^e the expected rate), U is the rate of unemployment, r is the discount rate (*positive* to reflect voter myopia), F, g are functions, ϕ is a positive constant, and D is the differential (rate of change) operator such that, e.g. $Dx = dx/dt$. Equation (8.1) is the government's objective function. Popularity, P, is maximized between the time of arrival in office (0) and the time of the next election

(T). Equation (8.2) is the augmented Phillips curve and equation (8.3) the adaptive expectations mechanism.

Clearly the optimal paths of unemployment and inflation will depend on the precise choice of function $F(\ )$ and $g(\ )$. Nordhaus specifies an objective function:

$$F(\ ) = -\alpha p - \frac{\beta}{2} U^2 \tag{8.4}$$

and a linear augmented Phillips curve:

$$g(U) = a - bU \tag{8.5}$$

where α, β, a, b are positive constants.

The mathematics required to solve this problem is outside the scope of this book (see e.g. Cass and Shell, 1976). It turns out that the path of the unemployment rate between elections implied by its solution has the form shown in Figure 8.1.

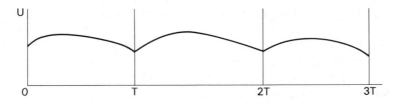

Figure 8.1 *The political business cycle*

The essential implication then of this work is that governments deliberately cause a business cycle so that, at the date of election, they are in the most favourable position *vis-à-vis* voters' preferences; hence on arriving in office, they raise unemployment to initiate a reduction in inflation, then after two years or so they stimulate the economy to reduce unemployment in time for the election date, leaving their successor to cope with the rise in inflation that is the lagged result of this policy.

While the optimal pattern of inflation or unemployment does depend on the precise choice of functional forms, the essential insight of Nordhaus, that governments may have a vested interest in creating business cycles, will survive these and other changes (such as endogenizing the electoral period T, see Chappell and Peel, 1979). The assumption that government popularity depends on variables such as the rate of inflation or unemployment has received some empirical support. In particular Frey and Schneider (1978a, 1978b) have reported empirical work for a variety of different countries, such as the United Kingdom, USA and West Germany, in which a measure of government popularity, typically based on opinion polls, is found to be significantly related to such economic variables.

However, more recent work (e.g. Borooah and Van der Ploeg, 1982; Chrystal and Alt, 1981; Minford and Peel, 1982a; Harte, Minford and Peel, 1983), shows that the work of Frey and Schneider is not statistically robust with respect to changes in the sample period or the economic variables chosen.

This is perhaps not too surprising. Economists, when analysing agents' choice between alternatives are concerned to stress the appropriate relative prices. This point has typically been neglected in the empirical work on government popularity. The alternative hypothesis is best outlined by Tullock (1976) who writes:

Voters and customers are essentially the same people. Mr Smith buys and votes; he is the same man in the supermarket and in the voting booth. There is no strong reason to believe his behaviour is radically different in the two environments. We assume that in both he will choose the product or candidate he thinks is the best bargain for him.

When we also recognize that voters are expressing preferences for different policies over the lifetime of a government, it is clear that the relevant choice should reflect *expectations* of future policy differences between parties. From this perspective the most charitable interpretation of the conventional work is that the future paths of economic variables under the party in power are formed adaptively and that the paths of economic variables under the non-governing party are considered by electors as fixed.

A RATIONAL EXPECTATIONS MODEL OF VOTERS AND PARTIES

We have developed an alternative model (Minford and Peel, 1982a) in which the expectations of both voters and the authorities are assumed to be formed rationally. We argue that the marginal costs of information gathering can be regarded as sufficiently low for the representative voter to develop an informed opinion of the future path of economic variables. One simple mechanism (and there are probably some others) by which this can occur is via public forecasts. Forecasts of inflation and output from major forecasting institutions (for instance, in the UK the Treasury, the London Business School, the National Institute and Liverpool) will represent informed opinion and are given widespread publicity by newspapers and television, which the voter obtains at negligible marginal costs. While these public forecasts will differ to some extent, they will tend to be correlated and voters' expectations, as conditioned by them, will more closely approximate rational expectations than some mechanistic adaptive alternative.

Although the typical voter may face low costs of gathering information and opinions this does not explain why he votes. The direct marginal benefits of voting, in the sense that the individual vote will influence the electoral outcome, appear *a priori* to be less than the marginal costs of voting. However, the most attractive rationale for rational voting is the 'civic' recognition by voters that democracy cannot function unless many people vote (see Mueller, 1979, for a fuller discussion of these issues).

Given these assumptions about the information set of agents, we follow a number of different authors in supposing that political parties wish, in part, to pursue economic policies which are broadly in accordance with the objective economic interests and subjective preferences of their 'class', defined as their core political constituency. For instance, H. Johnson (1968) writes:

From one important view, indeed, the avoidance of inflation and the maintenance of full employment can most usefully be regarded as conflicting class interest of the bourgeois and proletariat, respectively, the conflict being resolvable only by the test of relative political power in the society.

J. Robinson (1937) also writes:

In so far as stable prices are regarded as desirable for their own sake, as contributing to social justice, it must be recognised that justice to the rentier can be achieved only by means of the injustice to the rest of the community of maintaining a lower level of effective demand than might otherwise be achieved. We are here presented with a conflict of interests . . . and actual policies are largely governed by the rival influences of the interests involved.

(Clearly we do not accept the assumption made in both these comments that output is demand determined.)

We assume that there are three relevant sets of voters; Labour (Democrats), Conservatives (Republicans) and Floating Voters. The supporters of each party come from different parts of the electorate (for example, 'labourers' and 'capitalists', see Hibbs, 1978). The stylized assumption is that Labour voters primarily hold human capital and that Conservatives primarily hold financial capital.

The current utility function of the voters is written in quadratic form as:

$$c = c_1 p + c_2 p^2 + c_0 \qquad (8.6)$$

$$V = v_1 p + v_2 p^2 + v_3 y + v_4 y^2 + v_0 \qquad (8.7)$$

$$L = l_1 y + l_2 y^2 \qquad (8.8)$$

where c_1, c_2, v_1, v_2, v_4, l_2 are negative and c_0, v_0, v_3, l_1 positive constants; y is disposable labour income.

The floating voter who determines the election outcome is assumed to express his voting intentions (up to and including the time he votes in the election) according to which party is expected to give him greater utility from the time of the next election onwards. Formally he takes the expectation EV (which is taken as a proxy for his expected utility for all time beyond the election) conditional on each party's policies in turn, EV_T^L, EV_T^C (Labour and Conservative respectively); he casts his vote for Labour if $EV_T^L > EV_T^C$ and *vice versa*. In aggregate it is assumed that aggregate votes are distributed around the typical floating voter, yielding a cumulative voters' balance function of the form:

$$B = b(EV_T^G - EV_T^O) + h \qquad (8.9)$$

where G denotes 'government' and O 'opposition'; h is an error process for non-economic omitted variables. Taking expectations of (8.7), for government this yields the hypothesis that:

$$EV^G = v_1 Ep + v_2 Ep^2 + v_3 Ey + v_4 Ey^2 \qquad (8.10)$$

Doing the same for the opposition and subtracting from (8.10) gives:

$$EV_T^G - EV_T^O = \beta_1(Ep - \bar{p}) + \beta_2(\text{var } p - \overline{\text{var } p})$$
$$+ \beta_3(Ey - \bar{y}) + \beta_4(\text{var } y - \overline{\text{var } y}) \qquad (8.11)$$

where var p, var y are the variances of p and y around their expected values and $\bar{p}$, $\bar{y}$, $\overline{\text{var } p}$, $\overline{\text{var } y}$ reflect the relevant expectations and variances of the opposition.

Unlike previous voting functions, therefore, our formulation is explicitly forward-looking in inflation and income and it includes variances of the relevant economic variables. In our empirical work we use the perhaps unsatisfactory proxy of time trends for the opposition party's policies and there is clearly scope for use of more subtle alternatives in future work. Using Gallup data for the United Kingdom over the period 1959–75, we produce evidence that (8.11) performs in a more satisfactory manner than the conventional Frey–Schneider alternative.

With respect to party policy, we assume the authorities are faced with an economy in which there is no long-run trade-off between inflation and output, but where, in the short run, fiscal and monetary policy can stabilize the economy by appropriate choice of feedback rules; these are assumed to be effective on the grounds, such as, for example, contracts, discussed in Chapter 3. The absence of a long-run trade-off does not, however, avoid a choice of the long-run budget deficit and, of course, the implied monetary growth rate. It might seem that all parties would have as their long-run target zero inflation, and hence choose targets for the budget deficit and money supply growth to go with this. This is clearly not the case, however, once we recognize that a budget deficit with inflation implies a different incidence of the existing tax burden than zero inflation, since an unanticipated shift to higher inflation on the accession of a new government will lower the capital value of nominal government debt. This will expropriate debt holders to the advantage of the general taxpayer who now pays less tax.

We assume for formal purposes, very simply, that each party maximizes the expected value at the next election date of a weighted average of the utility of its own supporters and that of the floating voter. The expectation is formed at time $t = 0$, the time of strategy choice, and it is supposed that this choice occurs only once in each period between elections and then cannot effectively be changed. We suppose that a party has had its 'honeymoon' period, has had to react to the pressures of office and after about half a year of its term has settled down and then chooses its strategy. The other party has by this time settled in opposition and also chooses its strategy. Once chosen the parties cannot with credibility change them.

Formally then, for example, the Conservative party maximizes:

$$\lambda \mathop{E}_{0} C_T + (1 - \lambda) \mathop{E}_{0} V_T \qquad (8.12)$$

where λ is the weight given to its own supporters. The function will be expected to be maximized at time T, the time of the election. In principle it ought to be expected utility from this date onwards, with a suitable discount factor, however, for empirical purposes this is considered needlessly complicated, given that we have ruled out expected future changes in policy programmes.

(8.12) is maximized subject to the voters' preferences (8.6), (8.7) and (8.8) and the model of the economy. The formal mathematics of this is somewhat complicated and is relegated to the Appendix to this chapter. However, the implication of the analysis is important. This is that different political parties, who represent different class interests, will pursue different policies. In particular party policies will differ significantly, not only in budget and money supply targets but also in feedback coefficients, according to the interaction between voter preferences and the model structure. Labour reaction functions will, relative to Conservative reaction functions, embody a higher steady state budget deficit and be more responsive to real rather than nominal shocks.

Quite clearly the precise form of reaction function will be dependent on the true model of the economy and the nature of voter preferences (which may not be constant), However, the point of our study remains valid, namely that in an economy with rational expectations on the part of both government and voters, there is scope for systematic policy differences between different political parties.

Empirical results on UK reaction functions for the period 1959–75 support the model in that significant differences between the political parties were discovered. More recent work by Harte, Minford and Peel (1983) has confirmed the fruitfulness of the type of approach, and found significant statistical differences in reaction functions between the parties in the UK, Sweden and West Germany.

The results obtained by Harte and ourselves for the rational approach to the voting functions are, however, at conflict with our earlier evidence. It appears now that the functions based on equation (8.11) are statistically unstable between different sample periods. This also applies to the conventional specifications. This could, of course, be due to the unsuitable proxy for the opposition parties, which are based on a time trend. However, it seems more likely that the problems lie in the omission of non-economic factors from the analysis which can probably not be treated as stable error processes for the purposes of statistical estimation (consider the effects of the wars over Suez, Vietnam, and the Falklands). There are also some difficulties in generating adequate expectations series for future variables a long way ahead.

Such considerations have led to some further empirical work on voting related to Hall's (1978) specification of a rational expectations consumption function, which we now examine. This work has useful implications for voting functions which we return to below.

RATIONAL EXPECTATIONS AND 'PERMANENT' VARIABLES – THE
CONSUMPTION FUNCTION

According to the permanent income hypothesis of consumer
behaviour (Friedman, 1957):

$$C = kY^p \qquad (8.13)$$

where C is real consumer expenditure and Y^p is permanent
income. Permanent income is defined as the discounted value
of the stream of all current and future real income, Y
(including income from assets), therefore:

$$Y^p = \sum_{i=0}^{\infty} \frac{EY_{+i}}{(1+r)^i} \qquad (8.14)$$

where r is the constant real rate of interest at which agents
are assumed to be able to lend and borrow.

From the definition of permanent income, and independently of the question of how expectations are formed:

$$\underset{-1}{E} Y^p = Y^p_{-1} \qquad (8.15)$$

(8.15) follows because, from the very definition of permanent
income, agents do not expect it to change, for it is the constant steam of income which they envisage over their lifetime
or planning horizon.[1]

Taking expectations of (8.14) conditional on the information set at $t-1$ and subtracting from (8.14) we obtain:

$$Y^p - \underset{-1}{E} Y^p = \sum_{i=0}^{\infty} \frac{\left(EY_{+i} - \underset{-1}{E} Y_{+i}\right)}{(1+r)^i} \qquad (8.16)$$

Since, given the assumption of rational expectations, all the
right-hand side variables in (8.16) are innovations (or news),
we have:

$$Y^p - \underset{-1}{E} Y^p = \varepsilon = \text{news} \qquad (8.17)$$

Consequently from (8.15):

$$Y^p - Y^p_{-1} = \varepsilon \qquad (8.18)$$

The above argument is simple to understand. If expectations are rational, then, given the definition of permanent income, the only reason agents will raise their view of their permanent income is due to new information or news. If this were not the case, it would imply that expectations were significantly biased since agents should have revised their permanent incomes in previous periods.

(8.18) in conjunction with (8.13) implies that:

$$C = C_{-1} + k\varepsilon \qquad (8.19)$$

In other words, real consumer expenditures follow a random walk.

Equation (8.19) has the testable implication that all previous information, as embodied, for example, in lagged values of consumption, inflation or indeed any variable, should not add any significant explanatory power to (8.19). This is the result first discovered by Hall (1978). Allowance for factors such as growth in incomes over time or the seasonal pattern of consumption does imply slight modification to (8.19) but allowing for this the empirical results have been impressive (see e.g. Bilson, 1980; though for an alternative view see Davidson and Hendry, 1981).

VOTING AND 'PERMANENT' POLICIES

The idea that the 'permanent' variables under rational expectations will follow a random walk forms the basis for an alternative model of voting intentions.

Assume that voters' evaluation of parties is based on their judgment of the difference in permanent income (or utility) between parties. This judgment can be based on non-economic as well as economic variables. It follows that under rational expectations the popularity of parties should follow a random walk. Consequently, appropriate testing of voting models under rational expectations will involve relating changes in popularity to innovations or news.

As with the consumption function, past rates of inflation or unemployment or economic variables in general should have no explanatory power. This idea is currently being tested empirically; preliminary results are not inconsistent with it. It can be seen as a logical extension of our earlier model, but where proper attention is given to non-economic factors and the time horizon for expectations is extended into the indefinite future.

CONCLUSIONS

Recent work in the public choice literature has considered the interaction of the preferences of the government and electors and the behaviour of the economy. This work has assumed that expectations are formed adaptively and has generated one key conclusion, namely that the authorities may deliberately create a business cycle. When expectations are formed rationally, the authorities are no longer able to generate a political business cycle.

Another key result of the public choice literature is the median voter theorem, according to which party policies should be essentially the same, because they are designed to capture the floating voter. We also showed how a simple theory in which parties attempt to maximize the expected future utility, not only of floating voters but also of their own class-based supporters, will give rise to systematic differences in the parties' reaction functions. This prediction commands some empirical support. One implication of this work is that political factors ought to be formally incorporated into future research on policy rules.

We also considered the way in which government popularity and voting behaviour has been modelled. We suggested that the conventional approach based on past economic indicators was deficient in ignoring expectations of future economic variables and the behaviour of the opposition. However, because of the importance of non-economic factors, it is unlikely that functions based solely on economic variables will generate statistically robust results; the evidence to date confirms this view. We suggested an alternative approach which borrows from Hall's formulation of the consumption function, and sees voters as formulating a view of rival 'permanent' policies. There is clearly, however, much scope for further work in this area.

APPENDIX: PARTIES' ECONOMIC POLICIES

In Minford and Peel (1982a) we wrote the model for the economy as:

$$p = \pi_1 d + \varepsilon + \pi\varepsilon_{-1} \tag{8.A.1}$$

$$y = w_1 d + \eta + w\eta_{-1} \tag{8.A.2}$$

$$d = (1 - \delta_4)\bar{d} + \delta_2\varepsilon_{-1} + \delta_3\eta_{-1} + u + \delta_4 d_{-1} \tag{8.A.3}$$

where d is the government instrument (the budget deficit, or the growth rate of the money supply – we assume these to be highly correlated) and $\bar{d}$ is its long-run value. ε is the nominal shock, η the real shock; both ε and η are white noise errors. u, the error process in d, may be serially correlated for non-economic reasons and $\delta_4(|\delta_4| < 1)$ is assumed fixed, again by non-economic forces (e.g. political pressure groups which, once having gained higher expenditures at the cost of a larger deficit, will campaign against their reduction).

(8.A.1) and (8.A.2) indicate in the barest manner possible that inflation and real disposable labour income are both positively related to the budget deficit (and money supply growth). Each variable also depends on a moving average process in nominal and real shocks respectively. The dynamics of the real world are clearly inadequately represented here, but these equations will nevertheless suffice for illustration of our argument.

The problem for each party is to choose $\bar{d}$, δ_2, δ_3. The parties are not allowed to 'fine tune' in the optimal control sense of changing their strategies from period to period, this has been shown to be inferior to fixed feedback rules (see Chapter 5). We assumed that parties would therefore favour fixed feedback rules, since the others would be penalized by voters.

The Conservative party maximizes:

$$\lambda \underset{0}{\mathbf{E}} C_T + (1 - \lambda) \underset{0}{\mathbf{E}} V_T \tag{8.A.4}$$

where λ is the weight given to its own supporters.

From (8.A.1) − (8.A.3) we have:

$$p = \pi_1 \bar{d} + (\pi_1 \delta_2 + \pi)\varepsilon_{-1} + \frac{\pi_1 \delta_3 \eta_{-1}}{1 - \delta_4 L}\varepsilon$$

$$+ \frac{\pi_1 u}{1 - \delta_4 L} + \frac{\pi_1 \delta_2 \delta_4 \varepsilon_{-2}}{1 - \delta_4 L} \qquad (8.A.5)$$

$$y = w_1 \bar{d} + \frac{w_1 \delta_2 \varepsilon_{-1}}{1 - \delta_4 L} + (w_1 \delta_3 + w)\eta_{-1} + \eta$$

$$+ \frac{w_1 u}{1 - \delta_4 L} + \frac{w_1 \delta_3 \delta_4}{1 - \delta_4 L}\eta_{-2} \qquad (8.A.6)$$

where L is the lag operator. Hence the Conservative problem is to maximize (assuming T is 'large'), approximately:

$$k_1^C(\pi_1 \bar{d}) + k_2^C \left[\pi_1^2 \bar{d}^2 + \left(\pi_1^2 \delta_2^2 + \pi^2 + 2\pi\pi_1\delta_2 + \frac{\pi_1^2 \delta_2^2 \delta_4^2}{1 - \delta_4^2} + 1 \right) \text{var } \varepsilon \right.$$

$$+ \frac{\pi_1^2 \delta_3^2}{1 - \delta_4^2} \text{var } \eta + \frac{\pi_1^2}{1 - \delta_4^2} \text{var } u \left. \right] + k_3^C(w_1 \bar{d})$$

$$+ k_4^C \left[w_1^2 \bar{d}^2 + \frac{w_1^2 \delta_2^2}{1 - \delta_4^2} \text{var } \varepsilon + \left(w_1^2 \delta_3^2 + w^2 + 2w_1 w \delta_3 \right.\right.$$

$$\left.+ \frac{w_1^2 \delta_3^2 \delta_4^2}{1 - \delta_4^2} + 1 \right) \text{var } \eta + \frac{w_1^2}{1 - \delta_4^2} \text{var } u \left. \right] \qquad (8.A.7)$$

where:

$$k_1^C = \lambda c_1 + (1 - \lambda)v_1, \quad k_2^C = \lambda c_2 + (1 - \lambda)v_2,$$
$$k_3^C = (1 - \lambda)v_3, \qquad k_4^C = (1 - \lambda)v_4$$

We obtain from the first-order conditions:

$$d = \frac{-(k_1^C \pi_1 + k_3^C w_1)}{2k_2^C \pi_1^2 + 2k_4^C w_1^2} \quad \text{Sign: ?} \qquad (8.A.8)$$

$$\delta_2 = \frac{-k_2^C \pi\pi_1(1 - \delta_4^2)}{k_2^C \pi_1^2 + k_4^C w_1^2} \quad \text{Sign: } <0 \qquad (8.A.9)$$

$$\delta_3 = \frac{-k_4^C w_1 w(1 - \delta_4^2)}{k_2^C \pi_1^2 + k_4^C w_1^2} \quad \text{Sign: } <0 \qquad (8.A.10)$$

For Labour we obtain the same expression substituting k_1^L for k_1^C throughout, where:

$$k_1^L = (1 - \lambda)v_1, \qquad k_2^L = (1 - \lambda)v_2,$$
$$k_3^L = \lambda l_1 + (1 - \lambda)v_3, \quad k_4^L = \lambda l_2 + (1 - \lambda)v_4$$

where we have assumed for convenience that Labour assigns the same weight λ to its own supporters as do the Conservatives.

The sign patterns are the same, but because:

$$|k_1^C| > |k_1^L|, |k_2^C| > |k_2^L|, |k_3^L| < |k_3^L|, |k_4^C| < |k_4^L|$$

we have the prediction that Labour governments will have a higher $\bar{d}$ than Conservative governments, a lower $|\delta_2|$, and a higher $|\delta_3|$. That is to say, just as we would expect, they will have a higher budget deficit or money supply growth target and they will stabilize nominal shocks less, real shocks more, than Conservative governments.

So simple is the 'model' used to extract these predictions that it should be regarded merely as illustrative of the main point: that parties' policy functions will differ significantly both in targets and in feedback coefficients, according to the interaction between voter preferences and the model structure.

NOTE

1. This assumes there is no systematic growth in y. But allowing for a growth trend does not alter the essential point of the argument that follows. It adds a constant into (8.15). (8.19) would then become a random walk 'with drift' (i.e. with a constant anticipated growth component).

9

Wealth effects and
Bond-financed deficits

We saw in Chapter 3 that the presence of wealth effects has important implications for stabilization policy in rational expectations models. In this chapter we consider their implications for the link between fiscal and monetary policy. We shall see that wealth effects provide a compelling logic binding fiscal and monetary policy; later we shall discuss what links survive if there are *no* wealth effects and we shall argue that there are still important ones. In an Appendix to this chapter we review the theory and (scanty) empirical evidence on the existence of wealth effects; the conclusion of this Appendix is that wealth effects are likely to exist.

A CONVENIENT REPRESENTATION OF THE GOVERNMENT BUDGET CONSTRAINT

Private sector net financial wealth consists, in a closed economy (which we assume in this chapter), of government bonds and high powered money (the 'monetary base', consisting of the notes and coins issue plus commercial banks' deposits with the Central Bank), i.e. government net financial liabilities. These are recognizable as the 'outside money' of an earlier literature (Patinkin, 1965; Metzler, 1951; Gurley and Shaw, 1960). Bank deposits are 'inside money' in that banks are a private sector institution; their deposits are therefore both assets and liabilities of the private sector, cancelling out in net terms.

Let f be the stock of government net financial liabilities (hence government debt), in real terms (i.e. deflated by the consumer price index). f will rise for two reasons: first, a

159

government deficit will create new liabilities, and second, the existing stock of liabilities will be subject to capital gains, as the price of bonds rises or the consumer price index falls. We write:

$$\Delta f = f\pi d - f(q\Delta R + \Delta p) \qquad (9.1)$$

where $d =$ government deficit as a fraction of GDP, $\pi =$ inverse of the ratio of government debt to GDP, $q =$ proportionate response of long-term bond prices to the long-term interest rate (R). The unit coefficient on Δp reflects our assumption that all government liabilities are denominated in money terms. We will view (9.1) with π, q held constant at some average value as an appropriate approximation. Hence:

$$\Delta\theta = \pi d - q\Delta R - \Delta p \qquad (9.2)$$

where $\theta = \log f$. (9.2) will be the form in which we represent the government budget constraint in what follows.

To (9.2) we add a relationship determining the supply of high-powered money (in logs), which we shall write as m, the same as total money, reflecting the convenient and conventional assumption that there is a fixed 'money multiplier' between the two. We write:

$$\Delta m = \Phi\pi(d - \bar{d}) + \Delta\bar{m} + \varepsilon_\mu \qquad (9.3)$$

where $\bar{d}$ is the equilibrium government deficit as a fraction of GDP, ε_μ is an error term, and $\Delta\bar{m}$ is the equilibrium rate of growth of money. (9.3) states that out of equilibrium money supply will have an independent random component (to which we could add other independent temporary determinants of money if we wished) as well as a component responding to the temporary component of the deficit. Given (9.2), (9.3) implicitly determines also the supply of nominal bonds ($= e^{\theta + p} - e^m$, e being the base of natural logarithms) as the difference between nominal financial assets and the monetary base.

(9.3) focuses on two aspects of monetary policy with which we shall proceed to deal. First, how far does the equilibrium growth rate of money reflect the government deficit? Second, how far is money supply growth rate varied ('over the cycle') as budgetary financing needs change? In other words, what are the links between fiscal and monetary policy, first, in and, second, out of steady state? This distinction is an important one in rational expectations models, as we shall see.

We begin with behaviour out of steady state.

STABILITY AND BOND-FINANCE OUT OF STEADY STATE

One issue that has been given great prominence since the early 1970s is the possibility of instability in models with wealth effects, if budget deficits are bond-financed. This can be illustrated in a simple fixed-price IS/LM model without rational expectations (a log linear adaptation of Blinder and Solow's, 1973, model). We use non-stochastic continuous time and abstract from the steady state relationship between money and deficits by setting $\bar{d} = \Delta\bar{m} = 0$.

$$y = \kappa\theta - \alpha r + \phi d \tag{9.4}$$

$$m = \bar{p} + \gamma y - \beta r + \mu\theta \tag{9.5}$$

$$\dot{\theta} = \pi d - q\dot{r} \tag{9.6}$$

$$d = \bar{g} - ty \tag{9.7}$$

$$\dot{m} = \Phi\pi d \tag{9.8}$$

where $\bar{g}$ = government expenditure as fraction of GDP (ty are all receipts as a fraction of GDP); ˙ denotes the time derivative; because prices are fixed at $\bar{p}$, r is both the nominal and real interest rate. (9.4) and (9.5) are the IS and LM curves with wealth effects; (9.6) and (9.8) are the budget constraint and money supply relationship for this model.

The model solves for y and r given θ. Using (9.8) and (9.6) gives $\dot{m} = \Phi(\dot{\theta} + q\dot{r})$ so that $m = \Phi(r + qr) + \kappa_m$ where κ_m is an arbitrary constant. Substituting for m from this into (9.5) and for d from (9.7) into (9.4) yields the equations for y and r. Substituting the solution of them for y and $\dot{r}$ into (9.6) yields the equation of motion for θ as:

$$\dot{\theta} = \frac{-\pi t(\kappa\beta - \alpha\mu + \Phi\kappa q + \Phi\alpha)}{[(1 + \phi t)(\beta + q\mu) + \gamma(\alpha + q\kappa)]}\theta \tag{9.9}$$

For stability we require $(\kappa\beta \cdots + \Phi\alpha) > 0$. Clearly if money supply is held constant regardless of the deficit, i.e. $\Phi = 0$ (bond financed deficits), then we must have $\kappa\beta > \alpha\mu$, which raises the possibility of instability if there are relatively strong wealth effects in the LM curve. $\Phi > 0$ reduces the possibility; Blinder and Solow and others have accordingly advocated money-financed deficits as a means of avoiding possible instability.

Under rational expectations, however, this argument carries no force. To convert the Blinder–Solow model into a rational expectations form, it is sufficient to recognize that the valuation of financial assets is forward-looking, i.e. depends on expectations of future interest rates; for convenience, now use discrete time. Replace (9.6) and (9.8) by:

$$\Delta\theta = \pi d - q\left(\mathsf{E}r_{+1} - \underset{-1}{\mathsf{E}} \, r \right) \qquad (9.6a)$$

$$\Delta m = \Phi\pi d \qquad (9.8b)$$

If the model is now solved by the methods of Chapter 2, we obtain a third-order characteristic equation in which one of the roots should be unstable for a unique stable solution. It turns out that the roots involve all the coefficients and there is no general requirement on Φ, κ, μ that will ensure uniqueness let alone stability. Nor is it in general the case that the likelihood of uniqueness or stability is increased by $\Phi > 0$.

We conclude this section negatively: there is no compelling reason within rational expectations models why the cyclical or short-run component of monetary policy should be influenced by fiscal policy. The decision, for example, whether to pursue a constant money supply growth rate through the cycle even though the budget deficit will be moving cyclically, can be taken on other grounds, notably those appropriate to stabilization policy. We now turn to the steady state component of the money supply rule, where the situation is quite different.

LONG-TERM MONETARY TARGETS

We now take the previous model, but abstract from short-run behaviour while reinserting the possibility of steady state inflation. We have in equilibrium (* values are equilibrium ones):

$$y^* = \kappa\theta^* - \alpha r^* + \phi\bar{d} \qquad (9.10)$$

$$m^* = p^* + \gamma y^* - \beta R^* + \mu\theta^* \qquad (9.11)$$

$$\Delta\theta^* = \pi\bar{d} - q\Delta R^* - \Delta p^* \qquad (9.12)$$

$$\bar{d} = \bar{g} - ty^* \qquad (9.13)$$

$$R^* = r^* + \Delta p^* \qquad (9.14)$$

$$\Delta m^* = \Delta\bar{m} \qquad (9.15)$$

The question we wish to ask is: can $\Delta\bar{m}$ be chosen independently of $\bar{d}$?

For simplicity assume a zero growth steady state ($\Delta y^* = 0$), though this does not affect the argument. Assume also that $\bar{d}$ and $\Delta\bar{m}$ are chosen to be constants.

The first thing to notice is that, if in steady state both real interest rates and inflation are constant, then at once we have $\Delta R^* = 0$ from (9.14), $\Delta\theta^* = (\alpha/\kappa)\Delta r^* = 0$ from (9.10); then from (9.11) and (9.15) we have $\Delta\bar{m} = \Delta m^* = \Delta p^*$, while from (9.12) we have $\pi\bar{d} = \Delta p^*$. It then follows that $\pi\bar{d} = \Delta\bar{m}$; monetary and fiscal policy have to be 'consistent', that is the rate of money supply growth has to be equal to the deficit as a fraction of financial assets, $\pi\bar{d}$. This in turn is equal to the rate at which *nominal* financial assets are growing ($\Delta\theta^* + \Delta p^*$); hence if money is growing at this rate, so also are bonds. Consistent monetary and fiscal policy hence implies that money and nominal bonds must be growing at the same rate.

Clearly we would like to ensure – as would any sensible government – that in equilibrium neither real interest rates nor inflation are moving. We have already imposed a terminal condition on inflation as part of our general solution procedure; this therefore by imposition will be constant in steady state. Assuming this, we may then derive by a similar procedure to the one already used:

$$\Delta r^* = \frac{\kappa}{\kappa(\beta + q) + \alpha(1 - \mu)} (\pi\bar{d} - \Delta\bar{m}) \qquad (9.16)$$

In other words, if the government wishes (given its terminal condition on inflation) to avoid steadily rising or falling real interest rates, then it must pursue consistent fiscal and monetary policy. This has to happen at some stage; otherwise eventually either (rising r^*) government expenditure would have to contract to zero (taxes rise to absorb the whole of GNP) or (falling r^*) real interest rates would become negative – neither of which is possible. Of course a sensible government will wish to stop any such tendency well before any such stage were threatened.

This argument has been conducted on the assumption that $\bar{d}$ is set, with changing interest payments on debt being offset by changes in government spending or taxes; if one assumes instead that government spending and tax rates are unaltered, then the steady state inflation rates, $\bar{d}$ and $\Delta \bar{m}$, depend on the level of government spending and taxes chosen; the algebra of this is more complex (see Minford, Brech and Matthews, 1980), and the inflation resulting from any initial rise in the deficit is much greater than in the analysis above, because the eventual deficit is compounded by the rise in interest payments, but the essential message remains that there must be consistency between fiscal and monetary policy in steady state.

To conclude, wealth effects imply a constraint across the steady state components of fiscal and monetary policy, though not the short-run components. Hence in (9.3) $\Delta \bar{m} = \pi \bar{d}$, whereas we are free to write any short-run response function or error process besides.

ARE WEALTH EFFECTS CRUCIAL TO A FISCAL/MONETARY LINK?

We have stressed the role of wealth effects in forming a steady state fiscal/monetary link. However, even if there are no wealth effects, there are still limits to the possible divergence of fiscal and monetary policy within rational expectations models.

Such limits are placed by ceilings on the stock of government debt that the private sector will hold. In a world with no wealth effects, rising debt implies no change in real interest rates; in effect, future taxes being substituted for current taxes leaves everyone's wealth, savings and investment unaltered, so requires no change in interest rates. Nevertheless, there are a number of natural ceilings on debt.

First, there is a ceiling imposed by the logic of intertemporal maximization (see e.g. McCallum, 1982); real debt *per capita* cannot grow faster than the rate of time preference. Hence deficits which imply a more rapid growth in real debt will require to be 'monetized'.

But this ceiling still appears too high when distribution effects are taken into account. Debt is raised from *one* group of citizens, in order to avoid taxing *another* group (probably the majority) now; in effect the second group promise to pay off the first (or their inheritors) with future taxes. Therefore public debt is a form of contract between two sets of citizens, the terms of which depend for their enforcement on the honesty of government (the contract broker). If the debt is in money terms, then there are two ways of defaulting; explicit default where the money amounts are not delivered and implicit default where the anticipated real amounts are not delivered because inflation is higher than anticipated.

One way of looking at wealth effects is therefore as proxying the increasing risk-premium required by the risk-averse lending group as government debt rises. In that model, as debt rises, the marginal utility both of consumption and of real money balances rise, and real interest rates are forced up.

If wealth effects are ruled out, it is still plausible to assume some upper limit to the debt holdings of the lending group, if only their total net worth. Such a limit has been suggested by Sargent and Wallace (1981) in a paper designed to investigate the upper limit on deficits when money supply growth is being held down by 'monetarist' policies.

Suppose that GDP, N (also standing for the population by an appropriate choice of indices), grows at the rate n and that the real rate of interest, r, is constant and greater than n. Let $\hat{}$ = rate of growth, $'$ = *per capita* value, π = rate of inflation, P = price level. Write the demand for high-powered money, H, in the quantity theory manner as:

$$H_t = hP_t N_t \qquad (9.17)$$

so that $\hat{H}_t = \pi_t + n$. Suppose now that at time $t = 1$ new policies are announced and carried out, for future fiscal and monetary policy; the announcement (fully believed) changes the present real value of bonds to b_1 as prices and interest rates react. There are then two phases of policy: 'transition' from $t = 2, \ldots, T - 1$, and 'terminal' from $t = T, \ldots, \infty$. During the transition phase policies may be different from their terminal phase when they must be in steady state. The government budget constraint is from $t = 2$ onwards.

$$b_t - b_{t-1} = d_t + rb_{t-1} - \frac{H_t - H_{t-1}}{P_t} \qquad (9.18)$$

Here b = real bonds and d = real deficit *excluding* debt interest, i.e. the change in real bonds equals the deficit including real debt interest less money financing (notice that on our assumption of no further policy change there are no unanticipated capital gains from $t = 2$ and anticipated capital losses from inflation are deducted implicitly by using the real interest rate).

Expressing (9.18) in *per capita* terms, dividing all through by N_t gives:

$$\frac{b_t}{N_t} = \frac{d_t}{N_t} - \frac{H_{t-1}}{P_t N_t}\left(\frac{H_t - H_{t-1}}{H_{t-1}}\right) + (1 + r)\frac{b_{t-1}}{(1 + n)N_{t-1}} \qquad (9.19)$$

Using $P_t N_t = (1 + \hat{H}_t)P_{t-1}$, this becomes

$$b'_t = d'_t - h\frac{\hat{H}_t}{1 + \hat{H}_t} + (1 + r - n)b'_{t-1} \qquad (9.20)$$

Since $r > n$ this is an explosive difference equation if interest-exclusive deficits and monetary targets are pursued independently. Suppose that during transition a constant $\hat{H}$ and d are chosen: these policies are monetarist so that $\hat{H}$ is 'low' but fiscal policy is 'expansionary', so that $d' > h\hat{H}/(1 + \hat{H})$. The set limit on this *per capita* stock of debt $\bar{b}'$, discussed above, is now bound to be reached at some point. At the date when this occurs, then policies have to change so as to ensure:

$$0 = b'_{t+1} - b'_t = d' - \frac{hH}{1 + \hat{H}} + (r - n)b'_t \qquad (9.21)$$

i.e. that real bonds do not change any more. However, the policies could have been chosen so as to change *before* this, so that $b'_t < \bar{b}'$ at this point. In general, the terminal date, T, for the switch to a sustainable policy with unchanging *per capita* debt can be chosen freely from $t = 2$ onwards, so that $\hat{H}_T$ and d_T, the terminal or steady state policies are governed by:

$$0 = b'_T - b'_{T-1} = d'_T - \frac{h\hat{H}_T}{1 + \hat{H}_T} + (r - n)b'_{T-1} \quad (b'_T \leqslant \bar{b}')$$

(9.22)

The point is that there is a trade-off between the transitional policies (including the length of time they are pursued) and the terminal policies because the transitional policies affect the terminal stock of debt:

$$b'_{T-1} = (1 + r - n)^{T-2}b'_1 + \sum_{i=2}^{T-1}(1 + r - n)^{i-2}\left(d' - \frac{h\hat{H}}{1 + \hat{H}}\right)$$

(9.23)

The trade-off implies each of the following:

1. If the government wish to maintain a constant interest-exclusive deficit $d' = d'_T$, than the smaller is current (transitional) money supply growth, the larger will *future* money supply growth $\hat{H}_T$ have to be. Given fiscal 'profligacy', there is therefore a trade-off between current and future inflation.
2. If the government wish to maintain constant money supply growth $\hat{H}$, then the higher are the transitional deficits the larger the future *surpluses* that will be required. Given monetary discipline, there is therefore a trade-off between current and future fiscal discipline.

The message is, in short, that tough monetary policies require tough fiscal policies.

The Role of Long-dated Nominal Bonds

We have so far neglected the term in b'_1, the value of real bonds after the policies are announced; implicitly we have suggested that b'_1 was quite small. This then allows scope for policy-makers to choose between trade-offs (1) and (2) above.

If however b'_1 is large, and close to $\bar{b}'$, then there is little scope for choice; the policy-makers are forced to go rapidly to steady state fiscal/monetary policies, hard as these must be.

If the government bonds are short-dated, then the revaluation due to policies of lower inflation will be small unless the change is drastic; hence for example on a one-year nominal bond, b_0, the change in value will be $-b_0(\hat{H} - \hat{H}^e_0)$ where $\hat{H}^e_0$ is the money supply growth expected before the policy change. If the bonds are indexed, then the revaluation will be nil (given the fixed real interest rate assumption).

However, if the bonds are long-dated, the revaluation effect can be very large. For example, take a bond paying a fixed money amount, M_K, on maturity at $t = K$. The present value of this at $t = 1$ expected at $t = 0$ was $b_0 = M_K/[(1 + R_0)^{K-1}]$ where $R_0 = \hat{H}^e_0 + r - n$ was the nominal interest rate at $t = 0$; the actual present value at $t = 1$ is then $M_K/[(1 + R_1)^{K-1}]$. Hence the unanticipated capital revaluation on such a bond is $-b_0(K - 1)(\hat{H}_K - \hat{H}^e_0)$ where $\hat{H}_K = [(T - 1)/(K - 1)]\hat{H} + [(K - T)/(K - 1)]\hat{H}_T$ (i.e. a weighted average of the transitional and the terminal $\hat{H}$). For a credible anti-inflation policy where $\hat{H}_K = \hat{H} = n$, this revaluation will be a $K - 1$ multiple of the one-year bond revaluation, and create the necessity for harsh fiscal discipline with much greater rapidity.

A Digression on Definitions of the 'Deficit'

Several definitions of the government 'deficit' are in use: inclusive or exclusive of debt interest, and if inclusive, inclusive either of nominal or real debt interest. We have used all of these definitions at different stages in the preceding analysis; all are useful in focusing on different aspects of the problem. However, it is obvious that a *definition* as such imparts no information. The information is of course in the *model*. We have looked at two models: one with wealth effects and one without wealth effects but with a ceiling on real government debt *per capita*. From the viewpoint of controlling inflation permanently, both have told essentially the same story: that both fiscal and monetary discipline are required on average, though with the possibility of varying time paths.

Given this overall policy requirement, the application in any situation will be largely a question of what is politically feasible. This is particularly true of the short-run time path immediately on announcement. It may well be wise, for example, to cut public spending rapidly as money supply growth is cut, even though this implies a 'real' budget surplus (i.e. inclusive of real debt interest) in the first few years because during this period debt interest on long-dated stock is still offset by high inflation. This real surplus will disappear as soon as inflation comes down, because the debt interest on long-dated stock will fall away only very slowly. Then, the spending cuts done, the budget deficit will be at steady state levels and some of the debt revaluation (on the long-dated stock) will have been worked off by the previous real surpluses; this is an illustration of the previous section's discussion.

CONCLUSIONS

We have seen that there are important links between fiscal and monetary policy with rational expectations. These links do not involve short-run behaviour, i.e. over the economic cycle; independent fiscal and monetary responses to the cycle do not in general cause instability (or non-uniqueness), even with wealth effects. By contrast with adaptive expectations and wealth effects, coordination may be necessary even in the short run to avoid instability.

It is in steady state that fiscal and monetary policy must be 'consistent', i.e. the growth rate of real government bonds must be reduced to the rate of growth of GDP (assuming this is the rate at which the demand for bonds will grow in steady state at constant real interest rates). This condition is enforced by wealth effects or else in most circumstances by a ceiling on the stock of debt that lenders can absorb. The key implication is that budget deficits must generally at some point be brought down in line with money supply growth if counter-inflation policies are to be sustained.

APPENDIX: ARE THERE WEALTH EFFECTS?

There are two components in our measure of 'outside money' or 'financial wealth of the private sector': high-powered money and government bonds.

Take high-powered (or 'base') money first. This liability of government causes no obligation of repayment in a *'fiat'* money system; the paper says 'Pay the Bearer £1' but this now means merely that the bearer may be given another pound note just like the one he has, if he wishes to change it, and not that he is entitled to exchange it for goods or gold worth £1 at the Central Bank.

Consequently, the government has no obligation to raise any future taxes in order to pay off the currency liability (this will be contrasted with the need to pay off interest and principal on bonds via higher taxes). From the private sector's viewpoint, there is therefore no countervailing liability associated with their money asset. Its present value is its face value.

However, it can be argued that it is not 'wealth' in the sense that the level of real balances would affect consumption or the disposal of other assets. It would not be if high-powered money is held solely for transactions purposes and if the market for it clears continuously (see Barro and Fischer, 1976). For then the amount held would entirely be required to be held, as part of the optimal technology for doing business at all, and would not enter into the intertemporal budget constraint of the private sector. It is therefore 'nondisposable wealth' which should not enter the decision to consume or allocate the portfolio of 'disposable' assets.

The argument fails if either the (base) money market is in disequilibrium (e.g. Laidler, 1982) or money is held partly as a store of value (as in the Liverpool Model). With a store of value role, it is convenient to treat money as part of financial wealth and treat the decision to consume, dispose the portfolio and choose transactions technology as a joint one.

There are problems with both these possibilities. In the first place it is hard to rationalize disequilibrium in the money market when there is a continuously clearing market in bonds, in which money may be obtained or disposed of continuously in return for bonds. Secondly, there are alternatives to base money (e.g. time deposits) which would appear to dominate it as a store of value. However, base money is partly held as bank reserves against savings and time deposits; hence the private sector is indirectly holding base money as a store of value, in the sense that these bank reserves are not required technologically for transactions. Furthermore, there is flexibility in transactions technology and cash may have a wealth elasticity; wealthy men will hold more cash because the looser transactions technology is more pleasurable. Hence a part of cash balances reflects a disposable non-technologically-determined wealth holding substitutable for a consumption stream. Therefore base money probably should be included in disposable net wealth, even though it is admittedly a very small component of such wealth and so of little consequence.

We now deal with government bonds, the vast bulk of financial wealth. The argument here turns on the present value of the stream of taxes required to pay off bond interest and principal. It is clear that in a world of no uncertainty with infinitely-lived individuals, a government transfer to individuals today financed by bonds, which will be paid off tomorrow from taxes on those individuals with the same incidence as the transfer, leaves everything unchanged. Each individual obtains a transfer, held in the form of bonds, whose value is offset exactly by his future tax liability; his wealth remaining the same, he will wish to consume the same and will therefore lend the government the amount of the transfer (i.e. continue to hold the bonds). Consumption and investment will be unchanged, and so therefore will the rate of interest.

The question naturally arises: why should the government bother to carry out this operation if it affects nothing and nobody? Barro (1974) has suggested the reason is the transactions costs of changing tax rates when there are transitory shifts in public expenditure (such as for wars); a temporary rise in tax rates would require more resources to implement (e.g. more inspectors, notifications to the populace) than making a bond issue (to the same people who would otherwise be taxed). Yet this seems tenuous; bond issuing and servicing carries a transactions cost which might be greater.

This answer also does not fit the case of sustained bond issue to finance a sustained rise in public expenditure; a case that has been exemplified frequently by post-war Western governments. Many governments have appeared in these cases to have viewed borrowing as a more attractive option politically than current taxation (and of course some have also viewed printing of high-powered money as a still more attractive option, at least within some limit set by the inflation consequence). Governments of 'conservatives' by contrast have typically proclaimed the aim of 'sound finance', i.e. budgets balanced except for 'below-the-line' capital expenditure on revenue-generating projects.

With this in mind, we may consider possible relaxations of the strong assumptions set out earlier. Firstly, there may be distribution effects between recipients of current transfers and the payers of future taxes; while this would obviously have real effects, they are not of interest to us here because they are not essentially involved in the act of borrowing – any current transfer financed by current taxes could also have distribution effects.

Secondly and more interestingly, we must drop the assumption of infinite life. But Barro (1974) has shown in a model of overlapping generations that, if each person leaves a bequest, then everyone acts as if he is infinitely-lived. The reason is that the transfer he receives diminishes the utility of his heirs while raising his current resources. Yet he already decided, having left them a bequest, that his optimal course was to give them their previous utility at the expense of his current resources; therefore he will raise his bequest in order to offset the government's action, in effect saving the whole of the transfer for his heirs. The transfer, by not changing his opportunity set, leaves his net wealth and behaviour unchanged.

If he had not planned a bequest, then the level of utility he desired for his heirs cannot be established; the transfer may or may not push their utility below his desired level. Hence we cannot establish how much, if at all, he will offset the transfer by saving.

It is of interest that, if the law provided for heirs to pay off their parents' debts, then this would not matter, because a bequest could be negative (parents could borrow against the collateral of their children) or positive, a continuous variable; hence the transfer would always be offset. However, the law prevents this in most societies, no doubt mainly because the rights of children require protection from selfish parents. This suggests that the issue of whether *planned* bequests are general is non-trivial (accidental bequests, e.g. because death comes unexpectedly early, are beside the point).

The key assumption however is that of no uncertainty. If we drop this, we are faced with two types of uncertainty: first, about the *aggregate* flow of future interest and principal, and the tax levies necessary to fund them – uncertainties such as those about formal default by the government and unexpected monetization (we might term this informal default); second, uncertainty about the individual *incidence* of future taxes.

With *aggregate* uncertainty, whatever the shape of the probability distribution over future interest/principal payments, it is the *same* distribution (by definition) as that over future tax levies. Therefore with rational expectations, everyone's expectation of the mean and variance of both streams will be the same. It follows that each person can leave himself with exactly the same risk-return combination on his portfolio of physical, human, and financial assets by investing his transfer in government bonds; this is a perfectly hedged operation and without a change in other risks or returns, he would do just this. Hence, as before, nothing would change.

When we turn to individual incidence, the picture changes however. Suppose for simplicity there is now no aggregate uncertainty. Yet each individual faces considerable uncertainty about how much tax *he* and *his* heirs will pay; he does not know future income, future family size, possibility of emigration, etc.

Let us ignore emigration, in which case the change in tax prospects will have no impact on him; this no doubt affects only a minority. Let us assume the tax system, as is typically the case in Western economies, is progressive; also assume that people are identical and risk averse. Suppose everyone receives the same transfer and holds it in the form of bonds.

Then the individual will perceive his and his heirs' potential net income after tax as follows: at the one extreme they will be poor, receive the bond interest, but pay little tax, from there progressing with higher income towards the other extreme where they will be rich, receive the bond interest, and pay a lot of tax. If taxes are raised they will pay little more if poor, but significantly more if rich. This effect of a high covariance between tax and income is illustrated in Figure 9.1 (for a simplified distribution with only 'poor' and 'rich' states of equal probability).

We are interested in the change in the 'certainty equivalent' of each man's future net income after tax; by this we mean the sure income that would yield him the same utility as the income possibilities he actually faces. Before the bond transfer and consequent future tax liability, let him have an expected net income of Ey, the average of his 'poor' and 'rich' states; the expected utility of this is EU_0 and the certainty equivalent is $\bar{y}_0$. After the bond transfer, everyone's expected net income remains the same because the tax payments averaged across the two states must equal the bond interest receipts for the government's budget to balance in the future. But now each person will be better off than before when poor (he receives the bond interest but his extra tax burden is less than this), and worse off than before when rich (his extra tax burden exceeds the bond interest); the arrowed line on Figure 9.1 joins these two states, and, because of the insurance he receives in effect, his expected utility rises to EU_1 and his certainty equivalent income to $\bar{y}_1$ so that the bond transfer increases private wealth. Barro (1974) has further pointed out that, if the tax *rate* is raised when taxes go up to pay for the bond interest, then this increases the progressiveness of the tax system and this insurance effect is enhanced, as illustrated by the dotted line with higher expected utility EU_2 and certainty equivalent income $\bar{y}_2$.

Clearly this insurance effect of bond issue would be eliminated if the private insurance market already provided full insurance. However, this is unlikely because of incentive-incompatibility (see e.g. Hart, 1983); full insurance gives the insured person an incentive to lie about his poverty or fraudulently to avoid trying to be rich. Of course, the bond

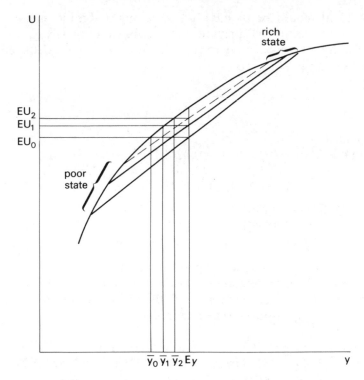

Figure 9.1 *Certainty equivalent and expected net income after tax*

issue may be incentive-incompatible at the margin, given existing private insurance; this, however, is relevant to the optimality of the bond issue, not to its net wealth effect (except in so far as it changes the probabilities of being poor and rich, which we ignore).

Empirical Studies of Debt Neutrality[1]

The debt neutrality argument suggests that the appropriate definition of disposable income is not simply $y - t$, where y is income and t is tax, but $y - t - (g - t)$ where g is government expenditure, i.e. government deficits are equivalent to explicit current taxes. A *weak form* of the debt neutrality argument would be to have $g - t$ having a significant negative influence on real private sector behaviour. A *strong form* of the hypothesis would require having the same coefficient on $y - t$ and $-(g - t)$.

Results on US data

Kochin (1974)

$$\text{CND} = 5.56 + 0.283\text{YD} - 0.224\text{FDEF} + 0.643\text{CND}_{-1}$$
$$\quad\quad\;\; (1.81)\quad (3.79)\quad\quad (2.56)\quad\quad\quad (5.12)\quad\quad (9.A.1)$$
$$R^2 = 0.9989; \text{SE} = 2.23; \text{DW} = 0.680; \text{ annual data } 1952\text{–}71.$$

$$\Delta\text{CND} = 2.88 + 0.392\Delta\text{YD} - 0.109\Delta\text{FDEF} + 0.218\Delta\text{CND}_{-1}$$
$$\quad\quad\;\; (3.44)\;\; (7.86)\quad\quad\quad (2.95)\quad\quad\quad\quad (2.42)\quad\quad (9.A.2)$$
$$R^2 = 0.892; \text{SE} = 1.26; \text{DW} = 1.79; \text{ annual data } 1952\text{–}71.$$

CND denotes consumer expenditures on non-durables and services. YD is personal disposable income and FDEF the federal deficit. Each variable is deflated by the implicit price index for consumption expenditures.

Buiter and Tobin (1979) – using revised data.

$$\text{CND} = 4.504 + 0.2498\text{YD} - 0.1781\text{FDEF} + 0.6981\text{CND}_{-1}$$
$$\quad\quad\;\; (1.26)\quad (3.45)\quad\quad\quad (2.43)\quad\quad\quad\quad (6.94)\quad (9.A.1a)$$
$$\bar{R}^2 = 0.999; \text{SE} = 2.66; \text{DW} = 1.21; \text{ annual data } 1952\text{–}71.$$

$$\Delta\text{CND} = 4.069 + 0.355\Delta\text{YD} - 0.086\Delta\text{FDEF} + 0.268\Delta\text{CND}_{-1}$$
$$\quad\quad\;\; (2.55)\quad (5.20)\quad\quad\quad (1.85)\quad\quad\quad\quad (2.10)\quad (9.A.2a)$$
$$\bar{R}^2 = 0.790; \text{SE} = 2.28; \text{DW} = 2.17; \text{ annual data } 1952\text{–}71.$$

Kochin's results give support for the 'weak form' of debt neutrality as FDEF is significant and has the correct sign. However, it does not support the 'strong form' of the hypothesis. Buiter and Tobin present the same regressions using revised data and report lower coefficients on FDEF. Econometric problems with Kochin's work stimulated Buiter and Tobin to carry out further investigations. The regressions are reported below.

$$\text{cnd} = -133.139 + 0.224y - 0.337t - 0.254\text{gdef} + 0.798\text{cnd}_{-1}$$
$$\quad\quad\;\; (1.57)\quad\quad (4.43)\quad (1.30)\quad\quad (1.04)\quad\quad\quad (13.46)$$
$$\quad\quad\quad\quad\quad\quad\quad\quad\quad\quad\quad\quad\quad\quad\quad\quad\quad\quad\quad\quad (9.A.3)$$

$\bar{R}^2 = 0.998$; SE $= 19.34$; SSR $= 8,604$; DW $= 1.73$.

$$\text{cnd} = -114.730 + 0.192y - 0.239g + 0.821\text{cnd}_{-1}$$
$$\quad\quad\;\; (1.38) \quad (4.64) \quad (0.98) \quad (14.81) \quad\quad\quad (9.A.4)$$

$\bar{R}^2 = 0.998$; SE $= 19.42$; SSR $= 9,050$; DW $= 1.78$.

$$\text{cnd} = -97.002 + 0.186(y - g) + 0.813\text{cnd}_{-1}$$
$$\quad\quad\;\; (4.48) \quad (6.11) \quad\quad\quad (20.68) \quad\quad\quad (9.A.5)$$

$\bar{R}^2 = 0.998$; SE $= 19.05$; SSR $= 9,068$; DW $= 1.75$.

$$c = -218.806 + 0.424y - 0.682t - 0.496\text{gdef} + 0.652c_{-1}$$
$$\quad\;\; (1.26) \quad (4.05) \quad (1.26) \quad (0.99) \quad\quad (6.24)$$
$$(9.A.6)$$

$\bar{R}^2 = 0.994$; SE $= 40.23$; SSR $= 37,218$; DW $= 1.44$.

$$c = -156.242 + 0.352y - 0.408g + 0.682c_{-1}$$
$$\quad\;\; (0.932) \quad (4.03) \quad (0.82) \quad (6.63) \quad\quad (9.A.7)$$

$\bar{R}^2 = 0.994$; SE $= 40.63$; SSR $= 39,621$; DW $= 1.51$.

$$c = -135.697 + 0.345(y - g) + 0.673c_{-1}$$
$$\quad\;\; (2.97) \quad (5.08) \quad\quad\quad (9.04) \quad\quad\quad (9.A.8)$$

$\bar{R}^2 = 0.994$; SE $= 39.82$; SSR $= 39,648$; DW $= 1.50$.

Variables Defined

$y = $ *per capita* real national income

$g = $ *per capita* government expenditure

$t = $ real *per capita* taxes

$\text{gdef} = g - t$

$\text{cnd} = $ real *per capita* consumption on non-durables

$c = $ total real *per capita* consumers' expenditure

The above equations suggest the debt neutrality hypothesis is not supported as the coefficients on t, gdef and g are insignificant. However, because of collinearity between the independent variables, Buiter and Tobin cannot reject the hypothesis at the 5 per cent level that the coefficients on y − t and −gdef are the same. Buiter and Tobin conclude that these results do not give much support for the debt neutrality hypothesis. One feature of their results which they fail to comment on is that the above regressions give little support for disposable income, as conventionally defined, as the appropriate independent variable because the coefficient on t is insignificantly different from zero. Thus, using their criteria for rejecting explanatory variables (i.e. a low t value) the appropriate variables are income and lagged consumption. Their results may therefore be regarded *not* as a rejection of the debt neutrality hypothesis, but as a rejection of any measure of disposable income as an explanatory variable in the consumption function.

Seater (1982)
Seater considers a life-cycle model of consumption and concludes that 'the results from the total consumption and financial asset demand equations support the hypothesis, whereas the results from the non-durable consumption demand equation reject it' (p. 388). A detailed summary of these conflicting results is omitted here. The US data used in these studies therefore, though they cannot actually reject strong neutrality, appear rather to support weak neutrality and so suggest that government bonds are net wealth but substantially less than 100 per cent of their face value; this conclusion is in line with our theoretical discussion.

NOTES

1. This section was written by Martyn Hill.

10

Interpreting the Evidence: The Problem of Observational Equivalence

As was shown in Chapter 3, it is a key implication of an economy embodying a Sargent–Wallace supply curve, rational expectations and identical information sets of public and private agents that, from a stabilization perspective, output (or the unemployment rate) will be invariant to anticipated rates of monetary change. Only unanticipated changes in the money stock will have any impact on output. Barro (1977) in a seminal paper attempted to determine empirically the relative impacts of unanticipated and actual rates of monetary change on the unemployment rate in the US over the period 1946–73.

Barro's empirical procedure involved two stages. First, a policy reaction function was determined for the authorities. This involved explaining the actual rates of change of the money stock in terms of variables previously known to the authorities.

The residuals, or unexplained part of monetary change, from this reaction function are interpreted as the unanticipated rate of monetary change.

Thus if the reaction function of the authorities is given by:

$$m = \lambda X + \varepsilon \qquad (10.1)$$

where m is the rate of monetary expansion, X is a vector of variables, λ = vector of coefficients, ε is a random residual. Then:

$$m - \mathop{E}_{-1} m = \lambda \left(X - \mathop{E}_{-1} X \right) + \varepsilon \qquad (10.2)$$

and assuming $X = \underset{-1}{E} X$:

$$m - \underset{-1}{E} m = \varepsilon \qquad (10.3)$$

Having obtained estimates of the monetary innovations, Barro proceeds to use these innovations (current and lagged) to explain (along with other postulated determinants of the natural rate of unemployment such as a minimum wage variable and a measure of military conscription) the rate of unemployment.

Barro's empirical results appear impressive. They suggest that the current and previous two years' monetary innovations are significant determinants of the rate of unemployment with the correct negative sign. Moreover, when Barro adds previous rates of change of the actual monetary change to his unemployment equation, they are found not to be statistically significant from zero at normal levels of significance.

The basic type of analysis conducted by Barro has been replicated by a large number of different authors for a number of different countries (see, e.g. Barro and Rush, 1980; Leiderman, 1980; Attfield, Demery and Duck, 1981a, 1981b; Mishkin, 1982). The results reported by almost all these authors (except Mishkin, 1982) are suggestive that real variables, either unemployment or output, are responsive only to unanticipated rates of monetary change and not the actual rate. Consequently, it would appear from this empirical evidence that there is powerful support for the joint hypothesis of the rational expectations hypothesis and independence of unemployment or output from anticipated rates of monetary change.

However, Sargent (1976b) in an important paper, showed that this interpretation of the empirical evidence may be incorrect. Sargent demonstrates that the reduced form for output or unemployment in a Keynesian model, in which systematic monetary policy will influence the variance of output, may be statistically indistinguishable from a classical model in which only unanticipated movements in the money stock impact on output or unemployment. The Keynesian and classical models are said to be observationally equivalent in their reduced forms.

Sargent's main point can be made most simply by consideration of the following model. Suppose the 'true' reduced form equations for an economy are given by the equations:

$$y = a\left(m - \mathop{\text{E}}_{-1} m\right) + \lambda y_{-1} + u \qquad (10.4)$$

$$m = gm_{-1} + \varepsilon \qquad (10.5)$$

where a, λ, g are positive constants, y is real output, and u, ε are random variables; all mean values of variables are put equal to zero for simplicity.

Since

$$m - \mathop{\text{E}}_{-1} m = \varepsilon = m - gm_{-1} \qquad (10.6)$$

equation (10.4) can be rewritten as:

$$y = am - agm_{-1} + \lambda y_{-1} + u \qquad (10.7)$$

It would appear from equation (10.7) that the current and lagged values of the money stock have an impact on real output, when in fact we know from equation (10.4) that this is not the case, since only unanticipated changes in the money stock have an impact on output.

It is obviously quite clear from Sargent's analysis that 'unrestricted' single equation reduced forms for output have no information content, at least with respect to the manner in which changes in the money supply impact on an economy. A single regression of output on current and past money supplies simply cannot inform us of the true nature of the impact of monetary change on these variables.

The point that Sargent is making is that two quite different types of model, Keynesian and classical, have indistinguishable reduced forms for output in terms of either actual or unanticipated money stock, current and lagged. This does not imply that the models *in toto* are not distinguishable; clearly they are, on the basis of a variety of tests on structural coefficients and also on reduced form equations for *more* variables than simply output. Therefore the point is a narrow but important one, related to this *particular* test carried out by economists (remember that there has been great interest in money supply-output relationships ever since the debate over Friedman and Meiselman, 1963).[1]

In particular, it needs to be stressed, because there has been some confusion on the point, that Sargent's point is not about 'identification' as such. Both the Keynesian and classical models may be fully identified; that is, the parameters of each may be individually retrieved by estimation of the full model (i.e. subject to all its restrictions). However, there is a useful potential connection with the concept of identification. If two models can be 'nested' in a more general model (usually, a linear combination of the two), then, provided the coefficients of each model can be identified in this general model, it is possible to test for their significance and accordingly that of each model. In this situation, if (and only if) the coefficients cannot be identified, the models will be 'observationally equivalent'.

Sargent's point has provoked a lively literature attempting to establish conditions under which a limited number of reduced forms *can* distinguish between the two models. These attempts have centred around identification within such a general model, in this case one which nests two distinct semi-reduced forms.

IDENTIFICATION

In order to discuss this issue more fully it is necessary first to set out the basic issues which arise in identification of an economic system. (For a comprehensive outline the reader should consult a standard econometric text such as, e.g. Cramer, 1969; Johnston, 1972).

Suppose that the demand and supply for a commodity is given by:

$$q = \alpha_{11} p + \alpha_{12} y \quad \text{(demand)} \qquad (10.8)$$

$$q = \alpha_{21} p + \alpha_{22} z \quad \text{(supply)} \qquad (10.9)$$

where the α's are constants, p is price and y and z are exogenous variables which affect demand and supply respectively. Demand and supply are assumed to be equal. Random disturbances and constants are omitted from (10.5) and (10.6) for simplicity. Equations (10.8) and (10.9), which specify the behaviour of demand and supply respectively, are called structural or behavioural equations and the α's are structural coefficients.

From (10.8) and (10.9) we can solve for p and q to obtain:

$$p = \frac{\alpha_{22} z - \alpha_{12} y}{\alpha_{11} - \alpha_{21}} \qquad (10.10)$$

and

$$q = \frac{\alpha_{11}\alpha_{22} z - \alpha_{21}\alpha_{12} y}{\alpha_{11} - \alpha_{21}} \qquad (10.11)$$

We can also write the equations (10.10) and (10.11) in their 'reduced form' as:

$$p = \pi_{11} z + \pi_{12} y \qquad (10.12)$$

$$q = \pi_{21} z + \pi_{22} y \qquad (10.13)$$

where

$$\pi_{11} = \frac{\alpha_{22}}{\alpha_{11} - \alpha_{21}}, \quad \pi_{12} = \frac{-\alpha_{12}}{\alpha_{11} - \alpha_{21}}, \text{ etc.}$$

When reduced forms are estimated, it is of course the π coefficients that are retrieved with the objective of deriving estimates of the structural coefficients. It is clear from sample estimates of these reduced form coefficients that all the structural parameters α can be uniquely retrieved (thus $\pi_{21}/\pi_{11} = \alpha_{11}$ etc.).

In these circumstances our structural equations (10.8) and (10.9) are said to be exactly identified.

Consider the next model:

$$q = \alpha_{11} p + \alpha_{12} z \qquad (10.14)$$

$$q = \alpha_{21} p + \alpha_{22} z \qquad (10.15)$$

The reduced form of this model is:

$$p = \pi_{11} z \qquad (10.16)$$

$$q = \pi_{21} z \qquad (10.17)$$

where

$$\pi_{11} = \frac{\alpha_{22} - \alpha_{12}}{\alpha_{11} - \alpha_{21}}, \quad \pi_{21} = \frac{\alpha_{11}\alpha_{22} - \alpha_{21}\alpha_{12}}{\alpha_{11} - \alpha_{21}}$$

It is clear that in this case, it is never possible to obtain estimates of the structural coefficients. The economic system (10.14) and (10.15) is said to be not identified and consequently there are an infinite number of parameter values in the equations (10.14) and (10.15) that are consistent with the reduced form (10.16) and (10.17).

Finally, consider the system given by:

$$q = \alpha_{11}p + \alpha_{12}y + \alpha_{13}x \qquad (10.18)$$

$$q = \alpha_{21}p + \alpha_{22}z \qquad (10.19)$$

where x is another exogenous variable.

The reduced form of (10.18) and (10.19) is given by:

$$p = \pi_{11}z + \pi_{12}y + \pi_{13}x \qquad (10.20)$$

$$q = \pi_{21}z + \pi_{22}y + \pi_{23}x \qquad (10.21)$$

where $\pi_{11} = \alpha_{22}/D$, $\pi_{12} = -\alpha_{12}/D$, $\pi_{13} = -\alpha_{13}/D$, $\pi_{21} = \alpha_{11}\alpha_{22}/D$, $\pi_{22} = -\alpha_{21}\alpha_{12}/D$, $\pi_{23} = -\alpha_{21}\alpha_{13}/D$, $D = \alpha_{11} - \alpha_{21}$.

In this case the system is identified but the parameters can be retrieved independently from alternative values of the reduced form coefficients; thus, two separate estimates of α_{21} are given by π_{23}/π_{13} and π_{22}/π_{12} while $\alpha_{22} = \pi_{11}(\alpha_{11} - \alpha_{21}) = \pi_{11}[\pi_{21}/\pi_{11} - \alpha_{21}] = \pi_{21} - \alpha_{21}\pi_{11}$ which gives two corresponding estimates of α_{22}. Here the system is said to be over-identified. If a system is identified or over-identified, then a researcher can, in principle, estimate its structural coefficients (methods of estimation do not concern us here).

IDENTIFICATION OF KEYNESIAN AND CLASSICAL REDUCED FORM COEFFICIENTS

We now return to the problem raised by Sargent. Let us initially suppose that there are no lagged effects; the salient points can be made for this case. We know that a classical model with a Sargent–Wallace supply curve can be written in the 'semi-reduced' form (semi because expectations have not been eliminated):

$$y = a_{c1} X + b_{c1}\left(m - \underset{-1}{\mathsf{E}}\, m \right) + u_{c1} \qquad (10.22)$$

and that a Keynesian model will have a reduced form:

$$y = a_{k1} X + c_{k1} m + u_{k1} \qquad (10.23)$$

where u_{c1}, u_{k1} are random errors (not necessarily independent).

We now combine these two equations into a linear combination ($\lambda = 0$ or 1):

$$y = [\lambda a_{c1} + (1 - \lambda)a_{k1}]X + (\lambda b_{c1})\left(m - \underset{-1}{\mathsf{E}}\, m \right)$$
$$+ (1 - \lambda)c_{k1} m + (\lambda u_{c1} + (1 - \lambda)u_{k1})$$

or

$$y = a_1 X + b_1\left(m - \underset{-1}{\mathsf{E}}\, m \right) + c_1 m + u_1 \qquad (10.24)$$

where $a_1 = \lambda a_{c1} + (1 - \lambda)a_{k1}$, etc. We would like to test whether b_1 or c_1 is significantly different from zero; if $b_1 > 0$, then $\lambda = 1$ and classical prevails. If $c_1 > 0$, then $\lambda = 0$ and Keynesian prevails (the other possibilities are disregarded here, though clearly if $b_1 = c_1 = 0$ or if $b_1 > 0 < c_1$, the problem must be reformulated if the test results are taken seriously).

Now suppose the rest of the model is a policy reaction function for money supply:

$$m = a_2 X + u_2 \qquad (10.25)$$

where u_2 is a random error independent of u_1. (Much of the discussion which follows is based on Buiter, 1983, to which the reader is referred for further analysis.)

Sargent's point can now be expressed as the impossibility of identifying c_1 and b_1 in this model. Assuming rational expectations, the reduced form of the model (10.24) and (10.25) is given by:

$$y = \beta_1 X + v_1 \qquad (10.26)$$

$$m = \beta_2 X + v_2 \qquad (10.27)$$

where

$$\beta_1 = a_1 + c_1 a_2$$

$$\beta_2 = a_2$$

$$v_1 = (b_1 + c_1)u_2 + u_1$$

$$v_2 = u_2$$

The effect of anticipated money on output is given by c_1, the effect of unanticipated money on output by $b_1 + c_1$.

We notice that the covariance between the error terms in the reduced form is given by:

$$\text{Cov}(v_1, v_2) = (b_1 + c_1)\sigma^2 \qquad (10.28)$$

where σ^2 is the variance of the money supply error, u_2. Consequently an estimate of $b_1 + c_1$ is obtained as:

$$\widehat{(b_1 + c_1)} = \frac{\widehat{\text{Cov}(v_1, v_2)}}{\hat{\sigma}^2} \qquad (10.29)$$

Even this requires independence of structural disturbances u_1 and u_2.[2]

However, to identify the crucial parameter, c_1, we must set one of the elements in a_1 to zero (if X is a single variable, $a_1 = 0$ is necessary); that is, at least one variable appearing in the monetary policy reaction function must *not* appear in the output equation. Suppose for instance our model is given by:

$$y = a_1 X_1 + b_1\left(m - \mathop{\text{E}}_{-1} m\right) + c_1 m + u_1 \qquad (10.30)$$

$$m = a_2 X_1 + a_3 X_2 + u_2 \qquad (10.31)$$

where X_1, X_2 are subsets of X, the exogenous variable set. The reduced form is given by:

$$y = (a_1 + c_1 a_2)X_1 + c_1 a_3 X_2 + (b_1 + c_1)u_2 + u_1 \qquad (10.32)$$

$$m = a_2 X_1 + a_3 X_2 + u_2 \qquad (10.33)$$

(10.30) is now identified.

This, however, is extremely hard to visualize in any model, because the reduced or semi-reduced form of output will generally contain all the exogenous variables of the model which are candidates for money supply reaction. Barro, in his work on the US, assumes, with this in mind, that government expenditure enters the money supply function but not the output function. This is totally implausible, given that government expenditure appears in the GDP identity.

Sargent has suggested that a model such as (10.24) and (10.25) may be identified if a structural break is known to have occurred in the policy regime during the sample period. If the world is classical (i.e. $c_1 = 0$), then the reduced form for output will be invariant to a change in the policy regime (when a_2 changes). Hence the coefficient β_1 will not change. Consequently tests for stability of β_1 across the samples before and after the break will allow for discrimination between Keynesian and classical models. Nevertheless, though clearly relevant (see p. 191), this has rarely been used to date.

This discussion can be extended to include lags. Write (10.24) and (10.25) generally as:

$$\lambda_1(L)y = a_1(L)X + b_1(L)\left(m - \mathop{E}_{-1} m\right) + c_1(L)m + u_1 \quad (10.34)$$

$$\lambda_2(L)m = a_2(L)X + u_2 \quad (10.35)$$

where L is the lag operator and $a_1(L)$, for example, is a polynomial in L; $\lambda_2(L) = 1 - \lambda_2^1(L)$ where $\lambda_2^1(L)$ are the terms for L^i ($i \geq 1$). The reduced form for y (obtained by substituting from (10.35); i.e. for $m - \mathop{E}_{-1} m = u_2$ and for $m = \lambda_2^1(L)m + a_2(L)X + u_2$) now becomes:

$$\lambda_1(L)y = [a_1(L) + c_1(L)a_2(L)]X$$
$$+ b_1^1(L)u_2 + c_1(L)\lambda_2^1(L)m + v_1 \quad (10.36)$$

which after substituting for lagged u_2 in terms of observables (i.e. $u_2 = \lambda_2(L)m - a_2(L)X$ from (10.35)) becomes:

$$\lambda_1(L)y = [a_1(L) + c_1(L)\widehat{a_2(L)} - b_1^1(L)\widehat{a_2(L)}]X$$
$$+ [b_1^1(L)\widehat{\lambda_2(L)} + c_1(L)\widehat{\lambda_2^1(L)}]m + v_1 \quad (10.37)$$

where $v_1 = (b_1^0 + c_1^0)u_2 + u_1$; b_1^0, c_1^0, are the leading terms, $b_1^1(L)$, $c_1^1(L)$ are the terms for L^i ($i \geq 1$) in $b_1(L)$, $c_1(L)$ respectively. $\lambda_2(L)$, $a_2(L)$ are hatted to show that they can be estimated from (10.35). The variance-covariance matrix will, as before, give an estimate of $(b_1^0 + c_1^0)$, provided there are no y innovations entering the money supply function. Even so, the $c_1(L)$ are not retrievable; they will only be retrievable if at least one of the X variables is excluded from (10.34), as before in the no-lag case.

Another possibility for discrimination when there are lags has been pointed out by McCallum (1979) which avoids the necessity of identifying the $c_1(L)$.

In the special case where the classical model contains only the current monetary innovation as a determinant of output, then it implies a testable relationship between the coefficients in the money rule and the coefficients obtained in the output regression on current and previous monetary expansion. This case corresponds to having $b_1^1(L) = 0$ in (10.37). In this case we retrieve $c_1(L)$ from the coefficients on lagged money supply; for the model to be classical, lagged money supply should not enter the output reduced form.[3]

However, the exclusion of past monetary innovations from the output equation may well not be valid; it places absolute reliance on the absence of a moving average process on the term $\left(p - \underset{-1}{\text{E}}\ p\right)$ entering the Sargent–Wallace supply curve. Yet it only acquires a one-period delay in *one* sector's observed response to such shocks to yield such a process; this surely cannot be ruled out, in view of decision and delivery lags.

There are further reasons for being sceptical of the possibility of discriminating on the basis of reduced forms between models in which systematic monetary policy influences output and those in which this is not the case. This is because there is a whole class of rational expectations models in which systematic monetary policy does influence the variance of output but which may be indistinguishable from the Sargent–Wallace reduced form for the impact of unanticipated money on output. Consider a model which embodies the simple 'Lucas' supply curve as discussed in Chapter 3. We take this supply curve as illustrative of a general class of classical supply models in which a variety of current and expected future variables may enter, and in which systematic monetary policy will influence the variance of output.

We suppose the structure of the economy is given by the following equations:

$$y = a(p - \mathsf{E}p_{+1}) + hy_{-1} + u \qquad (10.38)$$

$$m = p + y \qquad (10.39)$$

$$m = hy_{-1} + \varepsilon \qquad (10.40)$$

where u and ε are random errors.

Following the solution procedure outlined in Chapter 2, the solution for output in this model is given by:

$$y = \frac{a}{1+a}\left(m - \underset{-1}{\mathsf{E}}\ m\right) + hy_{-1}\frac{u}{1+a} \qquad (10.41)$$

(10.41) is of some interest, since it has the form given by (10.4). In other words, though the economy is described by a Lucas supply hypothesis, with consequent scope for stabilization policy, the authorities by choice of the monetary rule (10.40) have given rise to a reduced form equation for output which is indistinguishable from that generated by a Sargent–Wallace supply hypothesis. More generally an economy described by such a Lucas supply hypothesis can give rise to an economy with a reduced form where output is related to current and past monetary innovations and of course past output. (See Minford and Peel, 1979).

It will thus take the following form:

$$y = \pi_0\left(m - \underset{-1}{\mathsf{E}}\ m\right) + \pi_1\left(m_{-1} - \underset{-2}{\mathsf{E}}\ m_{-1}\right) + \pi_2 y_{-1}$$

$$(10.42)$$

However, in (10.42) the coefficients π_0, π_1 are not structural parameters, rather they are related to the parameters in the authorities' feedback rule.

Buiter (1983) gives a further example where equation (10.4) is observationally equivalent to models in which systematic monetary policy will influence the variance of output.

Consider a model in which expectations of future prices

are conditioned by information sets at different dates. This will occur for instance in models embodying overlapping contracts (or due to the Turnovsky, 1980, case where agents in goods markets have access to current macro data – see Chapter 3). In such models output is a function of, not only the current innovation in monetary policy, but also of the revision between periods of all forecasts of all future money supplies. Thus for example we could obtain:

$$y = a\left(m - \mathop{\mathrm{E}}_{-1} m\right) + a_1 \sum_{i=0}^{\infty} \pi_i \left(\mathrm{E}m_{+1+i} - \mathop{\mathrm{E}}_{-1} m_{+1+i}\right)$$

(10.43)

Clearly the terms in $\mathrm{E}\left(m_{+1+i} - \mathop{\mathrm{E}}_{-1} m_{+1+i}\right)$ are functions only of news. Consequently for any well-defined money supply process, (10.43) will collapse to:

$$y = a\left(m - \mathop{\mathrm{E}}_{-1} m\right) + a_1 \rho \varepsilon$$

(10.44)

where ρ is related to parameters of the money supply process, and ε is a random disturbance.

Only if there was a known change in policy regime could (10.44) be distinguished from (10.4).

There are three final points we would wish to make which make the interpretation of the reduced form evidence on monetary innovations even more difficult to interpret.

The first point is that all the empirical work so far conducted has implicitly assumed the absence of a global capital market. Clearly, as we note from Chapter 4, when there is a global capital market, unanticipated money will be a function of all random disturbances in the economy. Thus if:

$$m = \lambda X + \varepsilon$$

(10.45)

$$m - \mathop{\mathrm{E}}_{-1} m = \varepsilon - \mathrm{E}\varepsilon = f\left[\begin{array}{l}\text{all random disturbances} \\ \text{in model}\end{array}\right]$$

(10.46)

It is not as yet altogether clear what additional problems for identification or estimation are posed by recognition of global capital markets. However, we should note that a clear difference emerges between the impact of nominal errors on output (ε) and unanticipated money on output ($m - Em$).[4] We also note that the coefficient linking unanticipated output to unanticipated money will no longer be a structural parameter even in an economy typified by a Sargent–Wallace supply curve (see Chapter 4). Consequently, known changes in policy regime may not help in the statistical identification of the reduced forms.

The second point is an empirical one and concerns the interpretation of monetary innovations in annual or quarterly models. Given that monetary data is available either weekly (US) or monthly (UK), it is simply not clear what the appropriate interpretation of annual or quarterly monetary innovations are. This point is obviously related to our first point and concerns the appropriate specification of the information set facing agents.

Our final point is also empirical and also concerns the interpretation of the monetary innovations. No real attention has been paid in the empirical work to the possibility of changes in monetary regimes. Consequently all the work reported derives monetary innovations from one policy regime. *A priori* it seems most unlikely that there has only been one policy regime, given the change from fixed to floating exchange rates that has taken place in some countries, the changes in political regimes (see Chapter 8) plus the fact that the Central Bank authorities may have endeavoured to fix interest rates rather than the money stock in previous years. All these factors are suggestive that monetary innovations from one policy regime, as in the reported empirical work, may involve a serious mis-specification.

CONCLUSIONS

The empirical evidence presented by Barro and others on the impact of unanticipated or actual money on real variables appears to give impressive support to the view that systematic monetary policy will have no impact on real variables.

However, we showed that there are serious identification problems associated with these empirical studies which lead us to conclude that at this time it would be unwise to form a view as to the impact of monetary policy on economic activity based on this empirical work.

NOTES

1. The analogous point also turns out to be applicable to reduced forms for the exchange rate (see Chapter 7) as a means of distinguishing 'equilibrium' from 'disequilibrium' open economy models. It will also often be applicable when a reduced form on any single variable is appealed to as a means of distinguishing equilibrium from disequilibrium models; appeals to the 'stylized facts' about any single variable have accordingly to be treated with the greatest caution.

2. Buiter (1983) has further pointed out that if output or innovations in output enter the money supply reaction function (as might occur from micro responses of the banking system to changes in demand for money due themselves to anticipated and unanticipated changes in output), then too no estimate of any structural parameters can, in general, be derived from the variance-covariance matrix of reduced form residuals. This can be seen by rewriting (10.25) as:

$$m = a_2 X_1 + a_3 X_2 + b_2\left(y - \mathop{E}_{-1} y\right) + c_2 y + u_2$$

   In this case, c_1 will be identified (see next para.) but b_1 is not.

3. Alternatively, if we write the reduced form in terms of *current m* (exploiting the fact that it is recursively fixed), we obtain after substituting for current as well as lagged u_2:

$$\lambda_1(L)y = [a_1(L) + c_1(L)a_2(L) - b_1(L)a_2(L)]X$$
$$+ [b_1(L)\lambda_2(L) + c_1(L)\lambda_2^1(L)]m + u_1$$

   Here setting $b_1(L) = b_1$ implies that the lag coefficients on m should be $b_1\lambda_2(L)$, i.e. have the same pattern as the lag coefficients in the money equations, if $c_1(L) = 0$.

4. To the extent that the presence of a global market is important for the formation of monetary anticipations, this suggests that Barro's work would need to be reinterpreted, not as reflecting the impact of monetary surprises on output, but rather monetary errors.

11

The Liverpool Model

The object of this book has been to familiarize the reader with the uses of the rational expectations hypothesis in macroeconomics. In this chapter, the final use that we investigate is in a complete macroeconomic model of the UK; such a model has been built at Liverpool over the past six years by the Liverpool Research Group, of which the authors are members. Most of the issues already discussed have a bearing on construction of this model; so our discussion here should help to bring them into focus in a practical way.

Why build a rational expectations model of a whole economy? We have seen that a truly structural model, capable of policy simulation, would have as its coefficients the parameters of tastes and technology; any other model is vulnerable to the Lucas critique of policy evaluation. Yet the feasibility of a full macro model whose parameters are tastes and technology is doubtful. Our analysis also told us that there are many ways of representing a time-series system, not only by a structural model; the cheapest, and generally effective for forecasting under unchanged structure, is univariate time-series models. More expensive, but still cheaper than a full structural model, is the vector autoregressive time-series model. Such models are not structural, and cannot be used for policy evaluation or forecasting when regimes change, but they are relatively cheap for forecasting when regimes are constant.

All this might suggest that a truly structural model is not feasible, while a forecasting model can best be implemented by time-series methods, provided structure is constant; policy evaluation had therefore better be left well alone, and also forecasting when there is regime change. This would be a pessimistic conclusion for macroeconomists, though possibly correct.

The Liverpool model is an attempt to explore whether a 'half-way house' is feasible, which can carry out useful policy evaluation and forecasting under conditions of structural change. The model has as its parameters, not tastes and technology, but coefficients of demand and supply curves (or 'Euler equations' which represent the optimal plans of agents in response to expected events). In these equations, the expectations are separately identified and modelled by rational expectations methods (as opposed to the usual method where expectations are proxied by distributed lags of observable variables). If there is a regime change, the model allows for it by altering the expectations (computed by solving the model forwards in time and treating the result as the expected one), but the coefficients of demand and supply are *not* changed. Clearly the latter procedure is still vulnerable to the Lucas critique, but the assumption is made that the latter changes are likely to be of less quantitative importance than the effects on expectations themselves, perhaps because recomputation of optimal plans is likely to take some time as *everyone* must do it (in the light of *everyone else's* new plan), whereas expectations of the broad effects of new policies will be recomputed rapidly (each agent can do it easily enough on the assumption that other agents will maintain their reactions).

The justification for this half-way house can only be one of costs and benefits, when there is no satisfactory alternative. After all, policy-makers must have *some* guide to the quantitative effects of their policies, or they are unlikely to pursue new policies. Similar remarks apply to businessmen, money men, etc. faced with new policies. If it can be shown that these effects can be in practice calibrated within a useful order of magnitude, then the exercise is worthwhile. We look at the interim evidence from the Liverpool model experience below.

THE MODEL'S STRUCTURE UNDER FLOATING EXCHANGE RATES

The model has a basic structure that will by now be familiar. There is a demand (or IS) curve and a supply (or Phillips, PP) curve for goods; a demand (or LM) curve and a supply curve for money (MS). The foreign exchange market is cleared by 'efficient market' behaviour as in the Dornbusch model; the exchange rate and interest rates move until the expected return on foreign and domestic bonds is the same. The domestic bond market is eliminated by Walras' Law. It is assumed that all markets clear in each (annual) period. Hence the model belongs to the equilibrium or 'new classical' class of rational expectations models.

A stylized version is set out below, as is an illustrative diagram. As far as possible we preserve our previous notation. (Now $e = real$ exchange rate; rise = *appreciation*).

$$\text{IS} \quad y = \phi\bar{d} - \alpha r + \kappa\theta + \kappa'\Delta\theta - \eta e + x\overline{WT} + \varepsilon_d \quad (11.1)$$

$$\text{PP} \quad y = y^* + \delta\left(p - \underset{-1}{\text{E}}\, p\right)$$

$$+ \sigma(e - e^*) + \lambda(y - y^*)_{-1} + \varepsilon_s \quad (11.2)$$

$$\text{LM} \quad m = p + \mu\theta + \gamma y - \beta R + \varepsilon_\mu \quad (11.3)$$

$$\text{MS} \quad \Delta m = (1 - v)\pi\bar{d} + v\Delta m_{-1} + \varepsilon_m \quad (11.4)$$

$$\text{WW} \quad \Delta\theta = \pi\bar{d} - \tau(y - y^*) - \Delta p - q\Delta R$$

$$- \eta^* e - \mu' y + x^*\overline{WT} \quad (11.5)$$

$$\text{RR} \quad R = r + \text{E}p_{+1} - p \quad (11.6)$$

$$\text{EM} \quad r = r_F - \text{E}e_{+1} + e \quad (11.7)$$

We explain each equation in turn.

The IS curve has as its components $\bar{d}$, the fiscal deficit or PSBR (as a fraction of GDP and cyclically adjusted), real interest rates and the real exchange rate. In addition, there are wealth effects on consumption ($\kappa\theta$) and on investment in goods, fixed capital, consumer durables, and inventory ($\kappa'\Delta\theta$, an 'accelerator' effect because of stock-adjustment). In the full model, there are four equations from which this IS curve has been constructed: the GDP identity, the consumption function, an equation for the private sector's stock of goods and an equation for the real current balance. Consumption is related to private sector wealth, real interest rates and expected future real wages. The stock of goods is related to the stock of financial assets and real interest rates for portfolio balance reasons. The real current balance depends negatively on the real exchange rate and domestic income, and positively on world trade.

The main way in which this IS curve differs from those in other UK models is in the wealth effects. These are powerful and respond in turn to changes in expectations of real interest rates and inflation; these cause unanticipated changes in nominal interest rates which alter financial asset values.

The precise link is given in the WW equation (11.5), relating financial wealth to the PSBR, inflation, changes in interest rates, and the current balance. This utilizes the identity that changes in private financial assets equal the financial deficits of the public and foreign sectors plus valuation effects. The PSBR as a fraction of GDP represents the relevant public deficit (π, the ratio of GDP to financial assets, converts it into a fraction of financial assets); since $\bar{d}$ is cyclically adjusted, $\tau(y - y^*)$ is subtracted to give the actual PSBR. $-\eta^* e - \mu' y + x^* WT$ is the current balance as a fraction of financial assets. $-\Delta p - q\Delta R$ are the valuation effects; all financial assets are assumed to be nominal.

(11.6) is the Fisher identity defining real interest rates as the difference between the nominal interest rate and the expected inflation rate; we assume that the expectations used in computing the current real rate are based on full current information. This side-stepping of the signal-extraction problem (which creates substantial computational difficulties in a large model) is justified on the grounds that agents get close on average to having full information over the annual time period.

(11.7) provides the efficient market link between domestic and foreign real interest rates and the real exchange rate. Ee_{+1} will be related to e and, depending on the number of roots in the model, also to other current state variables. However, in practice the model's structure is such that we can approximate $(Ee_{+1} - e^*) \simeq \lambda(e - e^*)$; that is to say the real exchange rate returns to equilibrium at about the rate, λ, of 'persistence' in the Phillips curve. Consequently (11.7) can be rewritten as $r \simeq r_F + (1 - \lambda)(e - e^*)$.

This is a useful simplification, because we can now replace r in the IS curve by e and r_F, and draw it in (y, e) space as in Figure 11.1. The curve shifts rightwards with rises in $\bar{d}$, $\theta(\Delta\theta)$. $\overline{WT}$, ε_d, and falls in r_F. Next we can draw the WW curve as that combination of y, e for which there is no change in financial assets, i.e. $\Delta\theta = 0$ (stock equilibrium). To the right of this, θ will be falling and the IS curve will be shifting inwards; and *vice versa*. The WW curve will shift rightwards with a rise in $\bar{d}$, $\overline{WT}$, and y^* and falls in Δp and ΔR.

We have now described the apparatus regulating the demand for goods. We now turn to the supply side of the goods market, shown in (11.2).

Formally, it differs from the Sargent–Wallace supply curve only by the term in $(e - e^*)$. This term represents the effect on supply of the real exchange rate in an open economy. The real exchange rate is the domestic price level relative to the foreign price level converted into domestic currency; a rise in it implies that prices of UK products are higher relative to costs of imported inputs. Profits are accordingly increased, the demand for labour increases, real wages rise, and the supply of labour and output rises. (This effect will be most marked in the *non*-traded sector; the traded goods sector will tend to be depressed by this process because of stronger foreign competition.)

However, closer inspection reveals a further difference in (11.2) from the Sargent–Wallace supply curve. The term $\left(p - \underset{-1}{E} p\right)$, given our assumption above (11.6, 11.7) that agents have access to full current information, cannot arise from information lags as it does in Sargent–Wallace. It does not; rather it comes about because unions are assumed to enter into one-year nominal wage contracts, as a result of transactions costs in regulating their members' behaviour. The model assumes that there is a continuously clearing non-union sector (hence the equilibrium nature of the model), but given the unions' wage contracts, the supply curve shifts out-

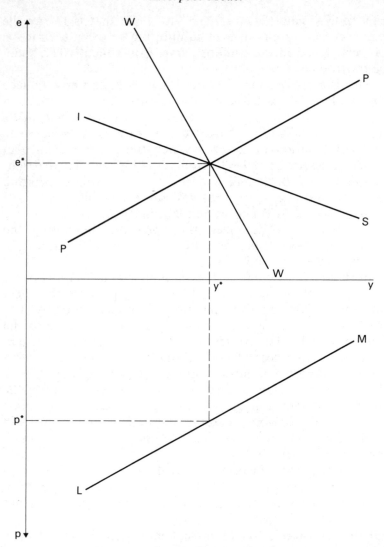

Figure 11.1 *The Liverpool Model Illustrated*

wards when prices are higher than expected the previous year. This is because now union employers find that profits are higher and employ more union labour; the additional labour is supplied at the contracted nominal wage by withdrawing it from the non-union sector where real wages rise, but because the union mark-up falls temporarily, there is a downward shift in the overall supply price of labour for any given labour supply.

The Phillips curve is shown in Figure 11.1 as an upward sloping relation in (y, e) space. It shifts rightwards with unanticipated inflation, rises in y^*, falls in e^*, and ε_s.

The intersection of the IS and PP curves represents the continuous equilibrium position in the goods market. An intersection to the right of the WW curve will induce a falling θ which will drive the IS leftwards until the IS/PP intersection reaches the WW curve; here will be stock equilibrium.

To complete the model, we turn to the money market. (11.3) is a standard demand for money (M1) function except for the presence of θ; this enters because holders of money are sensitive to the proportion of money in their overall financial assets, θ, even it is assumed for a narrow definition of money as here. This wealth effect implies that shocks to financial expectations affect the demand for money and so prices currently, even when output does not move, another feature distinguishing the model from most other UK models.

(11.4), the supply of money, has the property that monetary growth can be independent of the PSBR in the short term (and in the full model there is scope for a variety of short-term monetary responses). But in the long term it must be consistent with fiscal policy, for reasons discussed earlier in Chapter 9; that is Δm (long run) $= \pi \bar{d}$. The implication is that the expected cyclically adjusted PSBR determines the expected long-run inflation rate.

(11.3) and (11.4) are shown as the LM curve in (y, p) space in Figure 11.1. The price level, being fully flexible, can be regarded as moving to clear the money market. However, the full simultaneity implies that prices, interest rates and exchange rates all have impacts in each continuously clearing market – goods, money, and foreign exchange – and hence contribute to clearing each.

To explain how the model behaves, we consider the responses to, first, a monetary, then a 'reflationary' shock, using this diagrammatic apparatus.

An unanticipated rise in the money supply (once-for-all) shifts the LM curve outwards. This raises prices, which shifts the PP curve outwards and reduces the real value of financial assets, θ, shifting the IS curve inwards. The typical result is illustrated in Figure 11.2. There is an expansion in output, a sharp rise in prices, and a fall in the real exchange rate (the nominal exchange rate depreciates by this *plus* the rise in prices). Nominal interest rates fall. The expansion of output comes about in effect because of the fall in the real exchange rate (and so the real wage) brought about because unions underpredicted inflation in setting their nominal mark-up.

Subsequently, the economy settles on the stable path back to equilibrium shown by the arrows on Figure 11.2. Initially it wobbles because of the stock-adjustments effects of changing wealth ($\kappa'\Delta\theta$ in the IS curve). The stable path then is characterized by the PP curve shifting leftwards and the IS curve first shifting leftwards as θ falls, and then, once the IS/PP intersection is to the left of the WW curve, shifting rightwards up the PP curve. Meanwhile the LM curve first shifts further rightwards as now rising interest rates and falling real financial assets reduce the demand for money, and overshoots its long-run position (L^*M^*), before shifting back in as the effect of rising wealth dominates that of settling interest rates. In equilibrium the economy returns to exactly the same r, e, R, θ, y as before; p is higher by exactly the rise in m. In effect the shock reduced θ initially as p rose, and this loss has to be made good along the path back to equilibrium, along which there has to be therefore a public sector deficit and/or a current account surplus. Figure 11.3 shows this path in a simulation of the full model for a 10 per cent rise in the money supply, for the main variables.

This monetary shock simulation is relatively straightforward; a surprise expansion in money 'buys' a temporary rise in output at the cost of a temporary burst in inflation (a once-for-all rise in prices). We now turn to a more complex

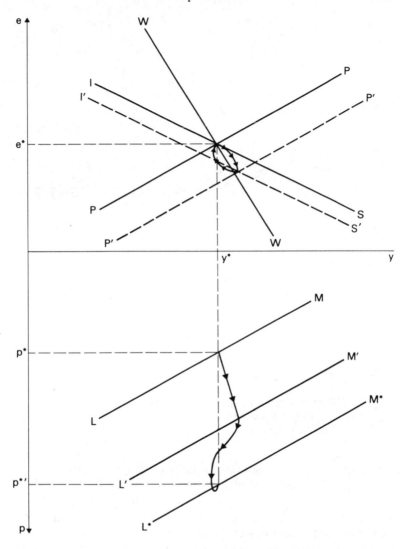

Figure 11.2 *Once-for-all rise in money supply*

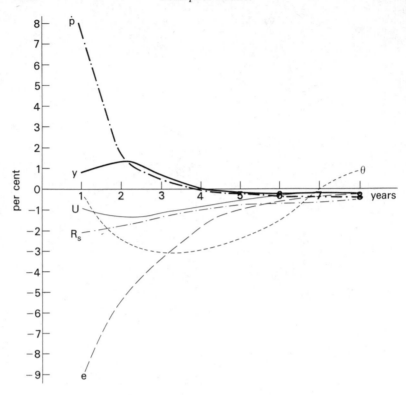

Figure 11.3 *Once-for-all rise in money supply by 10 per cent (unanticipated, in year 1)*

shock, that of a surprise 'reflationary package' consisting of a higher public sector deficit (resulting from higher public spending) accompanied by increased money supply growth, both intended to be permanent (in order to ensure that the economy, once 'stimulated', does not 'relapse'). In line with the model's logic, we assume consistency between the fiscal and monetary sides of the package, so that with $\pi \simeq 2$ a rise in the PSBR by 1 per cent of GDP is accompanied by a 2 per cent per annum rise in money supply growth; we also assume that the rise in the *PSBR* (and *not* the rise in public spending) is maintained, so that the rise in debt interest which must result from the stimulus is offset by reduced public spending.

There are two differences from the previous simulation. Here we have higher money supply *growth* as against a once-for-all rise in the *level* of money. Secondly here we have a fiscal as well as monetary stimulus.

Consider first the impact effects, shown in Figure 11.4. The current rise in the level of money shifts the LM curve outwards; this raises prices which shifts the PP curve rightwards and the IS curve leftwards as before. But the fact that higher future monetary growth is now expected raises expected inflation (not merely as before the expected price level); this *raises* nominal interest rates (even though as we shall see real interest rates drop). This rise strongly reinforces the depressing effect of higher prices on real financial assets, shifting the IS curve further leftwards. Furthermore, the fall in θ accompanying a rise in R depresses the demand for money sharply and shifts the LM curve rightwards by more than the rise in money alone would imply, so intensifying the upward pressure on prices. Finally, we can bring in the direct stimulative effects on demand of the higher public spending, which shifts the IS curve rightwards and *adds* to financial assets via the increased deficit.

Clearly, these direct effects on the IS curve work oppositely to the indirect effects through wealth arising from prices and expected inflation. The net effect within the model is to shift the IS curve leftwards; the wealth effects dominate, as illustrated in Figure 11.4. However, because the PP curve has shifted rightwards owing to the effect of unexpected inflation on real wages, the IS/PP intersection may either slightly expand or slightly contract output, while the real exchange rate unambiguously drops (the nominal rate again drops by this plus the rise in prices). Real interest rates accordingly drop too, but not enough to prevent a rise in nominal interest rates.

Subsequently, the model settles onto the stable path after again an initial wobble as the stock-adjustment effect of falling financial assets is unwound (the IS curve shifts back to the right in the second year as $\Delta\theta$ reverts to being slightly negative from having been heavily negative). As for inflation, we have conveniently drawn the LM curve in $(y, \dot{p})$ space, with inflation instead of the price level on the vertical axis,

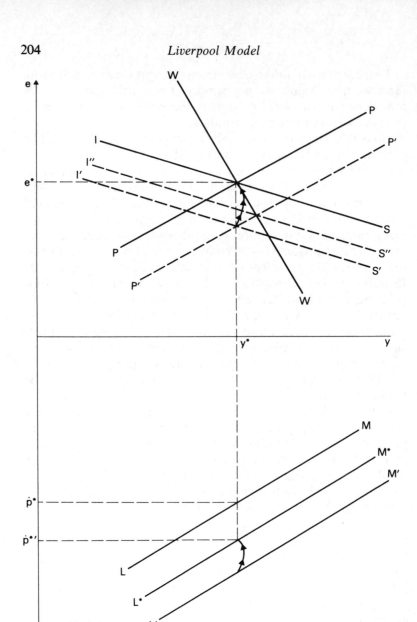

Figure 11.4 *Permanent rise in PSBR and money supply growth*

implying that lagged output is an argument of it as well as the rate of change of money, Δm; however, lagged output does not move very much in this simulation and $\Delta\theta$ becomes progressively more positive, raising the rate of growth of the real demand for money.

In equilibrium, inflation is higher by the rise in money supply growth (i.e. by π times the rise in $\bar{d}$), e, r, y are unaltered. However, because $\bar{d}$ is higher, there has to be some 'crowding out' of private demand; this is achieved by a fall in financial assets reducing private consumption (and also the stock of durables, so the rate of replacement expenditure on these). With lower θ and with higher nominal interest rates, real money balances are reduced, so that the cumulative rise in prices exceeds the cumulative rise in money supply. Figure 11.5 shows the time profile of the main variables' responses

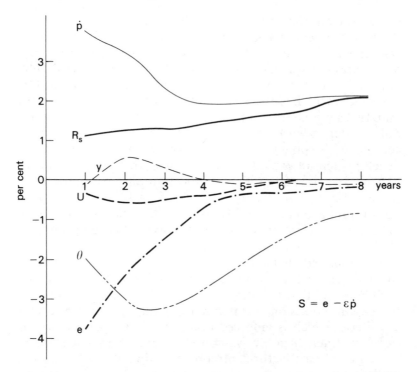

Figure 11.5 *Permanent unanticipated rise in PSBR by 1 per cent of GDP (balanced finance)*

to a reflation raising the PSBR by 1 per cent of GDP (and money supply growth by 2 per cent per annum).

THE 'NATURAL RATES' OF OUTPUT, EMPLOYMENT AND REAL WAGES – THE 'SUPPLY SIDE' OF THE MODEL

Surprising though it seems on reflection, very little of macroeconomics is devoted to explaining y^* and e^*, and the implied natural rate of unemployment. This has also been true of this book. In line with the usual focus of macroeconomics, we have taken y^* and e^* as given by 'underlying forces' outside the scope of our analysis.

Nevertheless, though a full treatment is in practice the subject of another book and belongs to another literature, the new classical analysis has, when confronted by UK postwar experience, driven the Liverpool Research Group into formulating an explanation of the natural rates and integrating it into the Liverpool Model. The reason is plain; UK unemployment has risen steadily and dramatically since the mid-1960s, apparently (and certainly according to the model) quite independently of the business cycle. A Group concerned with policy towards unemployment needs must develop such an explanation. Since it both forms part of the Model and is an application of rational expectations in its own right, it seems right to include a brief account here (for a full account see Minford, 1983, and for a policy-orientated description see Minford, Davies, Peel and Sprague, 1983).

It is assumed that industry is competitive and distributed into two sectors, unionized and non-unionized (or 'competitive') in a way that is outside firms' control. Firms are able to buy capital goods on an international market at a world real rental cost which is enforced domestically by perfect capital mobility. Each firm enjoys constant returns to scale but is limited by a fixed factor ('entrepreneurship'), so that marginal product declines as the industry expands. It buys imported inputs at a given world price. Accordingly, we write the demand for labour in each sector by profit-maximizing firms as:

$$L_u^d = (\overset{-}{w_u}, \overset{-}{T_F}, \overset{+}{e}, \overset{+}{k}) \qquad (11.8)$$

$$L_c^d = (\overset{-}{w_c}, \overset{-}{T_F}, \overset{+}{e}, \overset{+}{k}) \qquad (11.9)$$

where u, c subscripts stand for union and competitive sectors respectively, $L^d =$ labour demand, $w =$ real wage, $T_F =$ labour tax rate (as fraction of wage) paid by employer, $e =$ real exchange rate (price of domestic goods relative to price of imported goods, in common currency), $k =$ aggregate (positive) effect of technological progress, real rental on capital, and fixed factor supplies. The expected signs are indicated over the variables.

We complete the description of firms' activities by writing down their production function (we need only the economy's aggregate) as a supply of output equation:

$$Q = (\overset{+}{L_u^d} + \overset{+}{L_c^d}, \overset{}{k}) \qquad (11.10)$$

where $Q =$ total output of the economy. To avoid aggregation problems we assume the production functions of union and non-unionized industry are identical.[1]

We now turn to the behaviour of workers and unions. Unions maximize the present value of their potential members' aggregated real incomes by setting the union wage. This gives rise to a variable mark-up equation of the form :

$$w_u = m(\overset{+}{UNR}, \overset{+}{p^{ue}}, \overset{+}{k})w_c \qquad (11.11)$$

where m ($=$ one plus the mark-up) is a function of UNR ($=$ the unionization rate), k, and p^{ue} ($=$ unanticipated inflation). UNR enters as a proxy for the elasticity of demand for union labour, it being argued that the more unionized an industry, the greater the difficulty of substitution of non-union for union labour in that industry, whether in union firms or by the expansion of non-union firms. p^{ue} enters because unions find it convenient – in order to minimize the transactions costs of controlling work conditions – to draw up nominal wage contracts with only partially contingent price clauses, hence a surprise in prices will reduce the real union wage.

It is assumed that firms choose workers' hours given the union-set wage rates. Therefore unionized workers are rationed in their labour supply. We assume that total labour supply of hours in the economy is such that the marginal rate of substitution of leisure for goods equals the *marginal* net real wage available. This is, for union and non-union workers alike, the real wage in the competitive market (which is assumed to be continuously cleared), minus benefits lost and taxes paid through working extra. Because of the wide differences in individual tax/benefit circumstances, tight restrictions across the parameters of benefit, tax, and real wage variables are unlikely to hold and we write generally:

$$L^s = (\overset{+}{w_c}, \overset{-}{b}, \overset{-}{T_L}, POP) \tag{11.12}$$

where b = real unemployment benefit, T_L = tax rate (fraction of wage) paid by employee, POP = size of (registered) working age population (because this also acts as a proxy for demographic trends, the sign is left ambiguous).

The labour market equations are completed by the equilibrium condition in the competitive sector:

$$L^s - L_u^d = L_c^d \tag{11.13}$$

and by the unemployment relation:

$$U = POP - L^s \tag{11.14}$$

where U = unemployment. (11.14) states that those registered as potential workers will draw unemployment benefits if not working and will therefore under UK practice be counted as unemployed.

(11.13) taken with (11.8), (11.9), (11.11) and (11.12) yields a solution for w_c, w_u, L_u^d, L_c^d, L^s, in terms of e, T_F, T_L, UNR, k, and POP. Using (11.10) we can then solve for Q, and from (11.14) for U. The set-up, the economy's 'supply side', is illustrated in Figure 11.6. Quadrant (a) shows the equation of the production function (11.10), quadrant (b) shows SS, the equation of labour supply (11.12), and of total labour demand,

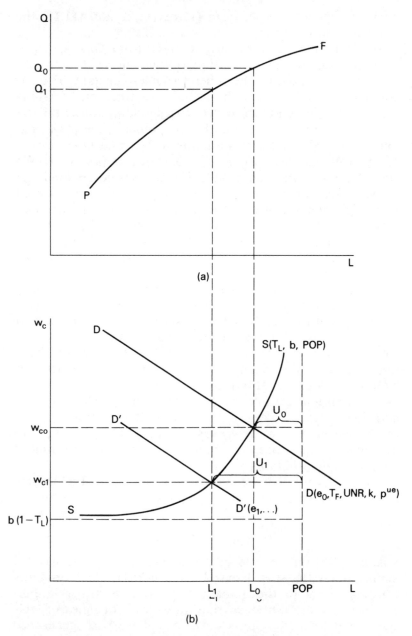

Figure 11.6 *Labour market and production functions*

$L_c^d + L_u^d$, in terms of w_c from (11.8), (11.9), and (11.11) the mark-up relation.

We may now conveniently extract from this an open economy supply curve, relating output supply to the real exchange rate, holding the other variables constant. Thus as we lower e, shifting DD to the left, we trace out a falling output path along the PF curve corresponding to the DD/SS intersection; this is illustrated by the points (e_0, w_{c0}, Q_0, L_0) and (e_1, w_{c1}, Q_1, L_1) corresponding to DD and D'D' respectively. This is shown in Figure 11.7, quadrant (a), as PP. We trace through in quadrants (b)–(d) the correspondence between real exchange rate, real wages, employment and unemployment, for given other variables. (Note that changes in all these other variables will shift both the PP and EW curves, and changes in T_L, b, POP will shift the LS curve. Also note that the shift in PP due to p^{ue} is the 'Phillips curve' effect.)

We now introduce the last relationship, required to close the open economy model in equilibrium. It will have been observed that the open economy aspect has added e, the real exchange rate, as a supply side determinant; were this a closed economy, e would be absent, and there would be a unique equilibrium supply, corresponding to that which can be produced given labour market equilibrium. This is the usual vertical aggregate supply curve set-up. However the addition of e has produced an upward-sloping supply curve; the reason being that as e rises, the terms of trade improve and with them profits, enabling firms to induce a higher labour supply profitably.

To close the model we specify an equation for the current account balance (x) and set it to equilibrium:

$$0 = x = (\overset{+}{WT}, \overset{-}{e}, \overset{-}{Q}) \qquad (11.15)$$

where $WT = $ the volume of world trade (or output). (11.15) simply states that the demand for imports by UK residents must be equal to the demand for UK exports by foreign residents, equilibrium occurring through e, our index of relative home to foreign prices. We can if we wish generalize (11.15) to allow for an equilibrium net capital transfer (e.g.

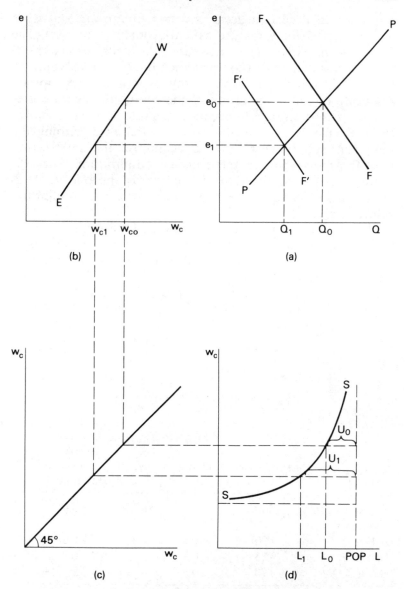

Figure 11.7 *The determination of the natural rate*

Liverpool Model

inwards and a current account deficit for an *ldc*, outwards and a surplus for a mature capital-exporting country). The FF curve in Figure 11.7, quadrant (a), illustrates (11.15). If this was a 'small' open economy, then the FF curve would be horizontal. But in this model this is not an appropriate assumption. Full equilibrium of the economy – with corresponding 'natural rates' – occurs at the intersection of the FF and PP curves. So one may think of PP as describing the short-run supply *curve* of the economy, the intersection FF/PP as determining the *point* of equilibrium. This PP curve is of course the same PP curve as the one in (11.2) discussed in the earlier section, which took the equilibrium values as given.

The natural rates are computed as the long-run solution of this system of equations at the current values of the exogenous supply side variables (i.e. benefit, tax and unionization rates, productivity trend, and world trade level). Responses of these natural rates to selected supply side variables on this basis are shown in Table 11.1.

Table 11.1
Effects of supply side policy shifts[1]

Fall of:	Unemployment ('000)	Real wages (%)	Output (%)	Available[2] for lump-sum transfers (£ billion at 1982 prices)
10 per cent in benefits	− 500	− 2.1	+ 2.5	+ 3.4
0.01 in T_F	− 90	+ 0.6	+ 0.5	− 0.6
0.01 in T_L	− 55	− 0.2	+ 0.25	− 0.9
0.01 in UNR	− 170	− 0.8	+ 1.0	+ 1.1

Source: Simulations of Liverpool Model (version of 8/7/83, see Minford, 1983)
Notes: [1] Computed on 1980 values.
[2] Includes extra revenue from rise in output. Negative figure denotes net drain on Exchequer. Assumes marginal overall tax rate of 0.4

While the fiscal and monetary shocks discussed earlier leave y^* and e^* unaltered and so have purely 'macro-economic' effects, shocks to supply side variables will not merely change y^* and e^*, but also the other 'macroeconomic' variables p, $y - y^*$, $e - e^*$, etc. Nevertheless, these effects are fairly straightforward, largely reflecting the adjustment lags built into firms' production decisions.

Figure 11.8 illustrates the effects of a once-for-all unexpected rise in real benefits. The effect on unemployment takes about five years to come through more or less fully. Prices rise, over a similar time scale, by 3 per cent as output and the demand for money falls.

The effect of including the supply side is to make the Liverpool Model capable of tracking not merely the business cycle but also the evolution of 'secular trends'. Nelson and

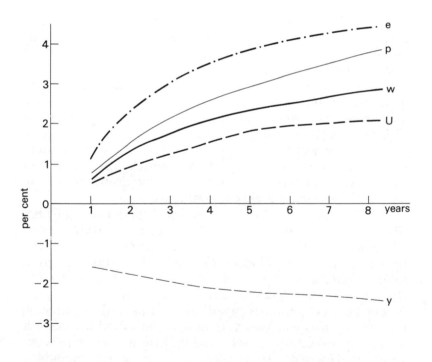

Figure 11.8 *Effect of unanticipated rise in real benefits by 10 per cent*

Plosser (1982) have shown that output and other macro-economic variables are not accurately modelled as consisting of a stationary autoregressive moving-average error process and a deterministic trend; rather they also include a non-stationary error component, arising from the cumulation of random walks in the exogenous variables generating the secular trends. This is precisely the implication of the Liverpool Model, since the supply side exogenous variables themselves have important random walk components. It would appear that macroeconomists generally ought to devote more resources to modelling the natural rates, instead of treating them as deterministic trends.

SIMULATION AND ESTIMATION – SOME TECHNICAL
ASPECTS OF PRACTICAL RE MODELLING

We have discussed the Liverpool Model (and indeed others earlier) as if it could be solved by the analytic methods described in Chapter 2 and as if its parameters could be imposed by *a priori* reasoning. Neither of course is true. The solution of a large rational expectations model is not easy with analytic methods; numerical (i.e. computer) methods are used in practice. And, while it is true that we *do* have a good idea from economic theory and earlier work of the range of values within which most of our parameters will fall, estimation is also clearly necessary. We now briefly discuss each of these matters in turn, but refer the reader elsewhere for full accounts of what are highly technical areas.

The Liverpool Model is solved by a computer algorithm (RATEXP, described by Matthews and Marwaha, 1981) which forces the expectations entering the model's equations to be equal to the model's forecasts. For example, given information for 1982, assumed to be available to all agents, the algorithm first 'guesses' a set of expectations, solving the model for 1983 onwards given this set; after then checking for equality between expectations and the solved forecasts, it alters the expectations set gradually into line until convergence. However, as we have seen, there are an infinite number of such consistent paths. Therefore, to ensure that the algorithm picks the unique stable path, the forecast values and expectations at the end of the forecast horizon are set at equilibrium, as terminal conditions. It was shown in Chapter 2 with a simple example how such terminal conditions select the unique stable path, since all others violate them; clearly the algorithm will also reject such paths, after numerical essays.

It may be asked whether setting terminal conditions at a point in time when they may well not yet be satisfied (e.g. we might be unsure that the economy would have reached equilibrium within the forecast horizon of 10 years) will distort the model solution, as compared with the true analytic solution discussed in Chapter 2 (where the terminal date is allowed to tend to infinity). The answer is provided by sensitivity tests which show that the solution for the period of interest is insignificantly affected, provided the terminal date is set well beyond it (e.g. for a five-year period of interest, we would set the terminal date at 15 years).

The numerical solution method also has the features discussed in the simple example with terminal conditions in Chapter 2: that if there is an infinite number of stable paths, it will select the one with the roots that are smallest in absolute value, and that if there are *no* stable paths, it will similarly select the one with the smallest roots. Thus it 'solves' the uniqueness problem in a way that leaves it to the modeller to decide whether the resulting model behaviour is sensible or not. The problem (as discussed in Chapter 2) in our view lies with the non-stable path case, which will be shown up clearly by the simulation path; the modellers will usually reject this behaviour and reformulate the model.

This and other numerical methods are now in widespread use. We have, however, found this method to be particularly robust in solving large rational expectations models (including the Liverpool Multilateral Model – Minford, Ioannidis and Marwaha, 1983a – which has 220 equations and 50 expectations variables).

Estimation is a more intractable matter. *In principle* one would wish to use 'full information maximum likelihood' (FIML) methods, estimating the whole model subject to the restrictions imposed by rational expectations (see Wallis,

1980). Unfortunately, for large systems such as the Liverpool Model, this turns out to be quite intractable. First, there are just too many directions in which to evaluate the likelihood function. Secondly, there are combinations of parameter values for which the model does not behave sensibly, and it is impossible to know which these are *a priori*; consequently any likelihood-maximizing algorithm would waste a lot of computer time investigating hopeless combinations. However, Fair and Taylor (1983) have described and researched such an algorithm, and though experiments they reported on a very small model took very large amounts of computer time, it will no doubt in time become possible to use such methods in practice.

Meanwhile, we and other researchers have tended to use variants of a single equation method due to McCallum (1976). In this method, the expectations variables are replaced by a prediction from a least squares regression on a subset of the information set available at the time of expectation. This can be regarded therefore as instrumental variables estimation, where the subset forms the set of instruments.

The variation in application arises from the choice of instruments. Provided they are independent of the error term in the structural equation being estimated, any subset will yield consistency (i.e. the coefficient estimates will tend in the infinite sample towards the true values). However, the closer the subset to the true subset determining the expectations and the more heavily restricted by the true model the coefficients used, the greater the efficiency of the equation estimates (i.e. the smaller the standard error of the coefficient estimates) and so the closer to FIML, the consistent and efficient estimator.

Wickens (1982) has shown that for models with expectations of current variables only, three stage least squares (i.e. where the subset of instruments used is the predetermined variable set) is under certain circumstances as efficient as FIML. However, this is not so when expectations of future variables are involved.

An alternative method that we have used repeatedly which appears to offer reasonable efficiency at relatively low cost is to estimate the model equations using the predetermined variable set as instruments, and then to re-estimate them using the predictions from the resulting model as expectations variables. One may then repeat the process if one wishes, until the parameter estimates have converged; but it is not clear how large a gain in efficiency this repetition will yield.

However one estimates a model, the parameters will need to be carefully restricted to obtain sensible simulation properties, since rational expectations models are extremely sensitive to changes in *any* parameter value for the obvious reason that the whole model determines the unique stable path and so the expectations. Clearly, in the iterative method, these restrictions must be satisfied *before* the model is used to generate expectations for re-estimation.

Good estimation methods are important, but in rational expectations models a failure of estimation is likely to be less damaging than a failure of specification because of this sensitivity. Remember that the model will have to be used in varying regimes; therefore sensible properties are more important than fine-tuning to past data. The overriding message from our experience is that an ounce of good theory is worth a ton of econometric sophistication.

INTERIM CONCLUSIONS FROM EXPERIENCE WITH THE
LIVERPOOL MODEL

We have built a machine for forecasting and analysis: but will it fly? To shed light on that question we have been publishing forecasts from the Model since March 1980, as well as running a number of related tests.

Our intensive experience of forecasting suggests first that the Model is not very good at forecasting output because this is dominated by surprises; but then no model is, for the same reason, very good at this either. True, the Liverpool Model has been worse than others since March 1980, but over other periods these other models did pretty badly too, and there is nothing so far to suggest any *systematic* difference of performance (particularly if one allows for the teething troubles of a new model).

The interim experience also suggests that the Model is rather good at forecasting inflation, because this is dominated by the *systematic* effects of government policies. Provided one can read this systematic part of policy well, then the model should be quite good at spelling out the effects on inflation. Of course there will be shocks which will disturb the path, but the broad path will be undisturbed.

Table 11.2 shows the forecasting experience since March 1980. Table 11.3 summarizes the equivalent experience since floating began of the NIESR, the well-known Keynesian forecasting body. These facts appear to be capable of the interpretation just laid out. But it is of course early days and they are but *interim* conclusions.

We have carried out two further pieces of analysis which are of interest. First, we have documented the errors the Model would have made had it been used to forecast the past; this is a weak test of a model, since it was constructed using the past, both formally and informally. However, it is of some interest.

Table 11.4 shows errors for the whole Model including the supply side. Hence errors in forecasting the 'natural rate' of output, unemployment, real wages etc. are embodied in them; possibly an unusually ambitious undertaking, particularly given that the Model's actual forecasts are heavily influenced by the 'natural rates'. 1972–80 was also a volatile period and difficult to forecast, as is well known to those who lived through it and attempted actual forecasting during it. Against this, these are of course *ex post*, and effectively within sample, dynamic forecasts, albeit with *forecasts* for exogenous variables.

An appropriate yardstick of comparison is hard to find. Simple time-series relationships appear the best available and these have been run for some of the variables; it would be interesting to have equivalent errors for other models, but these are not yet available. Output and inflation forecasts are comparable with time-series and interest rates not much worse. The real exchange rate and current balance are, however, quite a lot worse.

On other variables for which no time-series relationships have been estimated, most seem reasonable in order of mag-

Table 11.2
Liverpool forecasts made in February/March (year averages)

Forecasts for:

Year of forecast	GDP growth[a]				Inflation[b]				Unemployment[c]				Exchange rate[d]				3 Month Treasury bills[e]			
	1980	1981	1982	1983	1980	1981	1982	1983	1980	1981	1982	1983	1980	1981	1982	1983	1980	1981	1982	1983
1980	0.0	1.6	2.9	2.7	16.5	9.0	8.1	4.3	—	—			—	—			12.9	11.1	9.3	7.5
1981		−0.2	2.9	2.8		9.5	5.4	4.2		2.5	2.6	2.1		92.2	93.4	96.0		11.2	10.2	9.2
1982			2.5	4.4			7.6	4.0			2.8	2.4			91.8	90.9			13.0	11.1
1983				3.3[f]				4.4				3.1[i]				84.7				11.0
Out-turn (as estimated 8.7.83)	−2.5	−2.2	1.0	(3.7)[g]	16.0	11.0	7.7	(3.7)[h]	1.65	2.54	3.0	(3.0)[j]	96.0	95.3	90.5	(85.3)[k]	13.1	14.6	11.0	(9.5)[l]

Source: Quarterly Economic Bulletin, Liverpool Research Group in Macroeconomics

Notes:

a GDP at factor cost, average estimate, percentage change
b Consumer Expenditure Deflator, percentage change
c UK, Excluding school leavers, million
d Bank of England index, 1975 = 100 (Dec. 1971 = 100 index converted by factor 1.263)
e Interest rate, per cent per annum
f Expenditure estimate
g Growth in 12 months to 1983 1st quarter, expenditure estimate (average estimate 2.3)
h Percentage change in RPI, 12 months to May 1983
i New (claimants) basis
j May 1983, new basis
k Index on 8/7/83
l Rate on 8/7/83

Table 11.3
NIESR forecasts since 1980, made in February (year averages)

Year of forecast	GDP growth[a]				Inflation[b]				Unemployment[c]				Exchange rate[d]			
	1980	1981	1982	1983	1980	1981	1982	1983	1980	1981	1982	1983	1980	1981	1982	1983
1980	−0.5[e]	2.0[e]	—	—	15.8	13.0	—	—	1.58	1.84	—	—	90.9	90.9	—	—
1981		−1.3	0.2	—		10.5	8.2	—		2.67	2.99	—		104.7	109.8	—
1982			1.4	0.7			10.0	8.7			3.0[h]	3.2[h]			89.9	89.9
1983				1.4				7.6				3.2[h,i]				80.3
Out-turn (as estimated 8/7/83)	−2.5[e]	−2.3	1.0	(1.6)[f]	16.0	11.0	7.7	(3.7)[g]	1.9	2.6	3.0	(2.9)[j]	96.0	95.3	90.5	(85.3)[k]

Source: National Institute Economic Review, NIESR

Notes:
[a] GDP at factor cost, output estimate, percentage change
[b] Consumer Expenditure Deflator, percentage change
[c] GB, excluding school-leavers, fourth quarter, seasonally adjusted, million
[d] Bank of England index, 1975 = 100 (Dec. 1971 = 100 index converted by factor, 1.263)
[e] Average estimate
[f] Percentage change in 12 months to 1983 1st quarter, output estimate
[g] Percentage change in RPI, 12 months to May 1983
[h] UK converted to GB basis by deducting 0.1
[i] New (claimants) basis
[j] May 1983, new basis
[k] Index, 8/7/83

Model dynamic 'forecast' errors over the past, 1972–80[a]

	RMSE[b]			Mean error[c]			Serial correlation		
	1	2	3	1	2	3	1	2	3
Output level (%)	2.6 (3.1)	3.7 (3.8)	4.0	-0.1	1.0	3.1	0.09 (0.38)	-0.09 (0.15)	0.51
Inflation (% per annum)	5.2 (5.0)	5.8 (5.7)	6.3	0.5	-3.7	-4.2	0.05 (-0.35)	0.15 (0.15)	-0.06
Current account balance (% of GDP)	3.2 (1.6)	3.2 (1.6)	3.4	-2.1	-1.8	-1.8	0.62 (0.06)	0.54 (0.31)	0.43
Unemployment (% of labour force)	1.2	1.4	1.4	0.9	0.9	0.1	0.57	-0.20	-0.34
5-year interest rates (% per annum)	1.8 (1.4)	3.0 (1.9)	4.0	-0.5	-1.1	-1.4	0.25 (-0.08)	-0.02 (0.31)	-0.41
1-year interest rates (% per annum)	4.2	3.8	4.0	1.9	0.9	0.6	0.33	-0.20	-0.29
Real wealth total (%)	1.4	2.6	3.0	0.7	1.5	2.2	0.45	0.44	0.31
Real physical assets (%)	0.7	1.5	1.8	—	-0.2	-0.4	0.07	-0.33	-0.21
Real financial assets (%)	6.2	13.0	18.2	3.5	9.1	14.2	0.36	0.55	0.37
Real money balances (%) M1	8.2	10.1	7.6	-1.5	-0.6	-1.0	0.30	-0.92	-0.35
Real non-durable consumption (%)	2.6	5.4	7.6	1.2	2.9	5.1	0.26	0.14	0.08
Real government expenditure (%)	6.7	9.0	9.8	0.7	2.7	4.5	0.54	0.09	-1.00
Real exchange rate (%)	11.6 (5.9)	13.1 (7.8)	15.2	-0.8	-4.6	-7.6	0.48 (0.24)	-0.83 (-0.77)	-1.00
Real wage rates (%)	4.3	6.3	7.4	-2.8	-5.0	-6.5	0.22	0.39	0.28

Source: Minford, 1981, pp. 129–30.

Notes:

[a] The Model (the version as of 1/1/82) is simulated dynamically for information sets from 1971 to 1979, giving the 1 to 3 year-ahead errors summarized here. There are seven 3 year-ahead errors, eight 2 year-ahead, and nine 1 year-ahead errors. The serial correlation coefficients are first order for 1 year-ahead, 2nd order for 2 year-ahead, 3rd order for 3 year-ahead. Selected time series forecast errors are parenthesized

[b] Root Mean Square Error

[c] Predicted Minus Actual

Table 11.5
Comparison of the model with adaptive (AE) and rational (RE) expectations

	RMSE			Mean error		
	1	*2*	*3*	*1*	*2*	*3*
Part (1) Analysis of forecast errors 1957–71, for 1, 2 and 3 years ahead						
Inflation (% per annum)						
Years ahead						
RE	2.3	3.0	2.0	−0.5	0.6	0.1
AE	1.7	2.8	2.3	−0.8[b]	0.6	1.1[a]
Real GDP (%)						
RE	1.7	2.4	2.2	0.3	1.0	0.5
AE	2.8	3.1	2.1	1.6[b]	1.5[b]	−0.3
Part (2) Analysis of forecast errors 1957–77, 1972–77 for 1, 2 and 3 years ahead						
Inflation (% per annum)						
Years ahead						
1957–77 RE	2.8	3.8	4.6	0.0	0.1	−1.0
AE	2.8	5.9[d]	10.0[e]	0.6	0.0	−2.7[b]
1972–77 RE	3.7	5.3	8.0	1.2	−1.0	−4.0
AE	4.4	10.1[c]	18.2[c]	4.0[b]	1.3	−12.9[b]
Real GDP (%)						
1957–77 RE	1.8	2.9	3.2	0.1	1.3[a]	1.6[b]
AE	2.3	3.1	3.8	0.9[b]	1.0	1.4[a]
1972–77 RE	2.1	4.0	4.8	−0.2	2.1	4.4[a]
AE	2.1	3.6	6.5[c]	0.5	0.7	5.5[b]

Source: Minford, Ioannidis and Marwaha (1983b)
Notes:
[a] Significantly different from zero at 10 per cent level
[b] Significantly different from zero at 5 per cent level
[c] AE significantly higher than RE at 10 per cent level. Based on *F*-test errors, assuming normal and independent errors
[d] AE significantly higher than RE at 5 per cent level. See also last sentence of Note *c*
[e] AE significantly higher than RE at 1 per cent level. See also last sentence of Note *c*

nitude. Real financial assets and money stand out as bad, as does government expenditure. The former series, however, have been particularly volatile in these inflationary times; and so has government (especially capital) expenditure.

If the major interest is in output and inflation, however, one may perhaps conclude that the attempt to impose a lot of structure (especially on the natural rates) as in this modelling effort is not too unsatisfactory in terms of crude forecasting performance.

In our second test, we have checked out one of the crucial assumptions, rational expectations. It is a prediction of our theory that adaptive expectations should perform particularly badly after a regime change, because they do not incorporate the knowledge of this change. In 1972, the UK floated its exchange rate after fixed rates since the war, a major change of monetary regime. We ran the model using adaptive expectations based on average relationships up to 1976, and compared its performance for the floating period with the rational forecasts. Table 11.5 shows that indeed, particularly for inflation, the model with adaptive expectations performs much worse when floating period data is included. This test corroborates the model in a major respect.

In conclusion, the Liverpool Model has by no means failed in its chosen task of providing a useful tool for analysis and policy. It remains, it would appear, an interesting vehicle from which we may learn further about how to apply new classical macroeconomic analysis.

NOTE

1. (11.10) is derived from the following production function:

$$Q_i(1 - \mu) = f(K_i, L_i, \bar{T}_i)$$

where μ is the (assumed inflexible) share of imports in production and $\bar{T}$ is the stock of the exogenous factor ('entrepreneurship') which is assumed to be growing steadily over time. The derivation proceeds by substituting for capital (from the marginal productivity condition for capital) in terms of the cost of capital, labour, and the fixed factor.

12

Where Do We Go From Here?

Rational expectations has been frequently put in the class of such conceptual revolutions in economics as the marginalist and the Keynesian revolutions. It is easy to see why. It has turned a body of knowledge – macroeconomics based on the neo-Keynesian or neo-classical systems of the late 1960s – upside down; virtually every topic that was in 1970 regarded as conceptually settled and simply in need of more empirical work, has come under the new microscope and been found to be in need of rethinking. This book has dealt with a number of examples including: stabilization policy, the consumption function, asset market behaviour, the Phillips curve, the role of fiscal policy, the political business cycle. But the list could be lengthened virtually endlessly, as research proceeds on all areas of macroeconomics, putting Humpty Dumpty together again.

Beside the rational expectations revolution, the 'monetarist counter-revolution' appears more like the closing chapter, a clearing-up and completing, of the Keynesian revolution; the New Quantity theory of money demand and the Phillips curve, or natural rate hypothesis, were important modifications to the Keynesian system, but only modifications, not least in the sense that the resulting structure left the main Keynesian policy conclusion – that the state should intervene to reduce business fluctuations – conceptually unchallenged. (Milton Friedman's challenge, asserting that the state could not in practice do better, was empirical not conceptual.)

Given that the re-thinking has only recently begun, it is hard, probably impossible, to say where it will lead. In our first chapter (and throughout the book) we mentioned the variety of research and we will not repeat that here; nor will we foolishly attempt to predict its future outcome.

Instead, we will focus on just one issue. Among those macroeconomists – now the majority – who regard rational expectations as a good working hypothesis, the nature of the aggregate supply curve is the key area of disagreement today. Clearly there are disagreements over the aggregate demand curve also, such as the form and basis of the demand for money function (see, e.g., Kareken and Wallace, 1981) or on whether government bonds are net wealth, but at this point these appear to have somewhat less important implications both for policy and the overall behaviour of the economy.

We have two main theories of aggregate supply today: the 'New Classical' (or 'equilibrium') theory and the 'New Keynesian' (or 'disequilibrium') theory. In Chapters 3 and 6 we discussed the former at some length and in Chapter 3 we discussed the contract-based theory of supply which is the basis of the New Keynesian theory.

In the New Classical theory, suppliers confuse an unex- pected rise in the general price level with a rise in their own relative price and accordingly supply more output as the general price level rises unexpectedly; once they know what the true price level was, they correct their previous error, but because of adjustment costs they can only do so gradually (the error 'persists' for some time). Suppliers act as if any contracts they have entered into are either renegotiable or fully contingent on new information (so that their optimal reaction to this is already programmed into the contract); suppliers are therefore freely reacting to news in an optimal manner constrained only by historical data.

The New Keynesian theory, by contrast, stresses the exis- tence of price 'stickiness' owing to the existence of contracts, explicit or implicit, that are *not* fully contingent; in particu- lar, and crucially from the macroeconomic viewpoint, they are not fully indexed either to actual or to expected prices. Suppliers therefore supply more if the general price level rises because those suppliers whose output prices are rising (i.e. whose output contracts have run out) will profit from higher output at the margin, while those suppliers whose input prices are rising but whose output prices are fixed by contract cannot avoid supplying what they have already agreed to; this was illustrated in Chapter 3 with the Fischer labour contracts model. Output supply therefore depends positively on the price level relative to the *contract* price level, i.e. the price level expected at the time the contract was signed. The longer-dated the contracts, the longer the effect of a higher price level will last; and new information cannot affect this, because it cannot be utilized by those tied into their contracts.

This is a 'disequilibrium' theory, because the agents tied into contracts specifying supplies that are no longer optimal under the new price conditions, are frustrated from reacting optimally and are in disequilibrium.

We noted in Chapter 3 the different implications for stabilization policy of the two theories and also the different dynamic response patterns of output and prices to shocks (the π_i). Briefly, under the New Keynesian stabilization policy is a far more attractive option, while the effects of shocks are longer drawn out and have a bigger impact on output.

Modern macroeconomists who espouse rational expectations are ranged on either side of the equilibrium/disequilibrium debate. Can it be settled?

The answer is that presumably it can, but it is not nearly as easy as some have supposed.

Consider first the empirical evidence. Some have appealed to 'casual' empiricism (i.e. common observation) that people's optimal reactions are frustrated by prior contracts. Fischer, for example, claimed (1978) that non-contingent contracts were a 'fact'. Hahn (1982, p. 91) has asserted, as a fact 'we all know to be true', that some people are involuntarily unemployed, i.e. wish to work at the going wage but cannot get a job offer. Unfortunately, these appeals are of little use. The interpretation of these 'facts' themselves is controversial. On inspection, contracts turn out to be highly complex with implicit provisions even for renegotiation, and we just do not know what the typical contract really says; in the Hahn case we would need to know whether these workers were operating in the unionized or non-unionized sector, because if in the former of course they will be frustrated, and again we cannot say by inspection whether the typical worker in the non-unionized sector is or is not constrained.

At a deeper and more general level, we should notice that whether people are 'in equilibrium' (i.e. acting voluntarily) or not can only be settled in the light of a model of equilibrium behaviour. Casual empiricism therefore could never settle this issue.

Turning to more systematic tests, we discussed in Chapter 10 the reduced form tests proposed by Barro and subsequently widely copied. These unfortunately are, we concluded, incapable of settling this issue because of the problem of observational equivalence.

This leaves us with tests derived from structural estimation – e.g. models of labour, or product, supply. Here there has been not much progress as yet, though in principle there seems to be no reason why there should not be in the future. But it is bound to take time, as these tests involve more complicated hypotheses than the reduced form tests that have been popular hitherto.

There is one other way in which progress may be made: the theoretical one. Economists set great store by microfoundations, i.e. by being able to demonstrate that aggregate behaviour could be deduced from the optimizing actions of individual agents. This is a methodological principle which has a deep appeal because it means we can say such behaviour is 'sensible' or 'can be rationalized'; otherwise indeed why should we believe in it? A theory to underpin the New Classical supply curve exists, as described in Chapter 6, provided you accept that information lags do not need to be explained. However, this element is itself the result of optimizing behaviour; people or governments can collect information more frequently if it pays them. Therefore the assumption that the lags are of any particular length is '*ad hoc*', i.e. convenient but unexplained. Of course, everyone accepts there are costs in gathering information; but there are also (massive) costs to society in the supply errors which create the business cycle and, if collecting prices fast could avoid this business cycle, then surely society would pay the extra samplers' salaries. It seems a tenuous basis on which to rest the supply curve.

We also noticed in Chapter 6 that the way in which confusions about relative prices occur has to be very special in the New Classical theory; the supplier must not confusedly think his input prices have risen relative to his output prices, but there seems to be no compelling reason why he should not.

Nevertheless, at least we can see why confusion *could* lead to the New Classical supply curve, given that there *are* information lags. It is quite hard to see why information lags themselves should be permitted to continue for a significant duration; and indeed prices now are available with a lag of only a month in many countries.

One suggested approach to this problem has been that the general price level relevant to each person cannot be known perfectly (it is the underlying or 'permanent' price level, with temporary movements in relative prices stripped out) until all macroeconomic data has been collected; since the collection costs of this are very great, there will remain an element of signal extraction on the basis of less costly global information for a long time. This emphasis on the transitory/permanent confusion is due to Brunner, Cukierman and Meltzer (1980) and appears to be promising, though just why *permanent* nominal prices should matter to a supplier remains unestablished.

Turning to the New Keynesian theory, the theoretical problem is the basis of non-indexed long-term contracts. There is by now a large literature on implicit contracts (see Hart, 1983, for a survey) but nowhere in it is there a suggestion of why these contracts should not be in real terms, and hence of why there should be a supply curve with respect to the aggregate price level. Again, one may appeal (as have, for example, Barro, 1972; Mussa, 1981; Canzoneri, 1980) to transactions costs of changing prices; these, if large enough, could make it optimal for agents to endure disequilibrium for the sake of reducing repeated contracting costs. The problem is to see how indexing to a government index available with a short information lag could be costly, relative to the costs of individual supply errors. In asset markets, such transactions costs have been found to be relatively small.

Hence, at the theoretical level too, discrimination is hard. Both theories have problems which remain unsolved. Another school of thought, which still remains in a small minority, is that there is no supply curve of either variety, but rather causation goes the other way; there are real shocks affecting output which in turn cause money and prices to move unexpectedly, and the business cycle is not even partially caused by monetary shocks (e.g. Long and Plosser, 1983).

To conclude, it is around this as yet quite unresolved issue that our future understanding of the business cycle appears crucially to revolve. But even this assessment is tentative. The whole world of macroeconomics is currently in flux.

References

Aoki, M. and Canzoneri, M. (1979) 'Reduced forms of rational expectations models', *Quarterly Journal of Economics*, **93,** pp. 59–71.

Arrow, K.J. (1971) *Essays On The Theory Of Risk Bearing*, Amsterdam, North Holland.

Arrow, K.J. and Hahn, F.H. (1971) *General Competitive Analysis*, San Francisco, Holden Day; now reprinted, Amsterdam, North Holland.

Attfield, C.L.F., Demery, D. and Duck, N.W. (1981a) 'A quarterly model of unanticipated monetary growth, output and the price level in the UK 1963–78', *Journal of Monetary Economics*, **8,** pp. 331–50.

Attfield, C.L.F., Demery, D. and Duck, N.W. (1981b) 'Unanticipated monetary growth, output and the price level', *European Economic Review*, **16,** pp. 367–85.

Baillie, R.J., Lippens, R.E. and McMahon, P.C. (1983) 'Testing rational expectations and efficiency in the foreign exchange market', *Econometrica*, **51,** pp. 553–63.

Barro, R.J. (1972) 'A theory of monopolistic price adjustment', *Review of Economic Studies*, **39,** pp. 17–26.

Barro, R.J. (1974) 'Are government bonds net wealth?', *Journal of Political Economy*, **82,** pp. 1095–117.

Barro, R.J. (1976) 'Rational expectations and the role of monetary policy', *Journal of Monetary Economics*, **2,** pp. 1–33.

Barro, R.J. (1977) 'Unanticipated monetary growth and unemployment in the United States', *American Economic Review*, **67,** pp. 101–15.

Barro, R.J. (1980) 'A capital market in an equilibrium business cycle model', *Econometrica*, **48,** pp. 1393–417.

Barro, R.J. and Fischer, S. (1976) 'Recent developments in monetary theory', *Journal of Monetary Economics*, **2**, pp. 133–67.

Barro, R.J. and Rush, M. (1980) 'Unanticipated money and economic activity', in S. Fischer (ed.) *Rational Expectations and Economic Policy*, University of Chicago Press.

Beaver, W.H. (1981) *Financial Accounting: An Accounting Revolution*, Prentice-Hall.

Beenstock, M. (1980) *A Neoclassical Analysis of Macroeconomic Policy*, Cambridge University Press.

Begg, D.K.H. (1982) *The Rational Expectations Revolution In Macroeconomics – Theories and Evidence*, Oxford, Philip Allan.

Bell, S. and Beenstock, M. (1980) 'An application of rational expectations in the UK foreign exchange market', in D. Currie and W. Peters (eds.) *Studies in Contemporary Economic Analysis*, Volume 2, London, Croom Helm.

Bilson, J.F.O. (1980) 'The rational expectations approach to the consumption function', *European Economic Review*, **13**, pp. 273–99.

Black, S.A. (1973) 'International money markets and flexible exchange rates', *Studies in International Finance No. 32*, International Finance Section, Princeton University.

Blanchard, O.J. (1981) 'Output, the stock market and interest rates', *American Economic Review*, **71**, pp. 132–43.

Blanchard, O.J. and Wyplosz, C. (1981) 'An empirical structural model of aggregate demand', *Journal of Monetary Economics*, **7**, pp. 1–28.

Blinder, A.S. and Solow, R.M. (1973) 'Does fiscal policy matter?', *Journal of Public Economics*, **2**, pp. 319–37.

Borooah, V. and Van der Ploeg, R. (1982) 'British government popularity and economic performance. A comment', *Economic Journal*, **92**, pp. 405–10.

Brunner, K., Cukierman, A. and Meltzer, A.H. (1980), 'Stagflation, persistent unemployment and the permanence of economic shocks', *Journal of Monetary Economics*, **6**, pp. 467–92.

Buiter, W.H. (1981) 'The superiority of contingent rules over fixed rules in models with rational expectations', *Economic Journal*, **91**, pp. 647–70.

Buiter, W.H. (1983) 'Real effects of anticipated and unanticipated money: some problems of estimation and hypothesis testing', *Journal of Monetary Economics*, **11**, pp. 207–24.

Buiter, W.H. and Miller, M. (1981) 'Monetary policy and international competitiveness: the problems of adjustment', *Oxford Economic Papers*, **33**, pp. 143–75.

232   *References*

Buiter, W.H. and Tobin, J. (1979) 'Debt neutrality: a brief review of doctrine and evidence', Ch. 2 of G. Von Furstenberg (ed.) *Social Security vs Private Saving in Post Industrial Societies*, Ballinger.

Cagan, P. (1956) 'The monetary dynamics of hyperinflation', in M. Friedman (ed.) *Studies in the Quantity Theory of Money*, University of Chicago Press.

Calvo, G.A. (1978) 'On the time inconsistency of optimal policy in a monetary economy,' *Econometrica*, **46**, pp. 1411–28.

Canzoneri, M.B. (1980) 'Labour Contracts and Monetary Policy', *Journal of Monetary Economics*, **6**, pp. 241–55.

Canzoneri, M.B. (1981) 'Rational destabilizing speculation and exchange intervention policy', mimeo, Board of Governors, Federal Reserve System of the USA, International Finance Division.

Cass, D. and Shell, K. (eds.), (1976) *The Hamiltonian Approach to Dynamic Economics*, Philadelphia, University of Pennsylvania Press.

Chappell, D. and Peel, D.A. (1979) 'On the political theory of the business cycle', *Economics Letters*, **2**, pp. 327–32.

Chow, G.C. (1975) *Analysis and Control of Dynamic Economic Systems*, John Wiley.

Chow, G.C. (1980) 'Estimation of rational expectations models', *Journal of Economic Dynamics and Control*, **2**, pp. 241–55.

Chrystal, K.A. and Alt, J.E. (1981) 'Some problems in formulating and testing a politico-economic model of the United Kingdom', *Economic Journal*, **91**, pp. 730–6.

Copeland, T.E. and Weston, J.F. (1979) *Financial Theory and Corporate Planning*, Reading, Addison Wesley.

Cornell, B. (1977) 'Spot rates, forward rates and exchange market efficiency', *Journal of Financial Economics*, **5**, pp. 55–65.

Cramer, T.S. (1969) *Empirical Econometrics*, Amsterdam, North Holland.

Davidson, J.E.H. and Hendry, D.F. (1981) 'Interpreting econometric evidence: the behaviour of consumers' expenditure in the UK', *European Economic Review*, **16**, pp. 177–92.

Demery, D. (1981) 'Exchange rate dynamics – some efficient estimates', mimeo, University of Bristol.

Dickinson, D.G., Driscoll, M.J. and Ford, J.L. (1982) 'Rational expectations, random parameters and the non-neutrality of money', *Economica*, **49**, pp. 241–8.

Dornbusch, R. (1976) 'Expectations and exchange rate dynamics', *Journal of Political Economy*, **84**, pp. 1161–76.

Downs, A. (1957) *An Economic Theory of Democracy*, New York, Harper and Row.

Driskill, R.A. (1981) 'Exchange rate dynamics: an empirical investigation', *Journal of Political Economy*, **2**, pp. 357–71.

Fair, R.C. and Taylor, J.B. (1983) 'Solution and maximum likelihood estimation of dynamic nonlinear rational expectations models', *Econometrica*, **51**, pp. 1169–86.

Fama, E.F. (1970) 'Efficient capital markets; a review of theory and empirical work', *Journal of Finance*, **25**, pp. 383–417.

Fama, E.F. (1975) 'Short term interest rates as predictors of inflation', *American Economic Review*, **65**, pp. 269–82.

Fama, E.F. (1976) *Foundations of Finance*, Oxford, Basil Blackwell.

Fama, E.F. and Blume, M. (1970) 'Filter rules and stock market trading profits', *Journal of Business*, **39** (special supplement January), pp. 226–41.

Feige, E.L. and Pierce, D.K. (1976) 'Economically rational expectations: are innovations in the rate of inflation independent of innovations in measures of monetary and fiscal policy', *Journal of Political Economy*, **84**, pp. 499–522.

Finnerty, J.E. (1976) 'Insiders and market efficiency', *Journal of Finance*, **31**, pp. 1131–48.

Fischer, S. (1977) 'Long term contracts, rational expectations and the optimum money supply rule', *Journal of Political Economy*, **85**, pp. 191–205.

Fischer, S. (1977) 'Long-term contracting, sticky prices, and monetary policy – a comment', *Journal of Monetary Economics*, **3**, pp. 317–23.

Fischer, S. (ed.) (1980a) *Rational Expectations and Economic Policy*, University of Chicago Press.

Fischer, S. (1980b) 'Dynamic inconsistency, cooperation and the benevolent dissembling government', *Journal of Economic Dynamics and Control*, **2**, pp. 93–107.

Frankel, J.A. (1979) 'On the Mark, a theory of floating exchange rates based on real interest differentials', *American Economic Review*, **69**, pp. 610–22.

Frankel, J.A. (1982) 'The mystery of the multiplying marks. A modification of the monetary model', *Review of Economics and Statistics*, **64**, pp. 515–19.

234   *References*

Frenkel, J.A. (1977) 'The forward exchange rate, expectations and the demand for money: the German hyperinflation', *American Economic Review*, **70**, pp. 771–5.

Frenkel, J.A. (1981) 'Flexible exchange rates, prices and the role of the "news": lessons from the 1970s', *Journal of Political Economy*, **89**, pp. 665–704.

Frenkel, J.A. and Levich, R.M. (1975) 'Covered interest arbitrage: unexploited profits?', *Journal of Political Economy*, **83**, pp. 325–9.

Frey, B.S. and Schneider, F. (1978a) 'A politico-economic model of the United Kingdom', *Economic Journal*, **88**, pp. 243–53.

Frey, B.S. and Schneider, F. (1978b) 'An empirical study of politico-economic interaction in the United States', *Review of Economics and Statistics*, **60**, pp. 174–83.

Friedman, B.M. (1978) 'Discussion' of 'After Keynesian macro-economics' by R.E. Lucas and T.J. Sargent, in *After The Phillips Curve: Persistence of High Inflation and High Unemployment*, Federal Reserve Bank of Boston Conference Series No. 19, pp. 73–80.

Friedman, B.M. (1979) 'Optimal expectations and the extreme information assumptions of rational expectations macromodels', *Journal of Monetary Economics*, **5**, pp. 23–41.

Friedman, M. (1957) *A Theory of the Consumption Function*, Princeton University Press.

Friedman, M. (1968) 'The role of monetary policy', *American Economic Review*, **58**, pp. 1–17.

Friedman, M. and Meiselman, D. (1963) 'The Relative Stability of Monetary Velocity and the Investment Multiplier in the US 1898–1958', in Commission on Money and Credit: *Stabilisation Policies*, Englewood Cliffs, New Jersey, Prentice-Hall.

Gourieroux, C., Laffont, J.J. and Montfort, A. (1982) 'Rational Expectations in dynamic linear models – analysis of the solutions', *Econometrica*, **50**, pp. 409–25.

Graybill, F.A. (1961) *An Introduction To Linear Stochastic Models Vol. 1*, New York, McGraw-Hill.

Grossman, S.J. and Stiglitz, J.E. (1976) 'Information and competitive price systems', *American Economic Review*, **66**, pp. 246–53.

Grossman, S.J. and Stiglitz, J.E., (1980) 'On the impossibility of informationally efficient markets', *American Economic Review*, **70**, pp. 393–407.

Gurley, J. and Shaw, E.S. (1960) *Money in a Theory of Finance*, Brookings Institution, Washington.

Hacche, G. and Townend, J. (1981) 'Exchange rates and monetary policy: modelling sterling's effective exchange rate', *Oxford Economic Papers*, **33**, pp. 201–47.

Hahn, F.H. (1982) *Money and Inflation*, Oxford, Basil Blackwell.

Hall, R.E. (1978) 'Stochastic implications of the life cycle–permanent income hypothesis: theory and evidence', *Journal of Political Economy*, **86**, pp. 971–88.

Hansen, L.P. and Sargent, T.J. (1980) 'Formulating and estimating dynamic linear rational expectations models', *Journal of Economic Dynamics and Control*, **2**, pp. 7–46.

Hart, O.D. (1983) 'Optimal labour contracts under asymmetric information, an introduction', *Review of Economic Studies*, **50**, pp. 3–36.

Harte, C.P., Minford, A.P.L. and Peel, D.A. (1983) 'The political economy of government macroeconomic stabilisation policy', mimeo, University of Liverpool.

Hellwig, M.F. (1982) 'Rational expectations equilibrium with conditioning on past prices. A mean variance example', *Journal of Economic Theory*, **26**, pp. 279–312.

Hibbs, D.A. Jr. (1978) 'Political parties and macroeconomic policy', *American Political Science Review*, **72**, pp. 981–1007.

Hicks, J.R. (1939) *Value and Capital*, Clarendon Press.

Hoel, P.G. (1962) *Introduction To Mathematical Statistics*, 3rd edn., John Wiley.

Holden, K. and Peel, D.A. (1977) 'An empirical investigation of inflationary expectations', *Oxford Bulletin of Economics and Statistics*, **39**, pp. 291–9.

Holly, S. and Zarrop, M.B. (1983) 'On optimality and time consistency when expectations are rational', *European Economic Review*, **20**, pp. 23–40.

Holt, C.C., Modigliani, F., Muth, J.F. and Simon, H.A. (1960) *Planning Production, Inventories and Work Force*. Englewood Cliffs, New Jersey, Prentice-Hall.

Jaffe, J. (1974) 'The effect of regulation changes on insider trading', *Bell Journal of Economics and Management Science*, **5**, pp. 93–121.

Johnson, H.G. (1968) 'Problems of efficiency in monetary management', *Journal of Political Economy*, **76**, pp. 971–90.

Johnston, J. (1972) *Econometric Methods*, 2nd edn. McGraw-Hill.

Jordan, J.S. and Radner, R. (1982) 'Rational expectations in microeconomic models, an overview', *Journal of Economic Theory*, **26**, pp. 201–23.

Kalman, R.E. (1960) 'A new approach to linear filtering and prediction problems', Trans. ASME, *Journal of Basic Engineering*, Series D, **82**, pp. 35–45.

Kareken, J.H. and Wallace, N. (1981) 'On the indeterminancy of equilibrium exchange rates', *Quarterly Journal of Economics*, **96**, pp. 207–22.

Karni, E. (1980) 'A note on Lucas's equilibrium model of the business cycle', *Journal of Political Economy*, **88**, pp. 1231–8.

Keynes, J.M. (1936) *The General Theory of Employment, Interest and Money*, Macmillan.

Keynes, J.M. (1939) 'Professor Tinbergen's method', *Economic Journal*, **49**, pp. 558–68.

King, R.G. (1982) 'Monetary policy and the information content of prices', *Journal of Political Economy*, **90**, pp. 247–79.

King, R.G. and Plosser, C.I. (1981) 'The behaviour of money, credit and prices in a real business cycle', mimeo, University of Rochester.

Kochin, L.A. (1974) 'Are future taxes anticipated by consumers', *Journal of Money Credit and Banking*, **6**, pp. 385–94.

Koyck, L.M. (1954) 'Distributed lags and investment analysis', contributions to *Economic Analysis No. 4*, Amsterdam, North Holland.

Krugman, P.R. (1978) 'Purchasing power parity and exchange rates', *Journal of International Economics*, **8**, pp. 397–407.

Kydland, F.E. and Prescott, E.C. (1977) 'Rules rather than discretion: the inconsistency of optimal plans', *Journal of Political Economy*, **85**, pp. 473–91.

Laidler, D.E.W. (1982) *Monetarist Perspectives*, Oxford, Philip Allan.

Lawrence, C. (1983) 'Rational expectations, supply shocks and the stability of the inflation output trade-off. Some time series evidence for the United Kingdom 1956–1977', *Journal of Monetary Economics*, **11**, pp. 225–46.

Leiderman, L. (1980) 'Macroeconomic testing of the rational expectations and structural neutrality hypothesis for the United States', *Journal of Monetary Economics*, **6**, pp. 69–82.

Levich, R.M. (1978) 'Further results on the efficiency of markets for foreign exchange', in *Managed Exchange Rate Flexibility: The Recent Experience*, Federal Bank of Boston Conference Series.

Lipsey, R.G. (1960) 'The relation between unemployment and the rate of change of money wage rates in the United Kingdom 1862–1957: A further analysis', *Economica*, NS, **27**, pp. 1–31.

Long, J.B. and Plosser, C.I. (1983) 'Real business cycles', *Journal of Political Economy*, **91**, pp. 39–69.

Lucas, R.E. Jr. (1972a) 'Econometric testing of the natural rate hypothesis', in O. Eckstein (ed.) *Econometrics of Price Determination Conference*, Board of Governors, Federal Reserve System, Washington DC.

Lucas, R.E. Jr. (1972b) 'Expectations and the neutrality of money', *Journal of Economic Theory*, **4**, pp. 103–24.

Lucas, R.E. Jr. (1973) 'Some international evidence on output–inflation trade-offs', *American Economic Review*, **68**, pp. 326–34.

Lucas, R.E. Jr. (1975) 'An equilibrium model of the business cycle', *Journal of Political Economy*, **83**, pp. 1113–44.

Lucas, R.E. Jr. (1976) 'Econometric policy evaluation: A critique', in K. Brunner and A.H. Meltzer (eds.), *The Phillips Curve and Labour Markets*, Carnegie Rochester Conference Series on Public Policy No. 1, Supplement to the *Journal of Monetary Economics*.

Lucas, R.E. and Rapping, L.A. (1969) 'Real wages, employment and inflation', *Journal of Political Economy*, **77**, pp. 721–54.

Lucas, R.E. and Sargent, T.J. (1978) 'After Keynesian macroeconomics', in *After the Phillips Curve: Persistence of High Inflation and High Unemployment*, Federal Reserve Bank of Boston.

McCallum, B.T. (1976) 'Rational expectations and the natural rate hypothesis: Some consistent estimates', *Econometrica*, **44**, pp. 43–52.

McCallum, B.T. (1978) 'Dating discounts and the robustness of the Lucas–Sargent proposition', *Journal of Monetary Economics*, **4**, pp. 121–9.

McCallum, B.T. (1979) 'On the observational inequivalence of classical and Keynesian models', *Journal of Political Economy*, **87**, pp. 395–402.

McCallum, B.T. (1982) 'Are bond-financed deficits inflationary? A Ricardian Analysis', Working paper No. 905, National Bureau of Economic Research, June.

McCallum, B.T. (1983) 'On non-uniqueness in rational expectations models: An attempt at perspective', *Journal of Monetary Economics*, **11**, pp. 139–68.

McCallum, B.T. and Whittaker, J.K. (1979) 'The effectiveness of fiscal feedback rules and automatic stabilisers under rational expectations', *Journal of Monetary Economics*, **5**, pp. 171–86.

Macrae, D.C. (1977) 'A political model of the business cycle', *Journal of Political Economy*, **85**, pp. 239–63.

Markowitz, H. (1959) *Portfolio Selection: Efficient Diversification of Investment*, John Wiley.

Marshall, A. (1887) 'Minutes of evidence taken before the Royal Commission on Gold and Silver, Forty Third Day (19th Dec. 1887)', in *Final Report of the Royal Commission on Gold and Silver*, pp. 1–53, London, HMSO.

Matthews, K.G.P. and Marwaha, S. (1981) 'Ratexp Mk 2.', mimeo, University of Liverpool.

Meiselman, D. (1962) *The Term Structure of Interest Rates*, Prentice-Hall.

Metzler, L.A. (1951) 'Wealth saving and the rate of interest', *Journal of Political Economy*, **59,** pp. 93–116.

Minford, A.P.L. (1978) *Substitution effects, speculation and exchange rate stability*, Studies in International Economics No. 3, Amsterdam, North Holland.

Minford, A.P.L. (1980) 'A rational expectations model of the United Kingdom under fixed and floating exchange rates', in K. Brunner and A.H. Meltzer (eds.) *On the State of Macroeconomics*, Carnegie Rochester Conference Series on Public Policy No. 12, Supplement to the *Journal of Monetary Economics*.

Minford, A.P.L. (1981) 'The exchange rate and monetary policy', *Oxford Economic Papers*, 33, July 1981 Supplement, pp. 120–42.

Minford, A.P.L. (1983) 'Labour market equilibrium in an open economy', mimeo, University of Liverpool, forthcoming *Oxford Economic Papers*.

Minford, A.P.L. and Brech, M. (1981) 'The wage equation and rational expectations', in D. Currie, A.R. Nobay and D.A. Peel (eds.) *Macroeconomic Analysis*, London, Croom Helm.

Minford, A.P.L., Brech, M. and Matthews, K.G.P., (1980) 'A rational expectations model of the UK under floating exchange rates', *European Economic Review*, **14,** pp. 189–219.

Minford, A.P.L., Davies, D.H., Peel, M.J. and Sprague, A. (1983) *Unemployment: Cause and Cure*, Oxford, Martin Robertson.

Minford, A.P.L. and Hilliard, G.W. (1977) 'The costs of variable inflation', in M.J. Artis and A.R. Nobay (eds.) *Contemporary Economic Analysis*, Vol. 1, London, Croom Helm.

Minford, A.P.L., Ioannidis, C.E. and Marwaha, S. (1983a) 'Rational expectations in a multilateral macro model', in P. De Grauwe and T. Peeters (eds.) *Exchange Rates in Multi-Country Econometric Models*, pp. 239–66, London, Macmillan.

Minford, A.P.L. Ioannidis, C.E. and Marwaha, S. (1983b) 'Dynamic predictive tests of a model under adaptive and national expectations', *Economics Letters*, **11,** pp. 115–21.

Minford, A.P.L., Matthews, K.G.P. and Marwaha, S. (1979) 'Terminal conditions as a means of ensuring unique solutions for rational expectations models with forward expectations', *Economics Letters*, **4**, pp. 117–20.

Minford, A.P.L. and Peel, D.A. (1979) 'The classical supply hypothesis and the observational equivalence of classical and Keynesian models', *Economics Letters*, **4**, pp. 229–23.

Minford, A.P.L. and Peel, D.A. (1980) 'The natural rate hypothesis and rational expectations – a critique of some recent developments', *Oxford Economic Papers*, **32**, pp. 71–81.

Minford, A.P.L. and Peel, D.A. (1981) 'On the role of monetary stabilization policy under rational expectations, *Manchester School*', **69**, pp. 39–50.

Minford, A.P.L. and Peel, D.A. (1982a) 'The political theory of the business cycle', *European Economic Review*, **17**, pp. 253–70.

Minford, A.P.L. and Peel, D.A. (1982b) 'The Phillips curve and rational expectations', *Weltwirtschaftliches Archiv*, **118**, pp. 456–78.

Minford, A.P.L. and Peel, D.A. (1983a) 'Models of exchange rate overshooting' mimeo, University of Liverpool.

Minford, A.P.L. and Peel, D.A. (1983b) 'Testing for unbiasedness and efficiency under incomplete current information', mimeo, University of Liverpool, forthcoming *Economic Bulletin*.

Minford, A.P.L. and Peel, D.A. (1983c) 'Some implications of partial current information sets in macroeconomic models embodying rational expectations', mimeo, University of Liverpool, forthcoming *Manchester School*.

Mishkin, F.S. (1978a) 'Efficient markets theory: implications for monetary policy', *Brookings Papers on Economic Activity*, **3**, pp. 707–52.

Mishkin, F.S. (1978b) 'Simulation methodology in macroeconomics: An innovation technique', *Journal of Political Economy*, **87**, pp. 816–36.

Mishkin, F.S. (1981) 'The real interest rate: an empirical investigation', in K. Brunner and A.H. Meltzer (eds.) *The Costs and Consequences of Inflation*, Carnegie Rochester Conference Series on Public Policy No. 15, Supplement to the *Journal of Monetary Economics*.

Mishkin, F.S., (1982) 'Does anticipated monetary policy matter: An empirical investigation', *Journal of Political Economy*, **99**, pp. 22–51.

Modigliani, F. and Grunberg, E. (1954) 'The predictability of social events', *Journal of Political Economy*, **62**, pp. 465–78.

Modigliani, F. and Sutch, R. (1966) 'Innovations in interest rate policy', *American Economic Review*, Papers and Proceedings, **56**, pp. 178–97.

Mueller, D.C. (1979) *Public Choice*, New York, Cambridge University Press.

Mussa, M. (1981) 'Sticky individual prices and the dynamics of the general price level', in K. Brunner and A.H. Meltzer (eds.) *The Costs and Consequences of Inflation*, Carnegie Rochester Conference Series on Public Policy, No. 15, Supplement to the *Journal of Monetary Economics*.

Muth, J.F. (1960) 'Optimal properties of exponentially weighted forecasts', *Journal of the American Statistical Association*, **55**, pp. 299–306.

Muth, J.F. (1961) 'Rational expectations and the theory of price movements', *Econometrica*, **29**, pp. 315–35.

Nelson, C.R. and Plosser, C.I. (1982) 'Trends and random walks in macroeconomic time series: Some evidence and implications', *Journal of Monetary Economics*, **10**, pp. 139–62.

Nelson, C.R. and Schwert, G.W. (1977) 'Short-term interest rates as predictors of inflation: On testing the hypothesis that the real interest rate is constant', *American Economic Review*, **67**, pp. 478–86.

Nerlove, M. (1958) 'Adaptive expectations and cobweb phenomena', *Quarterly Journal of Economics*, **72**, pp. 227–40.

Nordhaus, W.D. (1975) 'The political business cycle', *Review of Economic Studies*, **42**, pp. 169–90.

Parkin, J.M. (1978) 'A comparison of alternative techniques of monetary control under rational expectations', *Manchester School*, **46**, pp. 252–87.

Patinkin, D. (1965) *Money, Interest and Prices*, 2nd edn., New York, Harper and Row.

Peel, D.A. (1981) 'Non-uniqueness and the role of the monetary authorities', *Economics Letters*, **4**, pp. 117–20.

Pesando, J.E. (1978) 'On the efficiency of the bond market: some Canadian evidence', *Journal of Political Economy*, **86**, pp. 1057–76.

Phelps, E.S. (1970) 'The new microeconomics in employment and inflation theory', in E.S. Phelps *et al.* (eds.), *Microeconomic Foundations of Employment and Inflation Theory*, Norton, New York, pp. 1–27.

Phelps, E.S. and Taylor, J.B. (1977) 'The stabilizing powers of monetary policy under rational expectations', *Journal of Political Economy*, **85**, pp. 163–90.

Poole, W. (1970) 'The optimal choice of monetary instrument in a simple stochastic macro model', *Quarterly Journal of Economics*, **84**, pp. 197–221.

Pratt, J.W. (1964) 'Risk aversion in the small and in the large', *Econometrica*, **32**, pp. 122–36.

Robinson, J.V. (1937) *Essays on the Theory of Employment*, London, Macmillan.

Saidi, N.H. (1980) 'Fluctuating exchange rates and the international transmission of economic disturbances', *Journal of Money Credit and Banking*, **12**, pp. 575–91.

Sargent, T.J. (1972) 'Rational expectations and the term structure of interest rates', *Journal of Money Credit and Banking*, **4**, pp. 74–97.

Sargent, T.J. (1976a) 'A classical macroeconomic model of the United States', *Journal of Political Economy*, **84**, pp. 207–38.

Sargent, T.J. (1976b) 'The observational equivalence of natural and unnatural rate theories of macroeconomics', *Journal of Political Economy*, **84**, pp. 631–40.

Sargent, T.J. (1978) 'Estimation of dynamic labour demand schedules under rational expectations', *Journal of Political Economy*, **86**, pp. 1009–44.

Sargent, T.J. (1979a) *Macroeconomic Theory*, New York, Academic Press.

Sargent, T.J. (1979b) 'A note on the maximum likelihood estimation of the rational expectations model of the term structure', *Journal of Monetary Economics*, **5**, pp. 133–43.

Sargent, T.J. (1981) 'Interpreting economic time series', *Journal of Political Economy*, **89**, pp. 213–48.

Sargent, T.J. and Wallace, N. (1975) 'Rational expectations, the optimal monetary instrument and the optimal money supply rule', *Journal of Political Economy*, **83**, pp. 241–54.

Sargent, T.J. and Wallace, N. (1981) 'Some unpleasant monetary arithmetic', *Quarterly Review*, Fall 1981, Federal Reserve Bank of Minneapolis, pp. 1–17.

Seater, J.J. (1982) 'Are future taxes discounted?', *Journal of Money Credit and Banking*, **14**, pp. 376–89.

Shackle, G.L.S. (1958) *Time in Economics*, Amsterdam, North Holland.

Shiller, R.J. (1978) 'Rational expectations and the dynamic structure of macroeconomic models – a critical review, *Journal of Monetary Economics*, **4**, pp. 1–44.

Shiller, R.J. (1979) 'The volatility of long-term interest rates and expectations models of the term structure', *Journal of Political Economy*, **87**, pp. 1190–1219.

Sims, C.A. (1979) 'Macroeconomics amd reality', *Econometrica*, **48**, pp. 1–48.

Taylor, J.B. (1977) 'Conditions for unique solutions to macroeconomic models with rational expectations', *Econometrica*, **45**, pp. 1377–85.

Taylor, J.B. (1979a) 'Estimation and control of a macroeconomic model with rational expectations', *Econometrica*, **47**, pp. 1267–86.

Taylor, J.B. (1979b) 'Staggered wage setting in a macroeconomic model', *American Economic Review*, Papers and Proceedings, **69**, pp. 108–13.

Taylor, J.B. (1980) 'Aggregate dynamics and staggered contracts', *Journal of Political Economy*, **88**, pp. 1–23.

Taylor, S.J. (1982) 'Tests of the random walk hypothesis against a price trend', *Journal of Financial and Qualitative Analysis*, **17**, pp. 31–61.

Tullock, G. (1976) *The Vote Motive*, Hobart Paper No. 9, Institute of Economic Affairs, London.

Turnovsky, S.J. (1970) 'Empirical evidence on the formation of price expectations', *Journal of the American Statistical Association*, **65**, pp. 1441–54.

Turnovsky, S.J. (1980) 'The choice of monetary instrument under alternative forms of price expectations', *Manchester School*, **48**, pp. 39–63.

Wallis, K.F. (1980) 'Econometric implications of the rational expectations hypothesis', *Econometrica*, **48**, pp. 49–72.

Walters, A.A. (1971) 'Consistent expectations, distributed lags and the quantity theory', *Economic Journal*, **81**, pp. 273–81.

Weiss, L. (1980) 'The role for active monetary policy in a rational expectations model', *Journal of Political Economy*, **88**, pp. 221–33.

Wickens, M.R. (1982) 'The efficient estimation of econometric models with rational expectations', *Review of Economic Studies*, **49,** pp. 55–67.

Author Index

Subject Index

252 *Subject Index*